"Anyone who is interested in structuring feelings and thoughts into words and story will find *Stealing Fire* stimulating and worthwhile. A lifetime's labor of love, it provides the reader with insight and an overview of the creative process through the history of story. I recommend it and congratulate Mr. Bonnet on his accomplishment."
— Elliott Gould, Actor, Academy Award nominee

"Challenging and provocative. Bonnet is a thoughtful and highly intelligent writer whose lifetime of experience has led him to an intriguing theory about how great stories are written. The Golden Paradigm is guaranteed to stimulate lively new debate on the age-old question."
— David W. Rintels, Emmy, Writer's Guild, Peabody Award-winning Writer, Producer

"James Bonnet's groundbreaking book, *Stealing Fire from the Gods*, is the fruit of more than four decades of intensive study of various areas — world mythology, depth psychology, literary classics, and successful modern novels and movies. Bonnet has been able to discover the secret of the psychological power and the emotional impact of effective storytelling of all ages and countries and come up with a true Rosetta stone for modern authors — a formula for creating masterpieces. A fascinating book and an extremely useful tool for creative individuals in various avenues of art!"
— Stanislav Grof, M.D., Consciousness Researcher, Author of *Psychology of the Future, Adventure of Self-Discovery*, and *The Cosmic Game*

"Employing psychological theory and his own hard-won insights, James Bonnet demystifies the magic of creative storytelling. *Stealing Fire from the Gods* is intelligent and fascinating."
— Robert Crais, *New York Times* best-selling Novelist

"James Bonnet isn't saying the same old thing. He's about challenging you to look deeply into your own fascination and attraction; to mine your story for the richness and texture that compels you to write; and to connect you to a noble lineage of storytellers. His tools will jump-start and intrigue you. Your connection to your craft will deepen, and your horizons will expand."
— Raymond Singer, Screenwriter of Disney's *Mulan*

"*Stealing Fire from the Gods* is like a rediscovered, ancient remedy for the ailing creative soul. Jim has tapped into a wellspring of lost knowledge that goes to the very core of the creative unconscious, unlocking the natural storyteller that is encoded in each and every one of us."
— Bob Camp, Artist, Writer, Director, and Co-creator of *The Ren and Stimpy Show*

"My advice to aspiring writers is simple: Read this book. There are some real pearls here."
— Billy Ray, Screenwriter of *Flight Plan, Shattered Glass, Hart's War*

"*Stealing Fire from the Gods* is a book that needs to be read and reread and a seminar of great value to all writers."
— Gene Hines, original Writer, Producer of *Cliffhanger*

"Bonnet is a brilliant man. He has drawn from the work of C. G. Jung and Joseph Campbell, then accomplished his own alchemy. The result is a personal transformation the reader can share. Everyone should read it."
— Darryl M. Diamond, M.D., Ph.D.

"Bonnet achieves what no one else has in moving beyond formulaic approaches to creating stories. Formulas don't work without the essence of true story which he has been able to depict in *Stealing Fire from the Gods*."
— Michael Elias, Writer, Producer, Director, Actor

"James Bonnet has drawn on his vast experience as a writer and knowledge of storytelling to create a bold, insightful journey into the creative process."
— Bill Ewing, Writer and Producer of *End of the Spear*

"Anyone who has come to love literature, drama, and just plain entertainment in their pursuit of enlightenment will love James Bonnet's *Stealing Fire from the Gods*."
— Don Murray, award-winning Writer, Actor, Producer of *The Hoodlum Priest*

"This book will certainly be a bible for writers."
— Jack Wiener, Producer of *FX* and *FX2*

"I recommend this book for every screenwriter. I also recommend it for producers, actors, and directors with an eye toward Hollywood."
— Pi Ware, Filmmakers Alliance

"The stories that really work, that go deep, that are universal, tap into the fractal nature of the archetypes of character and relationship. *Stealing Fire from the Gods* — the Promethean gift for storytellers — can be found by the faithful, assiduous seeker in James Bonnet's captivating, enlightening book."
— Lanny Cotler, Screenwriter, Director of *The Earthling* and *Heartwood*

"Page turner. *Stealing Fire from the Gods* is billed as 'a dynamic new story model for writers and filmmakers.' Like many other books, it covers the meaning and purpose of storymaking (i.e., myths and legends) through the ages and how understanding them leads to an understanding of self. It's an intriguing analysis that brings a unique look and insight to the creative process. And anything that does that is worth exploring."
— *Creative Screenwriting*

"James Bonnet throws convention to the wind when he offers screenwriters a new way to structure stories in his book *Stealing Fire from the Gods*. Bonnet offers his analysis of myths, legends, fairy tales, and such films as *Casablanca* and *Indiana Jones*. He discusses the link between all great stories and gives an in-depth explanation of the Golden Paradigm, his new story model."
— *Written By*, the magazine of the Writers Guild of America, West

STEALING FIRE FROM THE GODS

THE COMPLETE GUIDE TO STORY FOR WRITERS AND FILMMAKERS

∼ 2ND EDITION ∼

BY

JAMES BONNET

GRAPHICS BY
RICHARD BRASSAW
AND
DIANE TABBAN BONNET

MICHAEL WIESE PRODUCTIONS

Published by Michael Wiese Productions
11288 Ventura Boulevard
Suite #621
Studio City, CA 91604
(818) 379-8799, (818) 986-3408 (FAX).
mw@mwp.com
www.mwp.com

Cover design by MWP
Interior design by William Morosi
Copyedited by Paul Norlen
Printed by McNaughton & Gunn

Manufactured in the United States of America
Copyright 2006

Library of Congress Cataloging-in-Publication Data

Bonnet, James, 1938-
 Stealing fire from the gods : the complete guide to story for writers and filmmakers / James
Bonnet.-- 2nd ed.
    p. cm.
Includes bibliographical references and index.
ISBN 10: 1-932907-11-4
ISBN 13: 978-1-932907-11-7
1. Motion picture authorship. 2. Narration (Rhetoric) I. Title.
PN1996.B66 2006
808.2'3--dc22
                          2006003996

To my wife, Diane.

Without her love and support there would be

no book and I would have no life.

To my lifelong friend, Edward Cerny.

He introduced me to the books and ideas that

created the dream and the journey.

To my mentors,

Paton Price, Archer King, and Vincent J. Donehue.

To my daughters, Jean and Beth,

and to my grandchildren,

Katie, James, Max, and Sam.

The love and joy we share

are little tastes of paradise.

THESE ARE THE MYSTERIES THAT MADE FAIRY
TALES AND MYTHS AND ALL THE GREAT CLASSICS
SO POWERFUL AND ENDURING — THE SECRETS
THAT MADE THE TOP GROSSING FILMS SO
SUCCESSFUL — AND THE PRINCIPLES THAT CAN
GUIDE YOU TO A PROFOUND UNDERSTANDING OF
STORY AND THE CREATIVE PROCESS AND A TRUE
MASTERY OF THE STORYMAKER'S ART.

Contents

PART FOUR:
THE ART OF STORYMAKING

FOREWORD TO THE SECOND EDITION

Considered by many top professionals to be the most definitive and comprehensive guide to all things related to story and storymaking, this expanded, completely revised, and long awaited second edition of *Stealing Fire from the Gods* incorporates many of the advances evolved in James Bonnet's professional workshops over the last five years. These include new revelations concerning the essence of story (that without which there would be no story), the high concept great idea, the structures of the whole story passage, the antihero's journey, the threat (the cause of the problem), the value being pursued, the ultimate source of unity, and the use of the quintessential to make your characters not only memorable and merchandisable but truly charismatic. It also contains a critical assessment of the three-act structure, many new and completely revised illustrations, and the analyses of many important new stories and successful films.

With this new, deeper understanding of story, you will know how to tap creative sources deep within yourself and have the tools to use modern metaphors to create powerful and entertaining stories that have a significant impact on the world.

FOREWORD

The knowledge contained in this book is a continuation of the work begun by Carl Jung and Joseph Campbell and will introduce you to an important new model of the human psyche called the Golden Paradigm which was brought to light by intriguing new patterns discovered hidden in great stories. These new patterns reveal all of the psychic dimensions, their structure, their hierarchy, their conflicts, and their goals. These psychological models become story models when they are used to create new stories and will not only teach you how to create contemporary stories that are significantly more successful and real than stories currently are, they will reveal important new details concerning how the conscious and creative unconscious minds can interact to form a creative partnership which is applicable not only to storymaking, but to many different art forms, and can bring powerful inner resources to light.

Stealing Fire from the Gods will also introduce you to a new phenomenon called the Storywheel which brings all the different types of story together into one, grand design. All great stories, ancient or modern, have a place on this wheel, and when taken together in this way, they reveal their deeper, more amazing secrets, not the least of which are all of the life cycles we experience from birth to death. The archetypes, patterns of action and cycles of transformation revealed in story are the same archetypes, patterns and cycles which run through every individual and every group, and are being played out in all of life's important stages. If you understand these patterns, you can understand the world, your place in the scheme, and the paths which can lead you to higher states of consciousness and success.

A knowledge of story and the act of storymaking are essential links in a creative process that can reconnect us to our lost or forgotten inner selves. An understanding of story leads inevitably to an understanding of these dormant inner states and to a perception of the path which can lead us back to who we were really meant to be. In short, a vast, unrealized potential exists within us which a knowledge of story and storymaking can help to make real.

Because it contains important new knowledge about story that is not available anywhere else and is relevant no matter what kind of story, true or fiction, you want to create for whatever medium, this book will be of particular interest to writers and filmmakers, and those whose livelihood depends on an understanding of what makes a story great or successful. Its special emphasis is on how the great myths and legends were really created and how contemporary stories with that kind of magic and power can be created again. Armed with this new, deeper understanding of story, there is no limit to the power and art that can be created through them. You will know how to tap powerful creative sources deep within yourself and have the tools to use modern metaphors to create stories as significant for today as *The Iliad* and the legends of King Arthur were for their times.

Stealing Fire from the Gods will also be of special interest to psychologists and mythologists. Some important new discoveries have been made in their fields, most notably concerning the new phenomena revealed by the cracking of story's symbolic code. The secrets of great stories, it turns out, are the secrets of the human mind. And the study of story is the study of this remarkable phenomenon. Every great story reveals some small piece of that magnificent mystery. Unlocking the secrets of story unlocks the secrets of the mind and awakens the power of story within you. Work with that power and you can steal fire from the gods. Master that power and you can create stories that will live forever.

PREFACE

When I first came to Hollywood as a young writer more than thirty years ago, I wanted to do something really significant with my talent. I wanted to create novels and films that had the quality of authors like Dostoyevski and Tolstoy. So after working as a writer in television for several years, I decided I was ready to put everything else aside and write my first novel. I figured it would take about six months.

Two years later, after working eight hours a day, seven days a week, I found myself on page 600 with no end in sight. And I had the uncomfortable feeling that despite an already acknowledged skill I possessed concerning character, structure, and suspense, it wasn't going to work. Eventually, I had to admit there was much more to creating a great story than I thought. And the problem lay with an understanding of story itself. What was a story, really? And why hadn't I asked myself that question before?

I began talking to some of the important writers in town about story and was surprised to discover that no one seemed to know what a story really was. It was just something that was taken for granted. It was a knack. Part of your gift. You either had it or you didn't.

I asked Danny Arnold, an important writer-producer in television, what a story was, and he said, "You know, there are only seven basic plots: boy meets girl, boy loses girl, and so on." That sounded promising, so I asked him what the other six were. He gave me a disconcerted look and said, "I don't know."

Finally convinced that the answers to the questions I was asking about story weren't out there, I began to study stories and films in earnest on my own and to monitor what worked.

The first thing I realized was that everything that "worked," worked because of an emotional response that was triggered in the audience. Story communicated by feelings. And the accumulation of those emotional responses was the basis of both entertainment and meaning.

The second thing I discovered was that structure had power. You could intensify the emotional response by how you arranged the incidents. The more dynamic the arrangement, the more powerful the emotional effect.

"My God," I thought, "there's something very important going on here. A story really is a kind of magic." I got very excited. I rushed back into the house from the office I had built in the garage and told my wife what I had discovered. She seemed to share my enthusiasm, and in a moment of great inspiration, I raised my fist and declared "I'm going to figure out what a story really is, if it takes me twenty years."

Twenty years later, after countless hours of hard work, when things had finally begun to jell, I reminded my wife of that conversation. She looked at me and said, "I wish you had said ten."

For years during and after that time, whenever I ran into Julie Epstein, who wrote *Casablanca* and a number of other great films, he always asked me the same question: "How is your long-suffering wife?" And that mainly had to do with this very long and uncertain period of our lives.

Story and storymaking are the most important and misunderstood art forms in the world today. Important because there is a desperate need for real stories which isn't being met, and misunderstood because no one seems to know what to do about it. What stories actually are, how and why they evolved, the purpose they serve, and the mechanics of their creation has been largely misunderstood. And if it was ever known, that knowledge, like the meaning of dreams, was lost and is just now being rediscovered. The importance of story and the role it was meant to play in our lives is far greater than anyone has realized.

The goal of Astoria Filmwrights, the research project I founded, is to help rediscover and reveal this lost knowledge. The purpose of this book is to show the general reader and the professional storymaker how they can use this knowledge of story to dramatically transform their own and other people's lives.

Among the stories analyzed in this book you will find many of the most important myths, legends, and fairy tales (*The Iliad, The*

Odyssey, the King Arthur stories, the Greek myths of Amor and Psyche or Prometheus, "Rumpelstiltskin," "Cinderella," and "Jack and the Beanstalk"). You will also find many of the most important plays and literary classics (*Othello, Hamlet, Death of a Salesman, Macbeth, A Christmas Carol, The Count of Monte Cristo*, and *A Thousand and One Nights*); many of the most important classic and critically acclaimed films (*Grapes of Wrath, Casablanca, On the Waterfront, Dracula, Schindler's List, The Silence of the Lambs, All the President's Men, The Pianist, The Verdict, Braveheart, The Wizard of Oz, Snow White, Ordinary People, Shakespeare in Love, The Sixth Sense, Groundhog Day, A Beautiful Mind*, and *The Lord of the Rings*); and most of the all-time box-office hits (*E.T., Star Wars, Titanic, Pretty Woman, The Godfather, Armageddon, Superman, Jurassic Park, Indiana Jones, Mulan, Toy Story, Back to the Future, Ghost, Jaws, Gladiator, Shrek*, and *Harry Potter*).

The one thing all of these old great stories, modern masterpieces, and all-time megahits have in common is the Golden Paradigm, the story model that was created from the secrets hidden in their flesh and bones.

INTRODUCTION

The great myths, legends, and fairy tales were created in oral traditions, in a wholly natural and instinctive way by a very special but subtle collaboration between our conscious and creative unconscious selves. This natural storymaking process was so dynamic, well established and innate, there was no need for anyone to consciously understand exactly how or why they were being created. They were useful or pleasant to retell and that's all that mattered. There was no need to understand the principles and the principles were not known. That only became important after individual authors began to make up stories on their own and write them down.

A knowledge of principles and a good story model become critical when you create a story consciously. The principles guide you toward the real needs of the audience and line you up with the creative unconscious so you're both shooting for the same thing. The story model acts as a conductor drawing powerful hidden wisdom to the surface. Without a good story model, you can't get creative unconscious cooperation and support. Without unconscious cooperation and support, you can't get that vital information programmed into your stories and they won't have any real power or meaning. Whatever your story model is, that's your limitation. You can't rise above it. If you think a story is only: boy meets girl, finding a treasure, or solving a crime — or worse yet, a three-act structure, conflict, and turning points — that's all you're going to get because that's all you're going to be shooting for. Every idea will be pressed into that one mold. The better your story model, the better your story because you can access and accommodate more of that vital information.

Without solid principles and a knowledge of what stories really are, you're like a sailor who sets out to sea without rudder or compass and has almost no chance of reaching his destination. It becomes a strictly hit or miss, random process, which is basically the situation we have today — a lot of mildly entertaining but empty stories being created by a small number of specialized and polarized story models that are based on the few, obvious dimensions that have been discovered. The stories they produce don't make a psychological connection, they lack hidden wisdom and truth, they have no real power, and they aren't really that entertaining. The few exceptions become instant, super hits.

In short, there are six billion people in the world who, from early childhood to old age, have a desperate need for real stories which isn't being met. The old great stories are not being replaced. The intelligence and wisdom needed to guide us through life's passages isn't getting through to us. We're cut off from it. And the world is in desperate trouble.

On the PBS series they did together, Bill Moyers asked Joseph Campbell if we can get along without myth. And Campbell replied very emphatically, "No, we can't. All you have to do is read the papers. It's a mess."

There is simply no way the current Hollywood system of development, which is built on misconceptions about story and entertainment and what the public really wants and needs, can ever meet this need. Literally thousands of screenplays and story ideas are submitted to Hollywood each year. Two thousand or more are actively developed; four hundred or so are actually produced; and fewer than ten, in my opinion, are worth seeing. The same is true of novels and plays. Something is obviously wrong.

What is wrong is you have an entire industry manufacturing something it doesn't understand — story. If they did that in Detroit — manufactured cars without a clue to their real purpose — it would be a joke. The motor would be in the back seat and the wheels would be in the trunk. You'd have chaos. You'd have Hollywood.

In any case, if you're a screenwriter or filmmaker, don't be intimidated by the numbers I quoted above. The vast majority of the screenplays and stories that are submitted to Hollywood are created by complete novices — mariners who are hopelessly lost at sea without rudder or compass. If you came to this book to get the principles and tools you need to create powerful, successful stories, I am going to put that knowledge into your hands and give you a realistic chance of realizing your storymaking dreams.

I do this, first of all, by teaching you how to emulate the natural creative storymaking process and put all of your conscious and unconscious creative powers into your work. I do that by teaching you the nature and purpose of story. This is the compass that will orient you toward the real needs and desires of the audience. And finally, by showing you how to use the creative process, the language of metaphor, and a sophisticated story model to bring powerful hidden truths to the surface — all without compromising in any way the things you really want to write about.

PART ONE

THE NATURE AND PURPOSE OF STORY

"From women's eyes this doctrine I derive:
They sparkle still the right Promethean fire:
They are the books, the arts, the ademes,
That show, contain, and nourish all the world"
Shakespeare, *Love's Labour's Lost*

CHAPTER 1

THE STORY OF THE TWO POTATOES

A long time ago in far-off India there was a merchant who lived in one of the northern provinces. He was very successful, but he was living in a dog eat dog world, not unlike our own, and was very unhappy.

"My God," he thought, "there has to be more to life than this."

So one day he went into the mountains to consult a famous guru who lived in one of the remote caves. And he asked the guru: "What is our true destiny?"

The guru was impressed by his sincerity and said, "I'm going to show you." And he handed the merchant two potatoes and added, "But you have to do exactly what I say."

The merchant was eager to proceed and the guru gave him his instructions. "Take these two potatoes to the little stream at the bottom of the hill outside this cave. Very carefully wash both potatoes and eat them. Then return to the cave."

The merchant took the two potatoes and went down the hill to the stream. He very carefully washed the first potato and ate it. But while he was washing the second potato, an old woman came out of the forest at that spot and approached him. She was obviously very poor. She told him a sad story and begged him for something to eat. He was deeply moved. He gave her the second potato and she ate it.

The merchant felt rather good about what he had done and hurried back up the hill to the cave to report the incident to the guru. But much to his surprise when he told the guru what had happened, the guru was very upset.

"I told you to eat both potatoes," he admonished harshly.

The poor merchant was astonished. "I know, but...."

"No buts," the guru interrupted. "You were supposed to do exactly as I said." And he got so angry that he ordered the merchant out of his sight. Extremely despondent, the merchant went down the mountain and returned to his village.

Two years passed, and near the end of that time the merchant started a new business which turned out to be much more successful than the first. In fact, he became one of the richest men in all India. Two more years passed and he met the most beautiful woman he had ever seen in his life. They fell in love and were married. They had seven beautiful and healthy children, and everything these remarkable children did was a source of great pleasure and pride to their parents.

The merchant was held in such high esteem that he was elected governor of the entire province and people came from all around to seek his advice. He lived to be 120 years old and considered himself a very fortunate and happy man indeed.

And that was just the first potato.

~   ~   ~

Story is about those two potatoes. Story *is* those two potatoes. Story is the wisdom that can guide you to your true destiny — both temporal and spiritual. All of the great myths, legends, and fairy tales have that power. If you understand their secrets, they can guide you to a full realization of your self.

Where did they get that extraordinary magic and power? How were they created? Can stories with that kind of magic and power ever be created again? I will answer all of these important questions in the first part of this book.

Great stories are created by powerful and mysterious inner processes. They are designed to guide us to our full potential and are as necessary to our well-being as fresh air. Understanding great stories means understanding these inner processes. And understanding these inner processes can lead to a profound understanding of our selves and the world.

CHAPTER 2

HOW THIS KNOWLEDGE WAS DEVELOPED

The whole truth about story is like a large circle with a hundred dimensions. Each of these dimensions is so powerful that many of them can be isolated and made into a successful story or story film even if all of the other major dimensions are more or less unrealized. Character is one of these dimensions. Action, structure (plot), imitations of real life, metaphor, suspense, horror, and ironic comedy are others. But there are many more. And a number of important filmmakers and novelists have created major successes by excelling in or perfecting just one or sometimes two of these powerful dimensions.

Eddie Murphy's use of character in *Beverly Hills Cop* is a good example. Like Charlie Chaplin and Woody Allen before him, Eddie Murphy is a man who understands the character he plays, and Axel Foley, the character he created in this film, is brilliantly conceived, containing many of the delightful attitudes and qualities we saw being developed on *Saturday Night Live*. But the picture falls short in just about every other important dimension. The action is contrived, the plot and imitations of real life are extremely weak, metaphor is practically nonexistent, it lacks real suspense, and so on. But still the movie was a major box office success — a testimony to the power of that one dimension, character.

A similar case can be made concerning Alfred Hitchcock's use of suspense, Stephen King's use of horror, Jim Abrahms' use of ironic comedy, the novelist Emile Zola's use of imitations of real life, Sylvester Stallone's use of action in *Rambo, First Blood*, George Lucas' use of structure and special effects in *Star Wars* and Steven Spielberg's use of metaphor and special effects in *Close Encounters of the Third Kind*.

In all of these cases you will find one or two dominant dimensions brilliantly executed while many of the other important dimensions are more or less unrealized, and still they all enjoyed a phenomenal success.

Now, I am not putting down these storymakers because their work lacked the other dimensions, I am just trying to make clear how incredibly powerful the individual story dimensions are.

For instance, the structure George Lucas used in *Star Wars*, which was, by his own admission, modeled after the formula outlined in Joseph Campbell's book *The Hero with a Thousand Faces*, is so powerful and universal, that despite a number of other weaknesses, it remains one of the most successful series of films ever made.

Similarly, in *Close Encounters* Steven Spielberg's use of the metaphor — benign forces coming from outer space — made such a profound psychological impact that it set the stage for Spielberg to become the most successful filmmaker of all time.

So these individual dimensions are powerful indeed.

The problem is that each time someone discovers one of these important dimensions the effects are so tremendous they tend to think they have discovered the whole truth about story and not just a part. So their thinking becomes circumspect and they end up specializing in those few dimensions, i.e. creating stories and films that revolve around character, action, adventure, suspense, comedy, horror, and so on, rather than creating stories that incorporate all of the dimensions.

The same thing is true on the theoretical side where a hundred different schools of thought have sprung up based on the different dimensions that have been discovered. This is true from Aristotle and John Dryden all the way to John Howard Lawson, Lajos Egri and Joseph Campbell. Here again, because of the extraordinary effect of the dimensions, they tend to regard the part they have discovered as the whole thing. Their thinking becomes polarized. And rather than realizing they each discovered something valuable, they end up attacking each other. The result is a large number of one-sided, incomplete, and faulty story models.

In contrast, my strategy has been to make my thinking as non-specialized and non-polarized as possible, and to bring together as much information from as many different fields as I could to create one grand, unified theory of story. I have tried to accomplish this by assuming that the whole truth about story was, in fact, like a large circle with at least a hundred dimensions, and that each of these other important ideas was one of the dimensions in that much larger circle. The models I created from this knowledge became my reference points. Then I would use these reference points to develop new information. Each time I discovered something new, the current model would be adjusted and that would create a new reference point.

Then in March of 1989 something rather extraordinary happened and one of these elements tumbled into the center and the rest began to constellate around it. When this transformation was complete, a new model, the Golden Paradigm, had emerged. Previous models, like those of Aristotle and Joseph Campbell, had been created by the observation of the things that all stories had in common. This new model was being created by those things plus their differences. And the new patterns revealed by these differences were not only the key to story but the key to some important secrets about life as well.

CHAPTER 3

WHY THE OLD GREAT STORIES WERE CREATED

The element that tumbled into the center was "change" — the fact that our lives, like everything else in the universe, are in a process of continual evolution and transformation. Story has an important role to play in helping to guide and regulate that change.

According to story (which is to say, according to the hidden meanings being revealed by these new patterns), we all possess a vast, unrealized potential. There is a path to that potential, and a creative unconscious force that uses great stories (and also dreams) to guide us along that path. In a former time (perhaps as long ago as the cave paintings in Europe), communication between our conscious selves and this creative unconscious force was apparently excellent, we made these special passages easily, and everything was great. Then something happened, the world took a turn for the worse and communication between us and this creative unconscious force was cut off. We lost touch with our selves. We lost touch with the real meaning of story and dreams and we got stuck somewhere far from our full potential. Our lives became much less meaningful and far more difficult.

All of this is revealed in story. And part of what I intend to teach in this book, besides how to become a significant storymaker capable of creating great stories, is how to use this knowledge to mend these broken connections and recover that vast potential.

The Vast Potential

Recounting our evolutionary path, we evolved from reptiles to mammals to primates to early man to *homo sapiens*, man the wise.

According to story, this evolutionary path proceeded in cycles, in a series of advances and declines. At the top of every up cycle there was a psychological surge and a psychological paradise was achieved. This psychological paradise was not a lost civilization like Atlantis, but a brief moment in history when all of the talents and powers that had been so painstakingly evolved up to that point were being fully realized. But also contained in this paradise were the seeds and flaws that would bring about another decline, an alienation from the higher spiritual, mental and emotional dimensions that had been achieved. The old paradise had to be shut down, taken apart and rebuilt in order to advance to a new higher one.

I will describe the mechanisms revealed in story which bring about these declines when we talk about the dynamics of the passage, but I will outline one example here.

Commensurate with having achieved the last major advance was a knowledge of agriculture. The application of this knowledge led to an abundance of food and a sedentary life, which led to overpopulation, which led to a fierce competition for resources, which led to warring states — a downside condition from which we are yet to recover. The pressures of that decline helped transform us from fully awakened and enlightened spiritual beings into egocentric, patriarchal warriors with little need for higher powers. Or so we thought.

Today we find ourselves at the tail-end of the latest downside cycle in an age which the Hindus call Kali Yuga, the age of alienation and discord. This is the society we have to conform to, so this is where we get stuck. What we could gain if we chose to recapture the rest of this evolutionary cycle is the vast potential. It is our unrealized mental, emotional, physical, and spiritual genius, our hidden talents, our higher consciousness, a profound capacity to love, our extraordinary but latent intuitive, creative, and healing powers. Our power to influence the world, transcend duality, experience ultimate truth. In short, our charisma — who we were really meant to be. It is what the Indian merchant would have achieved if he had eaten the second potato. We get little tastes and inklings of it throughout our lives. Little tingling sensations that creep up our spines and tell us there's something more to life than we're experiencing. Much more.

The Path

The path is the journey of our lives, the cycles of change and growth that are necessary to reach this vast potential. These emotional, psychological, and spiritual passages correspond roughly to our physical growth cycles from birth to death. They last from three to five years and involve us in certain essential activities. As children, there are certain things that have to be experienced, if we are to mature properly. Then, as we get older, we have to be educated, establish our careers, find suitable mates, raise a family, serve our community, serve our country, serve our God, and so on.

If we fail to make these passages successfully, which most of us do, there are serious consequences. We get stuck. We stop growing. We feel lost and unfulfilled. But if we succeed, the rewards are tremendous.

The wisdom necessary to make these passages successfully is buried like a treasure deep in the unconscious. Great stories bring that wisdom to consciousness. The information contained in great stories is all about these passages and how to make them in such a way that you can achieve these higher states of being.

Our Conscious Self

By our conscious self, I mean all of the things we are consciously aware of — our thoughts, our feelings, mental images, etc. The ego is the center of consciousness, and it performs the conscious functions — rational thinking, creative thinking, decision making, and so on. The ego is that which we usually refer to when we say "I." And it is the conscious part of us that needs to be guided and directed along the path. It is the hero of our personal stories.

Our Unconscious Self

The unconscious self is the creative unconscious force that would guide us, if we weren't cut off from it. It goes by a lot of different names. Carl Jung called it the self or the collective unconscious. Freud called it the super ego, the libido and the id. Erich Neumann called it the creative unconscious. Buddhists call it Buddha Consciousness. Religions call it the God within, the Holy Spirit, the Devil or the soul. George Lucas called the negative aspect the Dark Side and the positive aspect the Force. Obi-Wan Kenobi (Alec Guinness) in *Star Wars*, an agent of the Force, is without a doubt a metaphor for this guiding self.

I usually call it the creative unconscious. The unconscious has a positive and a negative side, but when they are both working together to build consciousness, the negative unconscious becomes a reluctant ally and the creative unconscious is formed. I like that concept, so I like that term. I call the content of the creative unconscious the hidden truth or the self.

According to Carl Jung, the hidden truth is the ancient wisdom that has been accumulating in our psyches since the beginning of evolution. And that is basically what I mean when I talk about our evolutionary path and unrealized potential — that a record of this evolutionary path has been kept and stored deep in the unconscious like a treasure. It is probably stored somewhere in the DNA. It may be a manifestation of the DNA itself.

Whatever it is, or whatever you call it, doesn't matter. It is the creative unconscious source of all of the higher, universal intelligence, wisdom and truth we possess. And one of its main functions is to guide us along the path that will transform this vast unconscious potential energy into a useful conscious energy — in short, to a full realization of our selves. This process expands, strengthens, and elevates consciousness. It is what so-called "higher" consciousness and enlightenment is about, and when creative people say they have tapped into the source, this is what they mean. This is the source.

Great stories and dreams, as I said, are two important ways the creative unconscious self communicates its hidden knowledge to consciousness.

But why great stories and dreams?

Great stories and dreams are visual metaphors. They are symbolic languages. And the creative unconscious self uses these visual metaphors to express its hidden wisdom to consciousness.

The creative unconscious and its hidden treasure exist in the brain as energy. To be experienced consciously, this raw energy has to be translated into a form which the conscious mind can assimilate and understand. The forms of choice which the creative unconscious uses are feelings (which we'll talk about when we talk about the creative process) and the visual languages of fantasy, story, and dream.

There's nothing mysterious about this process. The brain is doing this all the time. It's a basic brain function. It's the way we see, for instance. When we look at an object like a person or a tree, photoelectric energy is reflected off that object, enters the eye, travels along the optic nerve, and is translated back into a visual image in the visual cortex of the brain. The creative unconscious simply utilizes this image-making mechanism to express itself to consciousness.

"Myths and dreams," according to Joseph Campbell, "are manifestations in image form (metaphors) of all of the energies of the body, moved by the organs, in conflict with each other."

In the movie *Star Man*, forgotten by most, but worth viewing for just one reason, you can see an excellent metaphor for this process. At the beginning of the film a bright ball of alien energy reaches the Earth from outer space, enters a house and, using a photograph from a family album, transforms itself into the dead husband of the lonely widow who lives in the house. This is a perfect metaphor for what I'm describing. The widow, like our conscious selves, could not relate to the alien in its energy form. So the alien, like the unconscious energy, translates itself into a form the widow can relate to and deal with, i.e. an image of her dead husband. The creative unconscious does exactly this when it translates its energy into a fictional visual form made up of everyday things we can consciously relate to and interpret.

I'll give you two simple examples. The first is a dream.

A year or two after Diane and I settled in Los Angeles, we were living in a small house in Studio City. I haunted the used book stores in the neighborhood and one day discovered a series of monographs by Jay Hambridge called *Dynamic Symmetry*. The premise of these monographs was that the extraordinary beauty achieved by the early Greeks in their art and architecture was due to a golden proportion which was based on a natural progression of numbers. The natural progression of numbers was found in nature and governed the distribution of leaves, the seeds of a sunflower, and the proportions of the human body. Called the Fibonacci series after the man who first described it, it begins with the number 1 and the next number in the series is formed by the addition of the two previous numbers: 1, 1, 2, 3, 5, 8, 13, 21, 34, 55, 89, and so on. I could find these special number ratios in the distribution of leaves and in the sunflower (34 counter-clockwise spirals overlaid by 55 clockwise spirals overlaid by 89 counter-clockwise spirals) but for the life of me I couldn't fathom where they were in the human body. It obsessed me like a riddle I couldn't solve. I fell asleep one night pondering this puzzle and had this dream. A muscular right arm reached into the darkness of the dreamscape and, slowly bending at each joint, formed this pattern and revealed that it was the bone lengths of the arm, hand, and finger digits that contained this golden proportion. Needless to say I was astounded that the unconscious mind had this ability to give me such a direct answer.

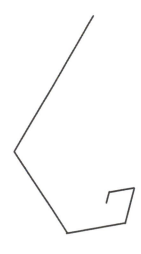

The second example is a story which I've known about since my mother began telling it to me when I was four or five years old. But I was well into my forties before I realized the hidden truth being communicated by this remarkable tale had to do with how these lost or unrealized potentials can be recovered.

JACK AND THE BEANSTALK

Jack lives with his mother in a remote valley and they are very poor. So poor, in fact, they have to sell the very thing they're living off — the family cow. And Jack's mother entrusts her son with that very important task.

On the way to town, he meets a man who offers to trade the cow for some magic beans. Jack is excited by the prospect of owning magic beans, so the deal is made, and he rushes home to tell his mother.

"Ma, Ma, look what I got for the cow." And he holds out his hand to show her the magic beans.

Not surprisingly, the poor woman is very upset. Any fool can see they're just ordinary beans. She grabs the beans, throws them out the window, sends the boy to bed without any dinner, and has a good cry.

In the morning when Jack wakes up, he discovers a remarkable thing. Outside the window, where his mother threw the beans, an enormous beanstalk has appeared during the night and grown all the way up to the sky. Jack climbs to the top of the beanstalk and discovers a gigantic house sitting on top of the clouds. He knocks on the door and it is opened by the giant's wife. He relates what happened and asks for something to eat. The giant's wife is sympathetic and offers to feed him, but on the way to the kitchen she warns him to be careful because her husband, the giant, likes to eat little boys like him for breakfast. And sure enough, while he's sitting at the kitchen table eating some porridge, he hears the giant approaching and exclaim: "Fee Fie Fo Fum, I smell the blood of an Englishman."

Jack panics and hides in the cupboard, just narrowly escaping detection and certain death.

The giant enters the kitchen. He looks around, sees nothing suspicious and relaxes. Then he takes several large sacks of gold from his hiding place of treasures, sits at the kitchen table to count his gold, and eventually falls asleep. Jack sees his chance, sneaks out of the cupboard, grabs the sacks of gold, and makes his escape down the beanstalk.

Jack and his mother share the gold with the other poor people in the valley, and for awhile everything is all right, but eventually the money runs out. So Jack makes a couple of more trips up the beanstalk. He gets the goose that lays the golden eggs and the magic harp. The last time the giant wakes up and almost catches him. There's a desperate chase, but Jack gets to the bottom of the beanstalk first. He chops it down and the giant falls to his death.

And so ends "Jack and the Beanstalk," the encoded message creative unconscious self.

The treasures — the bags of gold, the goose that lays the golden eggs, the magic harp — are the "manifestations in image form," representing some of the lost potential I've been talking about, and the story is a simple blueprint showing us how this lost potential (these lost inner psychic treasures) can be recovered by the skillful use of the creative imagination. It begins with a creative inspiration, represented by the magic beans. Jack is inspired by the idea of possessing magic. This creative inspiration leads to a nonconformist, impractical act — he sells the practical cow. The impractical act leads to consequences, the heat he gets from his mother. These consequences lead to isolation; he is sent to his room without any dinner. The isolation and hunger lead to the awakening of the creative imagination, the beanstalk. The creative imagination, which can bridge the gap between the conscious and unconscious worlds, puts him in touch with his creative unconscious self and the chance to recover some of that lost, unrealized potential, but it involves taking certain risks, and he has to confront, outwit, and destroy a big ugly giant to do it. The big ugly giant represents the negative energies which keep the potential treasures captive and prevent their easy recovery.

If you are an artist and you follow a real creative inspiration to its fulfillment, you will discover this trail. The creative inspiration will stimulate your imagination and make you aware of other worlds hidden in your soul. You will realize, if you are to be truly happy, there are other important things that have to be accomplished in life besides just making money. This will lead you to impractical acts. You will want to quit law school and go to Paris to study art, New York to study music, or Hollywood to break into film. These impractical acts will lead to consequences, the disapproval you are going to get from your parents, your spouse, or other well-meaning, interested parties. Whenever you try to step away from the mainstream, there will be conflict and resistance. These consequences can lead to alienation and isolation and you may find yourself alone in a garret in Greenwich Village or San Francisco with nothing to eat. Alone and hungry, your creative imagination will bridge the gap between the conscious and creative unconscious worlds (isolation, meditation, and fasting are well known avenues to the creative unconscious). Then if you have the courage to pursue these creative adventures, despite the difficulties, you can confront your ogres (negative energies) and one by one recover all of these lost treasures, until finally in the end all of these negative energies have been transformed and you have filled up the lost and missing parts of your self.

All of this is revealed in that simple story. It's a realistic look at what you will constantly face, if you choose a life of art, the good news and the bad. And if you reread the story with that in mind, you will realize it was always there waiting for you to discover its secret meanings. It is a special mirror that lets you look into your own soul. A story that can do that has real power and can live forever.

Great stories, then, are like collective dreams. They originate in the creative unconscious and have the same relation to society as a whole that the dream has to the individual. They both utilize the same archetypal symbols, but the meanings hidden in great stories are universal, whereas the meanings hidden in dreams are usually personal.

CHAPTER 4

HOW THE OLD GREAT STORIES WERE CREATED

Now, if the creative unconscious used these great stories to communicate with us, then it must have participated in their creation. And so it did. These old great stories, which really could change people's lives, were not authored by individuals the way stories are today but were evolved naturally and instinctively by unconscious processes in oral traditions. And whether or not they started out as made-up or true stories, revelations or dreams, they still ended up for long periods of time in oral traditions and that became the principal dynamic behind their creation.

The process goes something like this: It begins with a real or imagined incident or event that is worth repeating, something so intriguing that we're compelled to repeat it. It is passed along by word of mouth, from person to person and from generation to generation until it's been told and retold millions of times and exists in a hundred different versions around the world.

Each time the story is retold it changes. This is due to certain natural but curious tendencies of the mind — the tendency, for instance, to remember things that make a strong impression and to forget things that don't impress us very strongly. There is also a tendency to exaggerate or minimize, to glorify or ennoble, to idealize or vilify. Beyond that, there's a natural, unconscious tendency to analyze things, to take them apart and put them back together in different combinations (recombination), and a natural tendency to simplify or edit. The tendency to conserve energy in nature is very strong in everything we do, including how we organize and store our thoughts and memories. These are all things we're very aware of.

We've all heard about the three-foot-long fish someone caught that was, in reality, barely twelve inches, or seen someone make a minor problem seem like the end of the world, or recall something that was truly horrendous as being no big deal. Or we become convinced that someone we knew back then was a genius, a world-class athlete, the most beautiful girl in the world. I had a distant relative pass away who was, in reality, something of a bastard. But after his death, only the good things were being remembered and everyone began to believe he was one of the nicest guys that ever lived. Shakespeare reminds us that the opposite is also true. In *Julius Caesar* he tells us: "The evil men do lives after them, the good is oft interred with their bones." Hitler would be an obvious example. If he ever did a decent thing in his life, you're never going to hear about it. He's been completely and justifiably vilified.

We experience these curious tendencies constantly. They are a significant part of our everyday lives. We all know how hard it is to get a story straight or accurately remember something we've been told, or even experienced, if it hasn't been written down. You tell someone close to you something exciting that happened (an incident worth repeating) and when you hear it repeated later that week or even later that day it's been severely changed. It's the cause of many serious misunderstandings. Well, you can imagine what happens to a story that has spent hundreds of years in an oral tradition. It has been thoroughly and completely changed.

There have been numerous experiments documenting this phenomenon. I saw one not long ago on PBS on one of their science programs. In this particular experiment, twenty children were lined up on stage. A story was whispered into the ear of the first child and she was told to repeat it. She whispered it to the boy next to her and he whispered it into the ear of the girl next to him, and so on. Then everyone laughs when they hear the last child's version because of the way it's been completely changed.

The important thing to remember here is that these are unconscious, instinctual processes. These old great stories were being created by the creative unconscious mind, with the unwitting cooperation of the conscious mind, of course. The creative unconscious seized the incident worth repeating and slowly over time, using these curious tendencies, helped the storyteller sculpt it into a marvelous story that contained powerful bits of that hidden truth. No one actually had to do anything consciously but repeat the story. And even if there was conscious involvement (i.e. the desire to use the story to instruct or entertain or even to change it), those desires and changes were prompted by feelings, insights, and various other forms of inspiration, which originated in the unconscious, so the end result would be the same.

We can see how this works if we look at certain important historical figures and examine how the real incidents which surrounded their lives and were worth repeating were evolved by oral traditions into marvelous and even miraculous tales that contained important bits of this hidden truth.

The first involves Achilles and the Trojan wars. While there is no historical record of these events, most scholars, and most people for that matter, believe there really was a place called Troy and a war between the Greeks and the Trojans which took place on the western shores of Turkey some time around 1200 B.C. Many important archaeologists, Heinrich Schliemann among them, have devoted their lives to discovering the sites of these ancient events.

The real Trojan war, then, was the incident worth repeating, and Achilles, the greatest warrior fighting on the Greek side, was the Audie Murphy of his day (Audie Murphy being the most decorated soldier in World War II). It is controversial whether someone named Homer, the accredited author of *The Iliad* and *The Odyssey*, the famous legendary accounts of these wars, actually existed, but assuming he did, the true story of the Trojan war had already spent four hundred years in the oral tradition before he put his poetic stamp on it, and another three or four hundred years in the oral tradition after his contribution before it was actually written down. In that time it had evolved from the real incidents worth repeating into a truly miraculous tale in which the swift-footed Achilles has become the nearly immortal and invincible son of Thetis, a sea goddess — all of the other gods, including Zeus, have taken sides and are playing active roles in the war, and all manner of miraculous things are occurring. These immortal characters and miraculous occurrences have a psychological significance which goes far beyond anything a factual account of the real incidents could ever have conveyed. They do, in fact, reveal an excellent picture of the human psyche in transformation. And, more specifically, the consequences of anger on that transformation. All things we would have difficulty finding in a real account of that war.

Alexander the Great is another good subject to study in this regard because there is both a good historical record in the West as well as a rich tradition of legends in the East. In the West there are no real legends because there was always the real historical record standing as a reference to contradict them. But in the fabulous East, in places like India and Persia, where there was no historical record, he entered the oral tradition and all manner of fanciful and legendary stories evolved — "Alexander Searches for the Fountain of Youth," "Alexander Explores the Bottom of the Sea," and so on. These legendary stories, shaped and molded by these unconscious processes, contain the hidden wisdom we spoke of which the history does not. The historical record reveals reality, the legends that evolved in, and were sculpted by, the oral traditions contain the hidden, inner truth. The Fountain of Youth, for instance, like the goose that lays golden eggs, is another "manifestation in image form" (metaphor) of the lost potential. And Alexander's legendary adventures, like Jack's, are treasure maps that can, if followed, lead to its recovery.

King Arthur is another interesting case. Many scholars believe that this legendary English king was evolved from a real general named Arturis. General Arturis lived in the 5th century A.D. and won ten consecutive battles against the Saxons before he was finally killed. If these scholars are correct, then after only five or six hundred years in the oral tradition this real general Arturis had been transformed into the legendary King Arthur who wielded a magic sword named Excalibur, consorted with a sorcerer named Merlin, founded Camelot, established the Round Table, and sent his chivalrous knights on a quest for the Holy Grail. And, here again, like *The Iliad* and "Jack and the Beanstalk," the legends surrounding King Arthur have a great deal to tell us about our inner selves, our vast potential, and our true destinies, while the brief historical record of General Arturis has probably had very little effect on any of our lives.

The curious tendencies of the mind that drive this natural storymaking process, and which we tend to regard as shortcomings, turn out to be the artistic tools of the imagination. And the creative unconscious used these tools to create these great stories. This vital information was being programmed into them bit by bit with each of these changes. The tellers of stories were only having fun, but, in fact, they were helping to create and then pass this information along. And this is where these old great stories get their power. These little bits of hidden truth have real power and charisma.

Myths are stories that have evolved to such an extent that the truth they contain has become so charismatic and obvious that religions are formed around them. All of the great religions have mythological stories as their justification and the source of their truth.

There is no better example of this than Moses and Jesus. Again, no historical record, but most people believe, or are willing to concede, that a real historical Moses and Jesus did in fact exist. After six hundred years in the oral tradition Moses was turning staffs into serpents and performed any number of other miracles for the edification of the Pharaoh including the parting of the Red Sea. And after only forty to eighty years in the oral tradition, Jesus had become the result of a virgin birth, performed countless miracles, and rose from the dead. There's no way to calculate what effect a factual record of the real events surrounding these important figures might be having on our lives, but it's safe to say there have been very few things in life that have had a greater effect on the world than the miraculous stories that evolved from those real events.

It is, in fact, the function of religion to utilize the truth revealed in these great stories to help guide their charges back to their original nature. Religion, when it is not corrupt, is a conscious, organized effort to get people to go back up this path and they get their marching orders from stories. Instead of calling it individuation (Jung's term for the full realization of the self) or reaching your full potential, they call it recovering your lost innocence or reunion with God.

It may also be worth noting here that when the real incidents that were worth repeating entered the oral tradition and evolved into myths and legends, they became not less true, but more true, because now they contained some powerful bits of the hidden truth. The real incidents as they evolve become less reflective of the outer circumstances and more reflective of the hidden, inner reality. I leave it to the individual to decide which they think is more important.

CHAPTER 5

WHY THE OLD GREAT STORY TAKES THE FORM THAT IT DOES

The purpose of great stories, then, is to guide us to our full potential. Now let's talk about the nature of story — why the old great story takes the form it does and why its secrets have to be concealed.

The ego that would be guided through these passages presents the creative unconscious self with some pretty thorny problems, the principal one being it simply doesn't want to go through them. We have an incredibly strong, built-in resistance to change. In most cases, we would much rather hold on to some pleasant (or even unpleasant) current situation than give up everything and venture into the unknown. Real life is a serious and deadly game. It involves taking significant risks and facing unpleasant realities and truths.

Someone once asked a buddha about these truths and the buddha showed him a bowl of worms and said: "If you would understand these truths, then you would have to eat this bowl of worms."

The man shuddered with disgust and walked away. The point of the story being, of course, that the truths we have to face in life are sometimes like eating a bowl of worms. They can be that unpleasant.

Two days after I was thinking of using that little story in the seminars I was preparing, I had this dream: I was riding in the back of a convertible. We were approaching a crossroads and there was something there which I didn't want to see, so I covered my face with my hands and said: "No, no. I don't want to look." But then, to my credit, I peeked through my fingers, anyway, and this is what I saw.

There was a dinky little RV sitting at the crossroads. On the side of the RV, where the utilities are usually plugged in, there were four very organic looking holes. And while I was watching, a dozen or so very fat six-foot worms came sliding out of these holes onto the ground.

I woke up in a cold sweat. And it took several hours before I realized what the dream meant. The journey I was about to commence (i.e. taking the knowledge of story I had discovered to market) wasn't going to be a pleasant one. I could see that in the dream because I don't like traveling in RVs, especially this type, which was really just a pick-up truck with a small aluminum camper on it. And, furthermore, the worms I was going to have to swallow on this journey weren't itty bitty little worms like in the buddha's bowl, they were big fat ones that were six feet long. It's not the kind of thing you look forward to.

So we are reluctant to make these passages and we have to be lured or pushed into the process. The strategy that the creative unconscious uses to lure us is the same ingenious strategy nature always uses when it teaches. It covers its medicine with a sugar coat. It hides all of the secret wisdom and purpose of story in an irresistible package with a sugar coat. The sugar coat in story is, of course, the entertainment dimensions. And the recipient doesn't even know what's happening — like a mother secretly hiding vitamin pills in her child's Twinkie.

You can see this strategy very clearly in children's games, and for this reason they are very much like a great story. Games are fun to play and that's why children love to experience them, but they have an important and secret underlying purpose, i.e. to exercise the physical body, develop social skills, etc. In other words, they have an important purpose which the child is not aware of and a sugar coat. The sugar coat lures the child into the experience and he or she becomes better prepared for life while having fun. If you take the fun out of the game, the child loses interest. If you take the entertainment out of the story, the same thing happens. We lose interest.

Sex is another obvious example of nature's use of this strategy. We are lured into the experience by a seductive sugar coat (the promise of romance and pleasure), but the real, underlying purpose has to do with procreation and the continuation of the species.

Motherhood is another example. Women are lured into the experience by some very pleasant maternal instincts, then find out about morning sickness and teenagers later on, when it's too late to change their minds.

In all of these examples you will find a sugar coat (i.e. the promise of fun, fulfillment, or pleasure) that lures the person into an experience that has an important but hidden underlying purpose. In short, when nature wants something to happen, it doesn't rely on our having good judgment or common sense. It uses the promise of fun and pleasure to get the job done without any hassle.

The movie *Fatal Attraction* can give you a hint of how this process might work in a modern film. We were lured into the theatre by the promise of a great entertainment — a safe terror. That was the word-of-mouth on this picture. "You've got to see this movie. It is *so* scary." That was the sugar coat. Then we came out of the theatre with some very unsettling feelings about having affairs, as if there was a hidden message warning us of danger.

CHAPTER 6

HOW THE GREAT STORY DOES ITS WORK

The purpose of story, then, is to guide us to our full potential and the nature of story is to conceal that purpose in an enticing sugar coat that lures us into the experience. But if the purpose is concealed then how does it do its work?

The great story does its work in five important ways.

First, it stimulates our imaginations by provoking personal fantasies which lead to the desire for actions in the real world. Then it gives us a taste, by way of a special feeling, of what it might be like if we were actually to make one of these passages and accomplish some of these things.

When a young girl hears *Sleeping Beauty* for the first time, delicious feelings are awakened which that child has never felt before, and she begins to have fantasies about meeting a real Prince Charming of her own. And when the Prince kisses the Sleeping Beauty and she wakes up, the child feels a sensation which is like a taste of paradise — a taste of what it would feel like if this really happened to her. She wants that feeling again in real life. She longs for it and pursues it in life as a dream.

The same thing happens when we experience a story like *Lost Horizon*. Shangri-la, like paradise, Utopia, or any promised land, is another metaphor for the higher states of consciousness and bliss that can be realized. When we encounter these images in a story, we get chills and other special feelings which can convince us that such lofty places or spiritual states of mind actually exist and can be achieved. We long to experience those feelings and states again and pursue them in life as a goal.

Carl Jung explains it this way: "The auditor experiences some of the sensations but is not transformed. Their imaginations are stimulated: they go home and through personal fantasies begin the process of transformation for themselves."

And all of this happens automatically. The story recipient need not be consciously aware that the story is intentionally trying to influence and guide them.

Having lured us into the adventure by fantasies and a taste, the great story then provides us with a road map or treasure map, which outlines all of the actions and tasks we have to accomplish in order to complete one of these passages, and a tool kit for solving all of the problems that have to be solved to accomplish the actions and tasks. Every great story will divulge a little more of this truth, and bit by bit each step of the passage is revealed. Again, all of this is going on without the story recipient's conscious knowledge that it's happening.

How does it do that? By meaningful connections. If it's a great story, we will remember it, and, over time, we will make meaningful associations and connections with our real-life situations.

A lawyer friend of mine was recently telling me about a difficult case in which he was involved, and how he had suddenly realized why it was so difficult. He was acting quixotically. He was fighting windmills. Acting quixotically and fighting windmills, of course, comes from *Don Quixote*. Without even realizing it, my lawyer friend had suddenly made a meaningful connection with his real life situation. And once making that connection and having that realization, he was able to resolve the difficulty. He wasn't even aware that it was happening, that the metaphor in *Don Quixote*, which he hadn't read since college, was there waiting for him when he needed it.

Another friend came to me after seeing *Groundhog Day* and confessed, "This is my life. I'm constantly reliving the same day." A third friend confided he was like the beast in *Beauty and the Beast*. These are meaningful connections. And, if you will take the trouble to study them, you will find they are also providing you with the solutions to these very common problems. These lessons learned, we can transform ourselves back into princes and real human beings.

The more hidden truth the story contains, the more appealing it will be, the more relevant it will be to our lives, and the more likely we are to remember it. We'll cherish and work with it all of our lives, then we'll pass it on to our children.

No one story, as I've said, contains the whole truth. The process is accumulative. Each story contributes a little bit of this vital information. We can be affected by many different stories at the same time. We relate them to our lives when and if we need them and make the necessary course corrections.

It was more than thirty years from the time I first heard "Rumpelstiltskin" until I realized that the secrets hidden in that marvelous tale were about the creative process and how the mind is organized.

In "Rumpelstiltskin" and many stories like it, some endangered young girl or princess has to perform some impossible task like transforming a pile of straw into gold by morning or she'll lose her head. Then some miraculous helper like Rumpelstiltskin comes to her rescue and accomplishes the task for her while she sleeps.

Being a writer, I would often fall asleep at night worrying about certain difficult story problems I hadn't been able to solve during that work day. And just as often a marvelous solution to those problems would pop into my head as I was waking up the following morning. Naturally, I wondered who or what was solving those problems.

Suddenly, one day I made the connection. "My God," I exclaimed, "It's Rumpelstiltskin!" The miraculous little helper was a metaphor, a personification in image form of some unconscious problem-solving mechanism. The secret hidden in the marvelous story had something important to reveal about the creative process and how our minds function. Namely, that inside our minds there is an unconscious problem-solving mechanism (a Rumpelstiltskin) that continues to work, and transform our serious problems (the straw) into precious insights (the gold) while our conscious minds are asleep. Another little piece of the puzzle had been revealed.

And, finally, the great story guides this whole process with incredible insights and wisdom.

In *A Christmas Carol*, when the Ghost of Christmas Future is showing Scrooge his own tombstone, the kneeling, pathetic, nearly repentant Scrooge asks him: "Are these things that will be or things that may be?" The answer to that question, and the point of the whole story, is that these are things that "will be," if he does nothing, and things that "may be," if he does something about it, if he repents and changes his character. If he changes his character, he will change his future. In other words, at any given moment we have a certain destiny. And, if we're not content with that destiny, we can do something about it. We can transform our futures by transforming ourselves. If we change who we are, if we awaken our humanity, we can change our destiny. That's good news.

Believe it or not there's something similar and equally profound in the movie *Back to the Future*. Having seen *Back to the Future, Part II*, and having no desire to see *Part III*, I have concluded the profundity in the first film got there by accident, but nevertheless, it's there.

At the beginning of the story, we meet Michael J. Fox and his family. They're living in a hovel of mediocrity and despair. His mother is an alcoholic and his rather pathetic father a serious wimp and miserable failure.

When Michael J. Fox gets involved in his time machine adventure, he becomes entangled in the lives of his parents when they are still in high school, on the very day that they met. And they met in a curious way. His clumsy, painfully shy father was hit by a car in front of his mother's house while lurking there, trying to catch a glimpse of her. She took him into her house to nurse him back to health and fell in love with him out of pity. When Michael J. Fox arrives on the scene a moment before his father, he is hit by the car, and his mother falls in love with him instead.

He now has a very big problem. He has to make his mother fall out of love with him and in love with his geeky, future father or he isn't even going to exist. He accomplishes this one evening when his mother is being molested in the front seat of a car by the town bully. Fox goads his father into rescuing her, in the process of which, the father knocks out the bully with a lucky punch and his mother is saved. The mother immediately transfers her love from her future son to her new hero.

Now, that in itself is profound because it says that a love inspired by heroic deeds is stronger than a love brought on by pity. But there's more. When Fox gets back to the present, everything about the lives of his family has miraculously changed. His mother is no longer an alcoholic, his father is a big success and a real dude, and they're living in a magnificent, creatively appointed house — all because of that one change in the father's character.

The important bit of wisdom has to do with the incredible difference one courageous act can make on our lives. Standing up to that bully had an extraordinary and profound effect far into the future. We encounter numerous such challenges and opportunities to show our courage every day. The phone call we're afraid to make to ask for a date or a job. Little acts of courage that could be profoundly and irrevocably changing the rest of our lives. That's also very useful to know.

One final example. In a fairy tale called "Aga Baba," a young hero on an important adventure stops to rest at a witch's house. The witch, in cahoots with his enemies, tries to delay him by asking him some intriguing but difficult questions, like "What is truth?" "Does the universe ever end?" and so on. The wise young hero looks at her and says: "Shut up and get me something to eat."

The wisdom in this story is simple enough: Beware of imponderables when action is necessary. Don't while away the time worrying about infinity or other unanswerable questions when you should be out looking for a job.

So there you have three important bits of advice: change yourself and you change your destiny; little acts of courage performed today can have exponential effects on the rest of your life; and beware of imponderables when action is necessary.

Here again it's accumulative, each story contributing a little bit more of the hidden truth. When you've got a hundred such bits of wisdom working for you, it will give you a tremendous advantage.

So that's how the great stories do their work. They stimulate our imaginations and give us little tastes of paradise. These trigger fantasies, which lead us to desires for actions in the real world. Then, as we pursue these goals, the stories guide us through the passages using meaningful connections, each story revealing a little bit more of the hidden truth.

CHAPTER 7

HOW THIS NATURAL STORYMAKING PROCESS WAS CUT OFF

So what happened to this natural storymaking process? Why was it cut off? Why are stories with this kind of power only rarely, or accidentally, being created?

While I would be the last person to attack the virtues of the written word, the fact remains that when these old great stories were finally written down, a serious thing happened. They stopped changing and evolving. They stopped growing. This natural creative process came to a dead stop.

I have a copy of *Grimm's Fairy Tales* on my bookshelf. The stories in that book haven't changed in well over a hundred years, not since the Brothers Grimm took them out of the oral tradition and wrote them down. The Old Testament on my bookshelf hasn't changed in over twenty-five hundred years. In time these stories lose their relevance and their effectiveness. They still contain the same wisdom, if you take the trouble to hunt for it, but the average person no longer sees their relevance because the metaphors haven't been kept up to date. So they don't easily get the message. The knowledge they need to make these journeys is lost to them.

If "Cinderella," for instance, had remained in the oral tradition, it would have evolved into a modern, contemporary story like *Pretty Woman*, and people could see more easily how it relates to their lives.

Now, it is, in fact, true that this evolutionary process continues on today in a modified form. There have been dozens of different, written versions of "Cinderella," and Hollywood is constantly remaking or updating old movies, many of which are based on stories that originally came out of the oral tradition, but this represents only minor increments of change. And, furthermore, because of Hollywood's bias toward entertainment only, the stories are corrupted rather than advanced, their hidden wisdom is polluted or leached out rather than being enhanced or intensified. As a result they lose most of their power and meaning. Disney's *Snow White*, *Pinocchio*, *Aladdin* and *Beauty and the Beast* seem like happy exceptions. So, if the natural creative storymaking process is not, in fact, dead, it is very nearly so and desperately needs resuscitation.

My solution to this problem, as I mentioned earlier, involves teaching you how to emulate the natural creative storymaking process and put all of your conscious and unconscious creative powers into your work. I do this primarily by showing you how to use the creative process, the language of metaphor and a sophisticated story model to bring powerful hidden truths to the surface.

There are four great secrets hidden in this book. And this is the first: The author of the great myths and legends is inside you. And I don't mean that figuratively, I mean it literally. The intelligence and wisdom that created those old, great stories is inside you. You can get in touch with that source and make that precious knowledge and the power that goes with it come alive in your work. And, if you combine that power with a contemporary realism and character, you can create superpowerful stories that have a significant impact on the world. And you can make yourself very successful and perhaps even whole in the process.

PART TWO

THE SECRET LANGUAGE OF GREAT STORIES

"The poet's eye, in a fine frenzy rolling,
Doth glance from heaven to earth, from earth to heaven;
And, as imagination bodies forth
The forms of things unknown, the poet's pen
Turns them to shapes, and gives to airy nothing
A local habitation and a name."

Shakespeare, *A Midsummer Night's Dream*

CHAPTER 8

THE METAPHORS

As I indicated earlier, metaphor is the symbolic language that expresses the wisdom hidden in the creative unconscious self. And we'll use that hidden wisdom as a reference point.

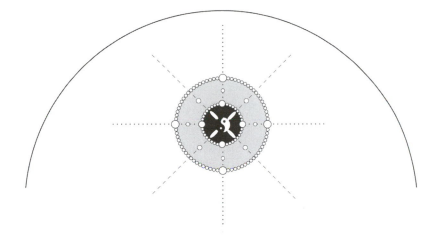

This hidden wisdom exists as raw energy and in order to be communicated to consciousness, it has to be translated into visual images — i.e. the characters, places, actions and objects, etc. that you actually encounter in a great story. These visual images are called metaphors. Metaphor literally means to "carry over," to substitute one thing for another. To describe one thing by means of another. To describe something that is unknown by the use of things that are known. In this case, to use everyday, visible, real things to describe (or express) these invisible, unconscious energies. And this is the second great secret revealed in this work, namely, that metaphors are made of real things that have been taken apart and artistically rearranged to represent these hidden truths.

For example: a certain Chinese dragon which represents some of these unconscious creative energies is made up of bits and pieces from a variety of other real animals. It has the head of a camel, the horns of a deer, the eyes of a rabbit, the teeth of a lion, the ears of a cow, the neck of a snake, the belly of a frog, the scales of a carp, the claws of a hawk, and the padded palms of a tiger. The same is true of Superman, Dracula, the time machine in *Back to the Future*, and the Hindu god, Shiva. They are all made up of bits and pieces of a variety of other real things that have been taken apart and artistically treated.

Superman wears a blue leotard and tights, a red cape, swim trunks and boots — all common everyday things put together in an unusual, rarely seen combination. And that gives them their other worldly character. He has X-ray vision. X-rays and vision are two real things that are combined here artistically to create a superhuman power. He can fly faster than a speeding bullet, leap over tall buildings in a single bound, and he has superhuman strength. Flying, leaping, and strength are all common everyday things which in this case have been greatly exaggerated — exaggeration being one of the important artistic treatments that help to reveal the hidden truth.

Dracula has a serpent's fangs. He sucks blood like a vampire bat. He can transform himself into a wolf or a bat. He sleeps in a coffin filled with Transylvanian dirt. His eyes turn a lurid red when he is excited or angry. He can only be killed if a wooden stake is driven through his heart or he's exposed to the sun. All everyday things in a unique combination.

The time machine in *Back to the Future* is a DeLorean car and a unique collection of artistically treated real parts.

The Hindu god, Shiva, is associated with the linga (phallus) and fire. Both everyday things. The real things that create these metaphors already have meanings attached to them which are the result of long association. And when they are artistically treated, they bring these qualities along. Fire means everything fire is and does. Fire is a source of light and heat that can be either creative or destructive. When fire is used metaphorically, as a symbol, it can mean any or all of these things. If you understand the nature of fire, you understand its symbolic meaning. Fire is one of the attributes of Shiva and this signifies that Shiva can be both creative and destructive. He also wears a crown of skulls. The long association with skulls is death. Many skulls mean many deaths, many deaths mean many rebirths. The linga is a sign of masculine virility and creativity. When you understand all of Shiva's qualities, and you see them in the context of a story, you can make meaningful connections and discover these dimensions in yourself.

Water means what water is and does. It is the source and matrix of life. Vampire bats suck blood. Lambs are meek. Fangs are venomous. Spiders are patient. Rabbits are prolific. Doors separate chambers. Keys open doors. These are the things storymakers and the creative unconscious have to work with. It's all that is available. And since nothing in the real world can by itself adequately express or represent these powerful unconscious energies, it has to utilize what is available and take a little bit from here and a little bit from there and fashion it into a new form which reflects as near as possible the hidden secrets.

The unique combination of these real things when brought together create the characters, gods, Shangri-las, haunted houses, monsters, and real people which express different attributes and dimensions of the hidden energies. The natural world is taken apart and rearranged to reveal the supernatural, unconscious, hidden world.

When the creative unconscious self wishes to express some aspect of itself, through stories created in an oral tradition, it takes a little bit of this real thing and a little bit of that real thing and artistically treats it using those curious tendencies of the mind we spoke of, which are really the artistic tools of the imagination. It prompts the conscious mind of the storymakers to idealize this, exaggerate that, minimize or vilify something else, take this apart and recombine it, keep this and discard that.

In Milton's *Paradise Lost*, when Satan is on his way to Paradise to corrupt Adam and Eve, he passes through the gates of Hell, which are so huge that their hinges create thunder and lightning storms when they move. By exaggerating the size of the gates and hinges, minimizing the size of the thunderstorm, and reversing their relative sizes a whole new world is created — a door between Heaven and Hell, a door between our higher and lower selves.

In the Biblical story of David and Goliath as well as in "Jack and the Beanstalk," the size of the adversaries are greatly exaggerated and fearsome giants are created. In the movie *Jaws*, the size of the man-eating white shark is exaggerated. These alterations create a certain effect. The new relative sizes and equations have special significance. They correspond to certain psychological states and provoke emotional responses from which meaningful connections can be made.

For example, the human mind has the unique ability to go back into the past or look into the future. And if you wanted to express those abilities in a story using visual metaphors, how would you do that? The stories evolved by the Greeks used Prometheus and his brother Epimetheus. Prometheus in Greek means forethought; Epimetheus, afterthought. Prometheus stole fire from the gods and gave it to man. And for this he was severely punished. The god, Zeus, had him chained between two great rocks and every morning a large eagle came and gnawed on his liver. During the night, the liver would heal. But then the following day the bird would return and gnaw on his liver again.

It doesn't take a great stretch of the imagination to realize that forethought, the ability to look ahead into the future, had a major role to play in Man's discovery of fire. It would simply not have been possible without it. Forethought was an important evolutionary step. But certain unpleasant side effects evolved along with it, among them, worry. The ability to look ahead means that you can anticipate certain unpleasant possibilities in the future and worry about them. A bird gnawing on the liver (the seat of anxiety) is an excellent way of expressing how worry behaves. But even serious worries can heal or be resolved during the night. But then when you wake up the next morning, you look toward the future again and there are new things to worry about. The bird returns. The truth hidden in the Prometheus stories reveal not only the nature and importance of forethought but also the relation of forethought to worry and the nature of worry itself.

What about Prometheus' brother, Epimetheus (afterthought)? He ignored his brother's warning to take no gifts from the gods and accepted the first woman, Pandora, together with her jar full of evils from Hermes, and lived to regret it. We can use this ability, after-thought, to analyze our past mistakes. We can also use this ability to go back into the past and correct mistakes, do psychological repairs. This is what psychoanalysis is all about.

And how might you express these abilities in a contemporary story using modern metaphors? Try *Back to the Future*, where the time machine is used to express these same psychoanalytic abilities. And because the time machine can go either into the future or into the past, it is a perfect modern replacement for the metaphors of old that expressed these mental abilities — forethought and afterthought.

In any case, using his extraordinary sports car, Michael J. Fox goes back into the past, identifies and corrects a serious weakness in his father which brings about a profound change in the present. That's psychoanalysis. The story is a little road map of these unique mental abilities. And because the story makes that psychological connection, whether done intentionally or not, is why, in my opinion, the film was so successful.

The haunted house story is another modern way of expressing that same psychological model. The house is a perfect metaphor for the human mind, because the human mind, like the house, is a dwelling occupied by living beings. The haunted house, then, is an excellent metaphor of a haunted mind. How do you cure a haunted mind? Well, that's the mind's psychoanalytic ability again. You have to look back into the past and understand the cause of the mental distur-bance (the haunting), which is often the result of some traumatically repressed natural instinct crying out for release. And you have to identify the cause of the repression before you can effect a release.

The ghost doing the haunting is usually the result of the murder of some innocent person in the house. Murder is an excellent way of metaphorically expressing acts of repression. In order to bring about the release of the ghost, the new occupant of the haunted house has to track down and identify the killer (repressor) of the innocent victim (repressed virtue). Once the killer is identified and punished, the ghost is released and mental health is restored.

CHAPTER 9

THE ARCHETYPES

Great stories, then, are complex metaphors, their different characters, places, actions and objects all reflecting different aspects of the wisdom hidden in the creative unconscious self. And if you analyze hundreds of great stories, certain patterns begin to emerge. These patterns are called archetypes.

Archetype means basic form or first type. These basic forms become an intermediate stage between the raw energy of the hidden truth and the metaphors. It is a first model from which the metaphors will spring. In fact, all of the symbolic elements we are going to meet in story represent one of these basic psychological forces — these archetypes.

For instance, let us say that the Spiritual Father Figure is one of these archetypes. Then Gandalf in *The Lord of the Rings* (an obvious father figure) is a metaphor of that archetype. Dumbledore in *Harry Potter*, Obi-Wan Kenobi in *Star Wars*, Jor-El (Marlon Brando) in *Superman*, and Mufasa in *The Lion King* are other examples. They are all metaphors of that same father figure archetype.

The model created from these archetypal elements or patterns is, in effect, a model of the hidden truth. And that's the third great secret, that a sophisticated model of the hidden truth can be made by analyzing the patterns found in great stories. These patterns are the source of *meaningful connections,* and seeing these patterns is the breaking of the story code.

To summarize: Utilizing the qualities of real things that have been artistically treated, the truth hidden in the creative unconscious is expressed in great stories as metaphors. The patterns found in these great stories can therefore be used to create an archetypal model which is, in effect, a sketch of this hidden truth. This sketch is our psychological model, the Golden Paradigm. It is also our story model. Later, when we are working with the creative storymaking process, we will use this model as a reference to help us communicate effectively with this creative unconscious resource.

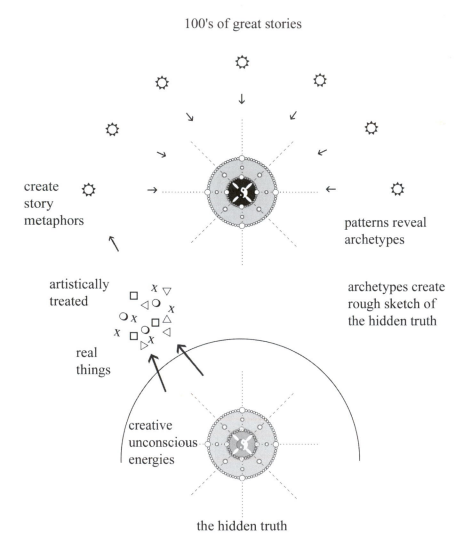

100's of great stories

create
story
metaphors

patterns reveal
archetypes

artistically
treated

archetypes create
rough sketch of
the hidden truth

real
things

creative
unconscious
energies

the hidden truth

PART THREE

THE NEW STORY
MODEL

"Whether we are describing a king, an assassin, a thief, an honest man, a prostitute, a nun, a young girl, or a stallholder in a market, it is always ourselves that we are describing."
Guy de Maupassant

CHAPTER 10

THE STORYWHEEL

I've divided the study of the hidden truth into four parts:

1. The Storywheel
2. The Golden Paradigm
3. The Story Focus
4. The Sugar Coat

The study of the **Storywheel** is the study of all of the cycles of change and growth we experience from birth to zenith and from zenith to death (or nadir). I illustrate the storywheel with this design:

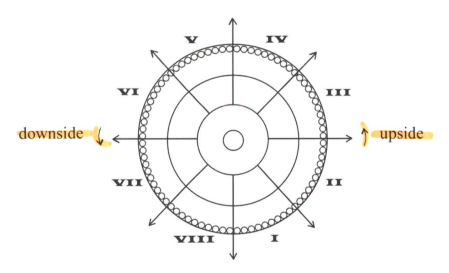

Every great story, ancient or modern, has a place on this wheel, and when you bring all of the different types of story together in this way, you begin to see how they are all really connected and have a common purpose, namely: they all have something to do with guiding us to higher states of being.

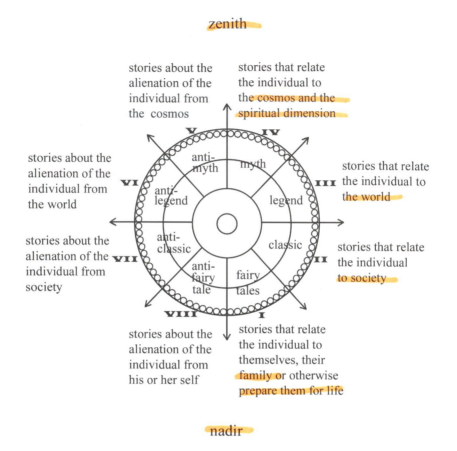

zenith

stories about the alienation of the individual from the cosmos

stories that relate the individual to the cosmos and the spiritual dimension

stories about the alienation of the individual from the world

stories that relate the individual to the world

stories about the alienation of the individual from society

stories that relate the individual to society

stories about the alienation of the individual from his or her self

stories that relate the individual to themselves, their family or otherwise prepare them for life

nadir

The four sections on the upside of the storywheel reveal the passages from birth to zenith, the four sections on the downside, the passages from zenith to nadir. Stories that end on the upside have happy endings. The heroes resist temptation and rise up to a higher plane. Stories that end on the downside have unhappy or tragic endings. The antihero gives in to temptation and slips down to a lower plane.

The stories in section I help relate the individual to himself or herself or their family, or otherwise prepare them for life. I call these stories fairy tales but they include all other stories of childhood and youth.

The stories in section II help relate the individual to society. They show us how to resolve an inauthentic state, how to establish our careers, how to raise a family, how to love, and so on. I call these stories classics.

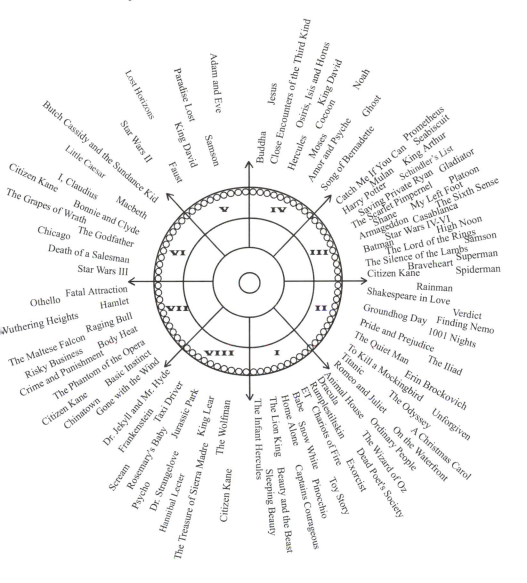

The Storywheel

The stories in section III relate the individual to the world at large. The heroes in this category sacrifice themselves for people they don't even know. They show us how to release our superhuman powers, how to become a great professional or a great success. I call these stories legends.

The stories in section IV relate the individual to the cosmos, to God or the spiritual dimension. In these stories the heroes transcend. They reach their full potential. I call these stories myths.

The stories in section V show us how the individual is alienated from the cosmos, from God or the spiritual dimension. I call these stories anti-myths.

The anti-legends in section VI show us how the individual is alienated from the world at large.

In section VII we see the anti-classics and learn how the individual is alienated from his society. Among these are anti-love stories like *Othello* which show us how lovers are alienated from each other rather than brought together.

In the final section VIII we see anti-fairy tales and learn about the alienation of the individual from himself.

The best example of the validity of the storywheel can be found in a famous Arabian tale.

A Thousand and One Nights

After discovering his wife in an orgy with her slaves, and similar infidelities on the part of his brother's wife, King Shahryar vows never to trust a woman again. And thereafter, to protect himself from future pain, he has a new young girl brought to him every night for his pleasure and then has her head chopped off the next morning. This goes on for several years and, much to the distress of the king's subjects, the population of eligible young girls is being seriously depleted. Now it just so happens that the king's vizier has a beautiful young daughter named Shahrazad, who he has, not surprisingly, been hiding from the eyes of the king. But then one day, Shahrazad tells her father that she intends to become the king's next concubine. Her father pleads with her to reconsider but she cannot be dissuaded and it comes to pass.

But Shahrazad has a plan and when she's alone with the king that night she puts her plan into effect. To begin with, she keeps herself alive by telling the king a marvelous story that reaches an intriguing and critical moment just at dawn, when the king's new mistress is usually executed. The king is so anxious to know what happens next in the story that he extends her life for another day. The following night, when King Shahryar returns from his public duties, and after he has ravaged her, Shahrazad continues her tale. She concludes this first story in the middle of the night and starts another marvelous tale which again reaches an intriguing point just at dawn, and again the king is anxious to know what happens next and so her life is extended. And by this stratagem she survives. After several hundred stories and a thousand and one nights King Shahryar has been completely transformed by the wisdom hidden in all of these marvelous tales and is brought back to his true humanity. And by this time he has had three children by Shahrazad and is more than ready to give up his former ways and settle down with her.

This wonderful story reveals in a most profound and delightful way how the great stories do their work. Each marvelous tale revealing a little bit more of the hidden truth, each story guiding one a little further along in the process of transformation.

Chapter II

The Golden Paradigm

The study of the **Golden Paradigm** is the study of one complete passage or cycle of the storywheel. It is the most important part of our model because it contains the basic patterns and blueprints that are repeated in all of the stages of the storywheel, like a genetic code.

I use this design to illustrate the Golden Paradigm:

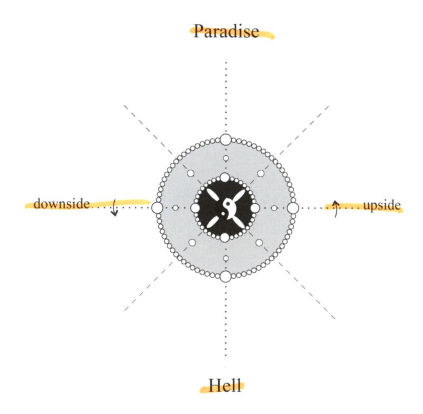

Each one of the ascending and descending circles on the circumference of the storywheel represents one of these Golden Paradigm models.

The metaphors and archetypes that describe the Golden Paradigm also describe the human psyche, the psyche being that part of the human mind that has been mapped. The Golden Paradigm is a way of looking at the psyche. It is a dynamic model of the psyche. A dynamic model of its structures and dimensions, showing how these structures and dimensions interact, evolve, and are transformed. It is also a way of looking at the groups and entities human beings form. It is a dynamic model of the psychology underlying these groups and entities as well. They all have the same basic structure and dynamics. And story, of course, is all about revealing these structures and dynamics. Each great story, as I've been saying, reveals a small part of this hidden truth, a little bit more of the Golden Paradigm. The stories build up and reveal the paradigm, and the paradigm repeats itself and creates the Storywheel.

There are three parts of the model which will be discussed throughout the book that I would like to introduce to you now. The first has to do with the archetypes that describe the different dimensions of our conscious and unconscious selves. These are the character archetypes, the major players and heroes of story. These archetypes help to reveal how the psyche is organized. They reveal how the mind functions, how the conscious and unconscious minds relate to each other and communicate, and how the creative unconscious archetypes interact, their relative hierarchy, rivalry, powers and goals. I illustrate them in our model as the large and medium sized circles and flower petals imbedded in the model.

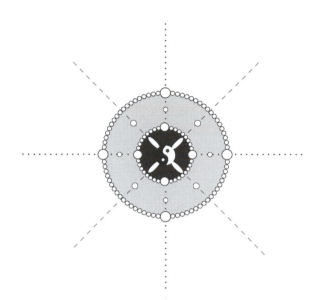

The second part concerns the archetypes that reveal the path. These are the actions and plots of story that reveal the creative actions and tasks which are necessary to awaken and release the extraordinary powers that bring about the shifts to higher consciousness. This larger whole story passage includes both the hero's and the antihero's journey. I illustrate this path in our model as the small ascending and descending circles bordering the circumference of the model.

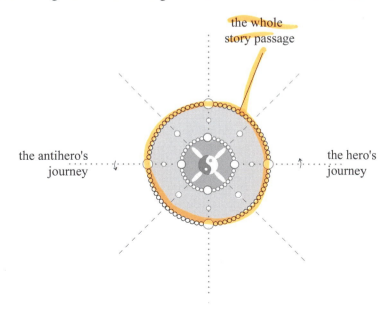

the whole story passage

the antihero's journey

the hero's journey

The third part concerns the story focus, which is the part of the whole story passage that is actually being focused on for the purposes of telling the story. I illustrate the story focus in our model as the little circles going around the circumference of the dark circle that contains the flower petals and the small yin and yang circle in the center of the design.

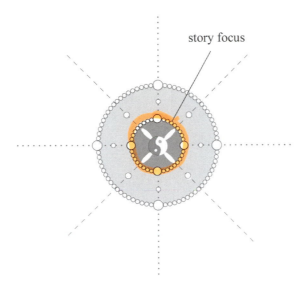

story focus

The Iliad (not to be mistaken for a movie called *Troy*) is a good story to illustrate the relationship of the larger, whole story passage to the story focus. *The Iliad* is really a whole, big story concerning the seduction of King Menelaos' wife, Helen, by the Trojan, Paris, and the war that was fought by the Greeks to get her back. The focus of that *whole story* is a single incident, the argument between Achilles and Agamemnon and its consequences in the ninth year of the war. The *whole story*, which is revealed in the exposition, is told in the context of this one dispute. The study of the Golden Paradigm is the study of the structures, dimensions, and dynamics of this larger, *whole story* (frame or backstory) while the study of the story focus is the study of the structures, dimensions, and dynamics of the smaller, foreground story itself, i.e. the dispute between Agamemnon and Achilles.

To give two other examples, the larger, *whole story* in *Casablanca* is World War II — i.e. Hitler's taking possession of Europe. The story focus concerns the transformation of one disillusioned patriot named Rick. The larger *whole story* of Dickens' *A Christmas Carol* has to do with London's poverty. The focus of that larger story is the transformation of one greedy miser, Ebenezer Scrooge.

The final and fourth part of our study will be the sugar coat, which is the entertainment dimensions that help to attract interest in the story and also to camouflage and conceal its hidden secrets.

The Principal (or Unifying) Elements

The best way to reveal the Golden Paradigm will be to describe the archetypal patterns that created it. I call these patterns the Principal (or Unifying) Elements. They are:

> The Subject
> The Value Being Pursued / The Scourge Being Avoided
> The Entity Being Transformed
>
> The Problem of the Larger, Whole Story
>> The Threat (the cause of the problem)
>> The Hook
>> The Inciting Action
>> The Terrible Element
>> The Victim(s)
>> The State of Misfortune
> The Real Cause of the Problem
> The Positive and Negative Character Archetypes (on the downside of the *whole story* passage, these are the Forces of Assistance and Resistance that are in play while the problem is being created).
>
> The Solution to the Larger, Whole Story Problem
>> The Anti-Threat (the hero, the one who opposes the threat)
>>> The Hero's Profession
>>> The Hero's Dominant Trait

The Hero's Handicap (Inauthentic State)

The Principal Action

Complications, Reversal, Crisis,
Discovery, Climax, Resolution

The Dominant Plot

The Subplots

The Marvelous Element

The Beneficiaries

The State of Good Fortune

The Real Cause of the Solution

The Positive and Negative Character Archetypes (on the upside of the *whole story* passage, these are the Forces of Assistance and Resistance that are in play while the problem is being solved).

The Details of the Larger, *Whole Story* Passage

The Problem of the Story Focus

The Central Character

The Theme

The Cause of the Problem of the Focus

The Inciting Action of the Focus

The Principal Action of the Focus

The Exposition

The Afterthought

The Structures of the Principal Action

The Solution Formula

The Genre Structures

The Dominant Plot

The Subplots

The Universal Structure

The Classical Structure

The Narrative Structure

The Sugar Coat

Why Great Stories Are About Problems

One of the main themes I will be developing throughout this book is the fact that great stories are about problems. The reason great stories are about problems is because life is about problems, and the great mission of story is to teach us how to analyze, cope with, and solve the problems that stand between us and our dreams — between us and paradise.

In truth, our lives are all about problems. We are bombarded daily by big and little problems — everything from lost keys or bugs in the pantry to a serial killer in our neighborhood. Then on top of that there are career problems, emotional problems, financial problems, health problems — threats to our lives, our well being, our welfare — threats to our families, our communities, our countries. But despite their prevalence, I'm not sure we really appreciate how much our lives are being dominated and controlled by problems — things that need to be fixed or solved because we won't be happy otherwise.

Story gets its structures from the problems we encounter in real life — from real serial killers, real diseases and disasters, real wars and raging fires. The structures found in great stories are the same structures that are ruling our lives — the principles of dramatic action being the structures of action in real life that have been isolated and artistically treated.

Story focuses on problems for the same reason the news only reports the bad things that are happening in the world and not the good — because the bad things are the things that need to be dealt with. They are the obstacles that stand in the way of the values we are trying to reach. Reaching those values will bring us a little closer to paradise, which is really where we are longing to be. When everything is in perfect harmony and there are no problems left to worry about — we'll be in paradise. And that's one of the functions of story: to help guide us to higher, more desirable, less problematic states of being. One of the ways it does that is by revealing the truth and nature of problems and their solutions. All of the professions, in fact — doctor, lawyer, accountant, plumber, police, psychologist, therapist, auto mechanic, etc. — are built around problem solving. They make their living solving problems for other people. Storymakers help solve the most dangerous problem of all — ignorance. Ignorance concerning who we really are and who we were really meant to be. Great stories help to overcome problems of ignorance by revealing their hidden wisdom.

Can any problem be a story? Technically, any problem can be a story if its solution contains a classical structure, i.e. if it's difficult to solve. But, generally speaking, an audience won't be interested in a story about some minor problem like finding your lost keys unless something truly funny or horrendous, like the end of the world, would happen if you didn't find them. Story is especially interested in problem-solving actions that involve crisis — critical events that threaten life, health, wealth, freedom, love, security, happiness, etc. while testing the limits of human endurance and ingenuity. Knowing how to manage crisis is the single most important thing we need to be able to do, if we are to survive and succeed. Seeing inside a great story shows us how problems are created and how problems are resolved. Knowing this gives us a working knowledge of both story and life.

We will now journey into the heart of a great story and begin mapping out this territory.

The Subject

The first of these archetypal patterns we will examine is the subject — and more specifically the connection of the subject to ultimate unity. Besides being the archetypal patterns that make up great stories, the principal (or unifying) elements I listed earlier in this chapter are the unifying threads that great stories are isolating and exploring in great detail. One of these unifying elements will be dominant and that dominant element will also be the subject of your story — what people will perceive your story is really about. Put another way, the subject of your story will be the dominant unifying element. And if that subject is explored in depth, which it is in all of the examples I will give you, it will become an ultimate source of unity — and an ultimate source of clarity, meaning, and power.

The ultimate source of unity and the subject of Homer's *The Iliad* is Achilles' anger, his dominant trait. More than anything else, the story is about Achilles' anger. *The Iliad* is, in fact, everything you ever wanted to know about anger — how it is created, its destructive power, how it is transferred and ultimately resolved. It is this clarity and singleness of purpose that has kept this story alive and relevant for over 3000 years. Anger is anger. If you isolated that one subject and described it perfectly 3000 years ago, that description would be relevant today. And this is where that story gets its enormous power, from its singleness of purpose. What is more, all of the other unifying elements support that dominant unity. They link the story to the larger whole and reveal its place in the larger scheme.

The subject and ultimate source of unity in *The Lord of the Rings* is the terrible element, the Ring of Power, and everyone in that story has their "will to power" tested by that ring. In *The Exorcist*, the subject and ultimate source of unity is the problem of demonic possession. In *Jaws*, it's the threat, the shark. In *Star Wars*, it's the anti-threat, Luke Skywalker, the hero. In *The Pianist*, it's survival, the value being pursued. In *Gladiator*, it's the hero's new profession, gladiator. In *Casablanca*, it's the love story which is the dominant plot. In *Atlantis*, it's Atlantis, the entity being transformed. In *A Christmas Carol*, it's Scrooge's greed, his dominant trait. In *The Sixth Sense*, it's the boy's fear, another dominant trait. In *The Silence of the Lambs*, it's the marvelous element — a profile of the serial killer. Each one of these stories is a puzzle piece that contributes more information to the larger picture — which, as I indicated earlier, is nothing less than a dynamic model of the human psyche. Basically, what I'm saying here is that if you make one of these puzzle pieces the subject of your story and you explore that puzzle piece in great detail, you will not only increase the power of your story and make a powerful artistic statement, you will be exploring those dimensions in yourself and using the creative process to bring forth the truth about those dimensions, which are locked inside you and waiting to be released.

The Value Being Pursued

Now, we'll look at the patterns that reveal the structures and dimensions of the whole story, and we'll begin with the value being pursued.

In real life, either as individuals or in concert with others, we are longing for and pursuing certain cherished values, such as life, health, wealth, justice, democracy, freedom, honor, wisdom, security, love, happiness, wholeness, equality, among others. At the same time, we are trying to avoid their opposites — scourges like death, disease, poverty, injustice, tyranny, ignorance, slavery, insecurity, dishonor, unhappiness, alienation, inequality, and so on.

Value

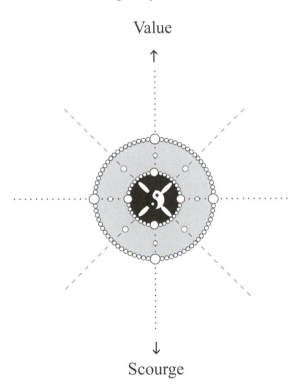

Scourge

These values and scourges played a major role in our evolutionary path and continue to govern our lives. In fact, we are pursuing all of these values more or less simultaneously. This makes real life appear, on the surface, to be extremely complex and difficult to analyze and understand. For clarity's sake, story likes to isolate these values (along with all of the other unifying elements), like threads from a complex skein, so that the pursuit of one of these values may be examined in great detail.

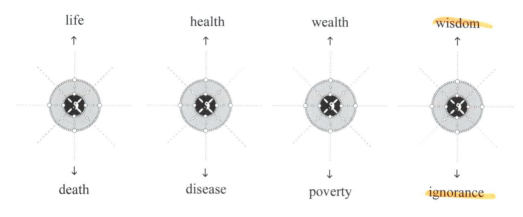

life	health	wealth	wisdom
↑	↑	↑	↑
↓	↓	↓	↓
death	disease	poverty	ignorance

These isolated components, these threads, are the stuff that great stories are made of and another source of their power. This is where it all begins. It starts with the pursuit of these values. And this is a constant in our lives.

In the larger *whole story* of The Iliad and The Odyssey, the value being pursued is honor. Everything in that larger whole story is related to that one virtue. It begins at the wedding of King Peleus and the sea goddess, Thetis. There is a contest to determine which of the three goddesses, Hera, Athena or Aphrodite, is the most beautiful. The Trojan, Paris, the handsomest living mortal, is chosen to judge the contest, and Aphrodite secretly offers to help him seduce the most beautiful woman in the world if he chooses her, which he does. Now Hera and Athena, sensing correctly that the contest was rigged, feel dishonored by Paris' choice, and they vow to take revenge on his father's kingdom. Later King Menelaos feels dishonored when Paris, with the help of Aphrodite, seduces his wife, Helen, and they run off together to Troy. Hera and Athena help Menelaos and his brother Agamemnon raise an army. During the ten-year war with Troy that ensues, Achilles feels dishonored when Agamemnon takes away the girl, Briseis, his prize from the sacking of the city of Lyrnessus. Then

Poseidon feels dishonored when Odysseus blinds his one-eyed son, the Cyclops, Polyphemus. As revenge, the god delays Odysseus' return home another nine years. Then Odysseus feels dishonored because the suitors who have taken over his estate in his absence are hounding his wife and son and squandering his wealth. And finally, Homer feels dishonored because of a movie they made of his story called *Troy*. In short, everything in that larger *whole story* is somehow related to the value, honor, and the avoidance of its scourge, dishonor. This value and its opposite have been isolated from all the other possible values and scourges and are being thoroughly and completely explored.

You will find this same pattern — the pursuit of some value that has been isolated and is being thoroughly explored — in many other great stories and films. In *The Silence of the Lambs* the value being pursued is justice. All of the actions of that story are designed to bring that about. In *Star Wars*, *Gladiator*, and *Casablanca*, the value being pursued is freedom from tyranny. In *The Lord of the Rings* it's power. In *The Sixth Sense*, it's the mental health of a young boy who is terrified of his psychic gift. In *Ordinary People*, it's the mental health of another young boy who has suicidal tendencies. In *Jaws*, it's life and the scourge being avoided is death. In *The Pianist*, it's also life. Everything Adrien Brody does has to do with survival, the avoidance of death. In *The Exorcist*, it's freedom from the slavery of demonic possession. In *A Christmas Carol*, it's wealth — the antidote to the poverty that is plaguing Cratchit, Tiny Tim, and London's poor.

In all of these examples, a single value has been isolated and is being examined in great detail which adds enormous clarity, meaning and power to the story and makes this value an important unifying force.

Now, all of the Golden Paradigm models associated with the different values in the previous illustration also represent the different entities we form to help pursue these values — i.e. we form governments to help us pursue life and liberty, hospitals to fight disease, schools to fight ignorance, armies to protect our freedom, police to prevent injustice, corporations to pursue wealth, and so on. And all of these entities, including the human psyche, as I've indicated, have the same structure. It is the fundamental unit — and this is our story model, the Golden Paradigm. And these different entities form the larger context which surround and support the stories being told.

The Essence of Story and the High Concept Great Idea

In order to reach these values, either as individuals or as part of the groups we form, we have to overcome the negative states being created by the scourges we're trying to avoid. In order to do that we have to overcome the problems that created them. The next several patterns have to do with that. I call them the essence of story — that without which there would be no story, and the high concept great idea. We'll start with the essence of story, and these are some of the critical elements:

The Change of Fortune
The Problem of the Story
The Solution to the Problem
The Complications, Crisis, Climax and Resolution
        of the classical structure
The Threat
The Anti-threat

Without these critical elements, there will be no story, i.e. without a problem and change of fortune, there is no story. If the story ends in the same place it began without some significant progress up or down, the audience will wonder what the point of it was. It will be a very unsatisfactory experience. So there has to be a problem. Similarly, if you have a problem without a solution, you have no story. If the movie *Jaws* begins with the shark eating a tourist, which establishes that as the problem, and Roy Scheider, the Sheriff, sets out to solve that problem — but then half way through the movie he loses interest in that problem and goes on to something else, the audience will be outraged. They'll demand their money back. So there has to be a problem and a solution. But then if you have a solution and that solution doesn't include complications and a crisis in its structure, there is no story. If Cinderella goes to the ball, falls in love with the prince and marries him without a single hitch, or if Indiana Jones goes after the Holy Grail and recovers it without running into any difficulty whatsoever, there is no story. The audience is left muttering: So what? Then if you have complications and a crisis but no climax and no resolution, you will have the same problem. You will leave your audience feeling completely unfulfilled. They will have the distinct feeling that the story was left unfinished.

So this is what I mean by the "essence" of story. These elements are essential. If you eliminate any one of them, you will have something less than a story. And if the story you're working on doesn't work, or it doesn't feel like a story, these are some of the elements you should look at first.

Now we'll look at these critical elements in a little more detail and examine their relation to the threat.

The Change of Fortune

The central character in a story is going through a transformation — but in a great story, that transformation is always in the context of the transformation of some larger entity. That larger entity can be a family, an institution, a town, a corporation, a government, or any of the other entities that we form to help achieve the values we're pursuing. In *Star Wars* the larger entity being transformed is an entire Galaxy. All of the actions in that story are having an impact on the fate of that entity. In *A Beautiful Mind, Independence Day, The Matrix*, or any James Bond film, that larger entity is the world. And the actions in those stories are having an impact on the world. In *Gladiator*, it is the Roman Empire. In *King Arthur, Braveheart* and *The Pianist* it's a country. In *Harry Potter* it's the Wizard World. In *The Lord of the Rings* it's Middle Earth. In *The Sixth Sense* and *A Christmas Carol* it's a city. In *On The Waterfront*, it's the working environment of a harbor area. In *Alien,* it's a space ship. In *Ordinary People,* it's a family.

In the course of the story, this entity goes from a desirable to an undesirable state or condition or the reverse. Or as Aristotle put it: "The proper magnitude (of a story) is comprised within such limits that the sequence of events will admit of a change from bad fortune to good or from good fortune to bad."

In *The Exorcist*, a little girl is possessed by the Devil and a state of misfortune exists. Then the principal action, casting out the Devil, brings about a state of good fortune. In stories that end unhappily, it's the reverse. In *Othello*, a state of good fortune exists at the beginning. Othello and Desdemona are in love. They get married. Othello, who is a general, wins a decisive battle at sea and is made governor of Cyprus. Everything is just great. Then the principal action, which is perpetrated by Othello's evil servant, Iago, destroys Othello with jealousy and a state of tragic misfortune is the result. So, in stories that end happily, you create a state of misfortune that has to be resolved — and in stories that end unhappily, you create a state of good fortune that is ultimately destroyed.

The Problem

The second critical element, the problem, brings about these changes of fortune.

This problem, as I indicated, is a prerequisite in all stories. You have a problem and that problem is resolved. It is the central event of the story. No matter how big or small the story, it will be focusing on, or related to, a problem. Everyone in that story will somehow be involved in that incident, and everything everyone does in that story will in some way affect the outcome of that incident. And revealing how that problem was created and how it can be resolved is at the very heart of a great story.

In *The Silence of the Lambs*, a serial killer is on the loose. That is the problem that brings about the change of fortune and that is the problem that has to be resolved. In *Harry Potter*, Voldemort is trying to get control of the Wizard World. In *The Lord of the Rings*, an even more powerful Voldemort-like dark force named Sauron is trying to take control of Middle Earth. In *Ordinary People*, a young boy is suicidal. In *Shrek*, fairy tale creatures have taken over Shrek's swamp and that is the problem the ogre sets out to solve. In *Gladiator*, a tyrant has usurped the Roman Empire, preventing the restoration of the Republic. In *The Sixth Sense*, a murdered child psychologist is stuck in limbo and the spirits of dead people are haunting a little boy's mind.

In *Independence Day*, aliens have invaded the Earth. In *Star Wars*, the Evil Empire has taken possession of the galaxy. In *The Iliad*, the Greek army is being decimated because Achilles, their best warrior, has dropped out of the fight. In *King Arthur*, the kingdom is in a state of anarchy and has to be reunified. In *Jaws*, it's a shark problem. In *The Mummy*, it's a mummy problem. In *The Perfect Storm*, it's a weather problem. In *Erin Brockovich*, it's an environmental problem. Each of these stories and hundreds of others I could name revolve around a problem that has to be resolved.

The Threat

The threat is the agent or perpetrator which creates the problem that brings about the negative state, the change of fortune. In *Kiss the Girls*, the serial killer is the threat and the act of murder is the inciting action which creates the problem that brings about the change to a state of misfortune.

Equally significant in a great story is the fact that this threat will become the principal source of resistance that opposes the action when someone tries to solve this problem and restore a state of good fortune. This resistance will create the classical structure that occurs when a problem solving action encounters resistance, for example, Indiana Jones goes after the Holy Grail and encounters no difficulties whatsoever. That action has no structure. He had a desire and fulfilled that desire. He went from point A to point B without any obstacles in between. But what if the Nazis don't want him to achieve that goal and stand in his way or try to prevent him? That resistance will create complications, a crisis, the need for climactic actions to resolve the crisis, and resolutions.

In *Harry Potter*, Voldemort is the threat. His efforts in the entire series of books to take possession of the Wizard World create the problem that brings about an undesirable state. He is also the source of the resistance that creates the classical structure whenever Harry tries to solve these problems and restore a state of good fortune. In *The Lord of the Rings*, Sauron is the threat. His desire to take possession of Middle Earth creates the problem which brings about a very unpleasant state of affairs. He is also the source of resistance that creates the classical structure when Frodo and his little Fellowship of the Ring try to solve that problem by destroying the coveted Ring of Power. The first movie is, in fact, a textbook of the complications and crises that result from Sauron's minions trying to prevent Frodo's success. In *The Exorcist*, the Devil is the threat. He takes possession of a young girl and that is the inciting action that creates the problem and brings about the change of fortune. He is also the source of resistance that creates the complications, crisis, climax, and resolution when the priest tries to solve that problem. In *Ordinary People*, the mother is the cause of the problem that has brought about the negative state, and she is also the main source of resistance when the psychiatrist, Judd Hirsch, and the boy's father, Donald Sutherland, attempt to solve the mystery of the boy's suicidal tendencies.

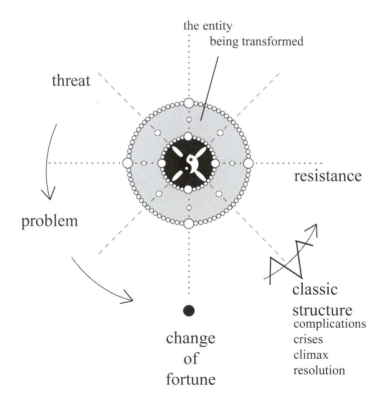

Having observed this pattern in story, you can easily see it at work in real life as well. In World War II, Hitler was the threat and his "taking possession" of Europe was the inciting action that created the problem and the state of misfortune. He was also the main source of the resistance that created the complications, crises, climaxes, and resolutions of the classical structure when the Allies got together and tried to solve this problem.

In the corporate debacle that ruined Enron, Ken Lay and his executive co-conspirators are the threat. Their cooking of the books created the problem that brought about a very serious change of fortune for their investors, who lost billions of dollars while they escaped with hundreds of millions of dollars in profits. And they were the main source of resistance that created the complications and crises for those who were, in their pursuit of justice, trying to solve this problem. In the 9/11 attacks, Osama bin Laden and his Al Qaeda terrorist network are the threat. Their attack on the World Trade Center was the inciting action which created the problem that brought a very undesirable state of fear to the United States. And they are the main source of resistance that is creating the classical structure as we try to solve this problem.

In all of these examples, the threat is the cause of the problem that brings about a change of fortune, and is the main source of the resistance that creates the classical structure when someone tries to solve the problem. The problem, change of fortune, and the components of the classical structure constitute the very essence of story — that without which there would be no story. So this component, the threat which is creating these essential elements, is obviously very important. In fact, it could be said that it is the very thing that brings the story into being. Without the shark in *Jaws* what would we know about the sunny little tourist trap, Amity Island? Not very much, I think. Without Buffalo Bill and Hannibal Lecter, what would we know about an FBI agent named Clarise? We are talking about Clarise and hearing about these events because of the problems they created. Without the iceberg what would we know about the maiden voyage of the *Titanic*? What do you know about the first flight of the 747 or the Concorde?

Very little, probably. Why? Because those flights were uneventful. We know so much about the *Titanic* because of the problem created by the iceberg.

You will, in fact, see the classical structure we just described in any problem-solving action, large or small, real or fiction, that encounters resistance. Story and our lives are defined by these elements. And again, like the value being pursued, we are dealing in real life with many different problems simultaneously, which makes it difficult to appreciate their underlying structure objectively. Story helps us do that by isolating that problem-solving structure from life's otherwise complex skein. The reward gained by a story that performs this service is clarity, meaning, and power.

The High Concept Great Idea

Now I'd like to show you how the threat relates to the high concept great idea — which, simply put, is an intriguing story idea that can be stated in a few words and is easily understood by all.

An asteroid the size of Texas is hurtling toward the earth. That's a high concept. Everyone knows exactly what that means. It arouses an emotional response and in just eleven words, everyone knows what the movie is about. Doomsday.

Creating a high concept implies an ability to formulate your idea in its most powerful and concise form — to make it as short and as marvelous as possible.

The fewer the words, the higher the concept.

Jack Nicholson is the Wolfman. The movie didn't turn out that well, but it was a great idea — a very effective high concept.

Now, is this idea of a high concept just something the studios cooked up to stifle art and increase profits? Of course. But does it also have merit? I think it has.

Whether you plan to create highly visible and commercial films like those created by Jerry Bruckheimer, James Cameron, and Steven

Spielberg, or highly acclaimed stories like *The Sixth Sense*, *Ordinary People*, *Schindler's List*, *The Pianist*, or *A Beautiful Mind*, I think this is important for you to know.

For one thing, being able to reduce your idea into something powerful that can be expressed in a few words forces you to come to terms with what the story is really about. In other words, to create a true high concept, you not only have to understand all of the important structural elements of your story, you have to get at the very essence of the story. And to do that, you have to come to terms with the threat. *An asteroid the size of Texas hurtling toward the earth* is exactly that. It's the threat that is causing the problem. And what about: *Jack Nicholson is the Wolfman*? What's happening there? What is the Wolfman? The Wolfman is the threat. He's a serial killer. The cause of the problem. And that's the thing that's making it possible to describe these ideas in a few words. The threat — which is at the heart of the story and is, in fact, bringing the story into being.

In the second place, the high concept is a valuable shorthand that can help facilitate communication. If your project is going to be sold to, or financed by, a major production company or publisher, then the idea behind that project not only has to be intriguing, it has to be brief. It has to move easily through the chain of command — and make everyone who hears it eager to listen to your pitch, read your script, or look at your film. Then after they've heard it, or read it, and loved it, they have to be able to explain it to others in the chain and intrigue them. If the idea is so complicated that it's difficult to explain, it may never get through the chain of command.

In the 1970s there was a very popular 90-minute TV show called *MacMillan and Wife* which starred Rock Hudson and Susan Saint James. Steven Bochco, whom you've no doubt heard of because of *NYPD Blue* and a lot of other important television shows he produced, was the story editor. I was introduced to the executive producer, Leonard Stern, by Julie Epstein, and Stern referred me to Bochco. So when I met Bochco he had never seen my work and had no idea what I could do. We had a meeting, discussed a couple of ideas, but nothing happened.

About a week after our meeting, I was in my kitchen making some coffee and an idea popped into my head. On an impulse I called Bochco. After the usual amenities, he asked me: "What've you got?"

"Susan gets lost in the Bermuda Triangle," I replied.

"I love it," he said, sounding delighted. "I'll get back to you."

Ten minutes later he called me back. "I hope you can write," he said. "You've got a deal."

Now, as it turned out, Bochco had called the producer and pitched the idea to him. The producer liked it and told Bochco to call their contact at NBC. Bochco called the contact and pitched it to him. He loved it and called his superior. The superior liked it and called Bochco, and Bochco called me. All within less than ten minutes. It was the highest-paying show on television, and, at that moment, *Susan gets lost in the Bermuda Triangle* was the sum total of what I knew about that idea. If anyone had asked me: "Then what happens?" I would've been stuck.

What is the heart of this idea? The Bermuda Triangle. And what is the Bermuda Triangle? A serious threat — a very bad place to get lost, if you're superstitious. And that's what made it possible to describe this idea in so few words. The threat.

The Inciting Action

The threat, as we indicated, is the cause of the problem. It has two parts: the agent or perpetrator and the inciting action. The inciting action is the action being taken by the agent. The virus is the agent. The spreading disease is the inciting action. That's the thing that's getting everyone so upset. The serial killer is the perpetrator, the act of murder is the inciting action.

You will know if it's an inciting action, if action has to be taken. If there's a problem and something has to be done about it — now. A huge asteroid is about to collide with the earth. Something has to be done. Action has to be taken. It has to be diverted or destroyed. A woman has been kidnapped. Action has to be taken. She has to be rescued and the kidnapper brought to justice. A baby is left on a doorstep. Action has to be taken. It has to be properly cared for. An invading army has to be confronted and defeated. An erupting volcano has to be escaped from. A man-eating shark has to be hunted down and destroyed. A raging fire has to be put out.

What characterizes these particular threats is the fact that they are so alarming that action has to be taken. When confronted by a threat of that magnitude, the mind fills in the rest of the story. Which is to say, the mind of the listener will begin to wonder how the problem is going to be solved. That activation of their imaginations will help to give them the sense that they just heard a good idea.

Besides the threat there are three other elements that can help you create an effective high concept: the hook, the fascinating subject, and a great title.

The Hook

The hook is the unique aspect of the threat which is alarming and suggests intriguing possibilities. It is the special circumstance surrounding the problem that raises the stakes and increases our interest.

Susan gets lost, not at the mall, but in the Bermuda Triangle. The asteroid that is about to collide with Earth is not the size of a trash can, it's the size of Texas.

A volcano erupts, not in some remote desert, but in the middle of the city, in Park LaBrea. A baby is left on the doorstep, not of a kindly nanny, but of three bachelors. A woman, Bette Midler, is kidnapped and her husband, Danny DeVito, refuses to pay the ransom. Star-crossed lovers meet, not at a church social, but on the *Titanic*.

The hook implies a difficulty which makes the threat more danger-ous and alarming – and it evokes intriguing possibilities. In *Fatal Attraction*, a successful lawyer has an affair, not with your average "other woman" but with a beautiful psychopath.

Finding the hook forces you to come to terms with what is unique about the threat, and this unique aspect will help to make the idea fresh, which in Hollywood, at least, is an obsession. They don't want to see anything they've seen before. Which is a bit of a paradox, since they also want to know that the film will be successful — and the only way they can do that is to compare it to something else like it that hit the jackpot. One solution to this paradox is to choose a subject like "serial killer" which everyone knows has been successful many times and then look at that subject from a new and unique angle. This was achieved in *The Silence of the Lambs*. It gave us our first look at profiling a serial killer.

The Fascinating Subject

What is a fascinating subject? A fascinating subject is just that, a subject that is in itself intriguing. Your story is about something that arouses our interest just because of the subject. That's a tremendous asset.

Not long ago, I walked into a bookstore. I walked past the first table and a book caught by eye. I walked another twenty steps, stopped, turned around and went back to look at it. The title of the book that caught my eye was: *Cleopatra's Secret Diaries*. The idea of reading about her most intimate secrets had gotten my attention.

What are some of the other subjects we're familiar with? Demonic possession, money, sex, power, dinosaurs, UFOs, infidelity, revenge, serial killers, extra-terrestrials, gangsters, lost treasure, seduction, eternal youth, and so on. I'm sure you can think of many others. Later, I will show you how to make any subject you like more fascinating.

Some of my favorites are: justice, mysteries, and mummies. Give me a mystery in a pyramid and it can be Indiana Jones, Brendan Fraser, or Donald Duck and I'm hooked. I can't resist it. And when the movie *The Mummy* first opened, I was there on the first day for the first showing, and I was first in line.

So you have to find the subjects that really fascinate you and will fascinate the audience you are trying to reach. Finding the fascinating subject is one of the things that forces you to discover what the story is really about. In any event, it's helpful if your story is about something that is in itself intriguing.

The Great Title

A great title is a title that not only tells you what the story is about — what the fascinating subject is — it reveals the genre, which is to say, it whets your appetite for the type of feelings associated with that genre. The feelings associated with a thriller, a mystery, a love story, an adventure. Each of these different genres will take you on a different emotional adventure.

Magic is a popular subject, and not long ago there was a mini-series entitled *Merlin,* which is a good title for a story with that subject because Merlin is associated with that activity. It tells you what the subject is and what the genre is. Harry Potter is gaining that same distinction. He is now synonymous with magic and wizardry. Doomsday is another popular subject. *Armageddon* is a good title for that subject. We immediately know it's about the end of the world and all of the activities and feelings related to that event. Catastrophes — what better title than *Titanic?* Murder — and this is one of my favorites — *The Black Widow.* What more do you need to know? It wasn't a very good movie but it's a great title. Another bad movie with a great title was *Original Sin.* One of the things you eventually come to realize is that Hollywood is much better at coming up with good high concepts and great titles than they are at making great movies.

What are some other good titles? *The Perfect Murder, Shakespeare in Love, The Da Vinci Code, The Sixth Sense, Roswell.* What is *Roswell* about? Aliens and UFOs, of course, because that's the association with that town in New Mexico. *ER* — you can see the gurneys flying down the hospital corridor heading for the operating room. *Kiss the Girls* and *Along Came a Spider* are, in my opinion, terrific titles for serial killer movies. *Star Wars, Gladiator, Jurassic Park, Bruce Almighty, Genghis Khan, The Perfect Score, Thirteen.* What more do you need to know?

You know it's a great title when it tells you everything desirable to know up front. And finding a great title forces you to discover the subject and the genre, which is to say, the source of the feelings you're going to evoke. And when you find a great title, it hits you like a revelation. You get very excited.

In any event, if you have a great title, a fascinating subject, and an intriguing threat, you very likely have a great idea.

So these are the four elements of the high concept: the threat, the hook, the fascinating subject, and the great title. All of which can be expressed in a few words. And if you're going to create a high concept, you'll find these four elements very useful.

The thing to remember, of course, is the important role being played by the threat, which, as we have just seen, is at the heart of both the high concept and also the six critical elements that constitute the essence of story. It is obviously an element worth thinking about and understanding. In fact, if you started out by creating an interesting threat, you couldn't go too far wrong.

Now, we'll talk more about the patterns that describe the entity being transformed and explore the archetypal forces inside that entity that create the problems and solutions that bring about the changes of fortune.

Our Conscious and Unconscious Selves

The first of these inner patterns reveals the relationship between the conscious and unconscious minds. I illustrate this relationship in our model as a small conscious circle surrounded by the larger black and grey unconscious circles.

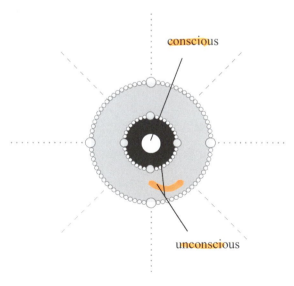

In real life, the conscious mind is the pilot in our heads who monitors the real world through our senses. It is the president, the governor, the king of our personal selves. The unconscious mind is the special intelligence that surrounds and supports the conscious mind and operates behind the scenes. In great stories, we see their relationship revealed by the contrasting of two worlds, i.e. the contrasting of some familiar, known, everyday, real world with an unfamiliar, unseen, mysterious, or supernatural world. In *The Wizard of Oz*, an obvious example, the known (conscious) world of Kansas is contrasted by the strange and fantastic (unconscious) world of Oz. In *The Iliad*, it's the everyday, real world of the Greeks contrasted by the supernatural world of the Olympian gods. In *The Sixth Sense*, it's the world of the living and the world of the dead. In *Harry Potter*, it's the world of the wizards and the world of the muggles. In *Peter Pan*, it's London and Never Never Land. In *A Beautiful Mind*, it's the world of reality and the world of delusion. In *E. T.* and *Independence Day* it's the earth and outer space. In *Armageddon*, it's the earth and the surface of the asteroid. In *Alien*, it's the control room and the remote, less familiar parts of the space ship. In *Jurassic Park*, it's the compound and the rest of the park. In *Being John Malkovich*, it's the real world and the world inside John Malkovich's head. In *The Matrix*, oddly, what we know as the real world is the illusion, contrasted with the alien world of Larry Fishbine, which, we are told, is the true reality.

These contrasts do not have to involve something that is fantastic or supernatural. It can be the juxtaposition of things in the real world. A contrast between the regular living quarters of a house and a spooky basement or attic; the everyday world of the detective and the shady underworld. In *Chinatown*, it's the everyday world of J. J. Gittes and the San Fernando Valley. In *Erin Brockovich*, it's the home and workplace of Julia Roberts and the community being poisoned by the electric company. In *Titanic*, it's the upper decks contrasted by the bowels of the ship, and later, after the iceberg, the sinking ship contrasted by the open sea. In *Jaws*, it's an island surrounded by the sea. The sea is an excellent metaphor for the unconscious because, like the unconscious, the ocean is a vast, mostly hidden domain that is teeming with mysterious life forms. And the island is an excellent metaphor for the conscious mind which is very much like an island surrounded by an unconscious sea.

Communication Between Our Conscious and Unconscious Selves

Another set of patterns reveals how the conscious and unconscious minds communicate. They work very closely together and information passes easily between the two worlds. The unconscious mind communicates with consciousness by means of insights, feelings, premonitions, mental images, intuitions, visions, dreams, and so on. They are visitors into consciousness. So in story we see these communications expressed as visitors or messengers from the remote, supernatural regions or as the hero venturing into these other worlds. E.T., Superman, and the aliens in *Independence Day* are visitors from outer space; George Burns in *Oh, God!* and Morgan Freeman in *Bruce Almighty* come from Heaven; the Devil in *The Exorcist* and the dark forces in *Ghost* come from Hell. Peter Pan visits from Never Never Land. Arnold Schwartzenegger in *The Terminator* comes from our own future.

The conscious mind can communicate with the unconscious mind as well. We do this when we use our creative imaginations, when we ask ourselves questions, say our prayers, meditate, create fantasies, or dream. When we dream, the conscious mind ventures into the strange and fantastic world of the unconscious. So in great stories, we see this as the hero venturing into these other worlds. Jack scurries up the beanstalk to the giant's house in the clouds. Jacob climbs the ladder into Heaven; Alice tumbles into a rabbit hole and ends up in Wonderland. Dorothy rides a tornado into Oz. J. J. Gittes heads for the San Fernando Valley and Sigourney Weaver searches the remote recesses of the space ship seeking the alien. John Cusack enters the portal into John Malkovitch's mind and Pinocchio journeys into the ocean and ends up in the belly of a whale. In *The Matrix*, Keanu Reeves goes back and forth between the two worlds. And so does Russell Crowe in *A Beautiful Mind*.

The Character Archetypes

The next set of patterns reveals the archetypes that describe the different dimensions of our conscious and unconscious selves. These are the character archetypes, the major players and heroes of story.

There are nine character archetypes or major players in our study — the Ego/Hero, the Spiritual, the Emotional, the Mental, the Physical, the Anima/Animus, the Trickster, the Threshold Guardian, and the Shadow.

The male and female heroes and antiheroes are the metaphors that personify the archetypes of the conscious self and all of the other characters in the story are metaphors representing the different archetypes of the creative unconscious self.

To recall an earlier quote from Joseph Campbell, "Myths and dreams are the manifestations in image form of all of the energies of the body, moved by the organs, in conflict with each other." The archetypes of the creative unconscious self are the personifications of these organic energies in conflict.

The basic divisions I use to describe these unconscious archetypes (these energies in conflict) are the four essential dimensions of ourselves, namely: the physical, the emotional, the mental, and the spiritual, so that we will have archetypes that describe the operating energies of the physical self, the emotional self, the mental self and the spiritual self. In our model, these are the larger circles at the cardinal points of the circumference.

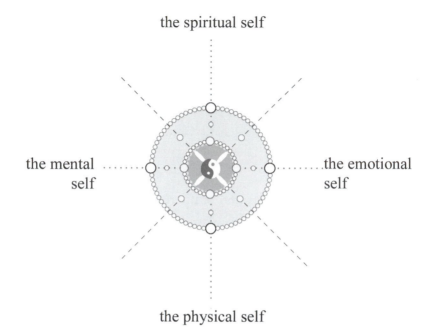

the spiritual self

the mental self

the emotional self

the physical self

I call the archetypes of these different dimensions the spiritual archetypes, the mental archetypes, the emotional archetypes, and the physical archetypes. In great stories, these are the forces that bring about the problems and the resolutions that bring about the changes of fortune. They are the forces of assistance and resistance — the allies, enemies, and other important characters that confront and surround the hero and the antihero and act as antagonists or guides. I will describe them all in great detail in Chapters 13 and 15 but I will introduce you to a few of them here.

The anima and animus are the love interests in a story and the ego/hero's guide to the soul. I illustrate these archetypes in our model as the flower petals linking the conscious center to the surrounding unconscious.

The tricksters are the troublemakers that goad the conscious arche-types forward when they get stuck. I illustrate them as the small circles imbedded in the lighter dotted spokes.

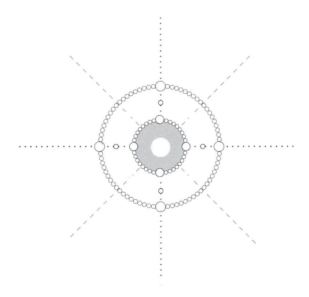

The threshold guardians act as obstacles and barriers. They stand in the way of the conscious archetypes and are there to verify their preparedness and test their resolve. I illustrate them as the larger circles embedded in the bolder spokes.

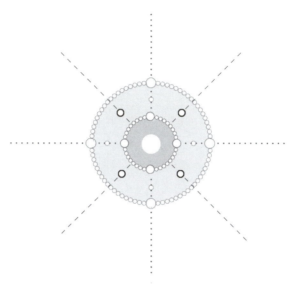

Each of these major sets of archetypes has a male and a female aspect which can be either positive or negative. By "positive" I mean favoring the creative goals of the higher, unselfish, spiritual self, and by "negative" I mean favoring the special interests and selfish motives of the lower, primordial, physical self. I illustrate these attributes as Yin and Yang, the Chinese symbol of opposites, which is embedded in the small circle of consciousness.

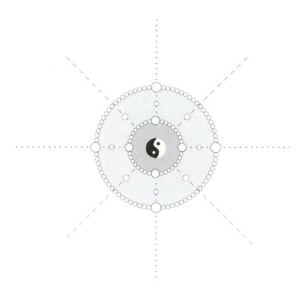

We experience these character archetypes, as we do all of the archetypes, in four ways. We experience them in story and dreams but we
also experience them psychologically and in real life. Psychologically,
we experience the archetypes as feelings, thoughts, physical sensations,
desires, fantasies, mental images, and so on. Feelings of aggression,
desire, and hunger, for instance, are all expressions of the lower, instinctual, physical self. In real life, we experience them as the different roles
we're called upon to play. For example, my students might experience
me as a mental or spiritual mentor. People who disagree with my poli-
tics might see me as a dangerous troublemaker or negative trickster.
One of my daughters may see me as a positive emotional father figure,
the other daughter as negative. The next week it can be the reverse; it
would all depend on my disposition at that moment. My grandson,
Jimmy, might experience me as a threshold guardian, when I'm trying
to prevent him from doing something foolish because he's not ready.
My wife might perceive me as a positive animus figure, when I'm being
supportive, and as a negative animus figure, when I'm being critical. I
might experience her as a positive anima figure in the morning, a guide
to my soul, a mental helper in the afternoon, when she's acting as my

editor, and a temptress at night. It's all relative. The archetypes being revealed in great stories are reflections of our inner and outer social selves — they are the source of the feelings and ideas that influence and motivate our actions and behavior.

The **shadow** is all of the repressed elements of our psychic selves that got stuffed into the trunks of the personal unconscious. They can be either spiritual, emotional, mental, or physical — conscious or unconscious, positive or negative.

In Freudian psychology, these repressed elements are all there is to the unconscious. After Carl Jung described the collective, archetypal unconscious we all share in common, he renamed the repressed elements the shadow. I indicate the shadow in my model as the dark, shadowy ring that surrounds consciousness.

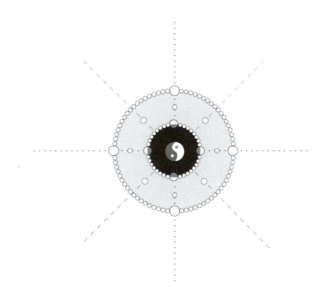

In story and dreams, these repressed elements become demons, mummies, ghosts and arch villains.

CHAPTER 12

INNER CONFLICT

Why are these creative unconscious energies in conflict? You can get a clue to that if you study our evolutionary development, whereby we evolved from reptiles to mammals to primates to early humans to *homo sapiens* (man the wise). Each new development of the brain superseded the previous one. The physical, instinctual reptile brain (the R-complex) was covered over by the emotional, mammalian brain, the limbic system, and the mammalian brain was covered over by the thinking, human brain, the neo-cortex. There's a spiritual brain in there somewhere but it hasn't been located yet.

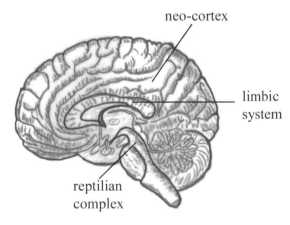

neo-cortex

limbic system

reptilian complex

You can see this development in the human fetus, in animated time-lapse photography, where the later, younger brains clearly seem to be overlaying the earlier, older ones. The lower, earlier forces are, in effect, being overthrown by the younger, higher forces.

Somewhere along the line, the ego, the center of the conscious mind, was developed to act as an administrator and mediator of all of these forces. There's been a struggle for power going on ever since. And the main objective of the principal opposing forces (the spiritual and the physical) has been to influence and control the conscious element (the ego) and use it as a power-releasing, consciousness-building resource.

Now, if you wanted to express these evolutionary ideas in story using visual metaphors, i.e. real things that have been artistically treated and arranged into stories, how would you do that? Two stories which illustrate this basic evolutionary situation come to mind — the Greek myth of the battle of the Titans and Milton's story in *Paradise Lost* about the battle between God and Satan.

In the Greek myth, the newer, younger, Olympian gods, led by Zeus, take on and overthrow the older, Titanic gods led by Cronus, his father. Zeus wins and becomes king of the gods and Cronus is sealed up in Tartarus, the Greek underworld. That is a perfect metaphor for what we have been describing — newer, younger, more powerful brain functions superseding older, lower forces.

In Milton's story, a similar, great battle is fought between God and Satan for control of Heaven. Satan loses and is condemned to Hades, the underworld — aka Hell. As part of Satan's counterattack, he turns himself into a serpent and goes up to the Garden of Eden to corrupt God's new favorites, Adam and Eve. He tempts them with an apple that can give them some of God's great power. They break God's law and are driven out of Paradise.

God, in this story, represents, of course, the higher spiritual self and Satan the lower, superseded, physical self which is shut up in the underworld. Adam and Eve represent the conscious self, the ego. This is made clear by the fact that they are naming things in the Garden. That's one of the things the conscious mind does, it gives names to things. And finally, the snake is a perfect metaphor of the lower, physical self, which is, in fact, a reptile brain, the R-complex, the source of our most basic physical instincts, appetites, and drives, the ones that control survival, hunger, sex, anger, aggression, power, and greed.

The two important structural patterns being revealed by these stories have to do with the fact that the conscious and unconscious energies are organized in a hierarchy — the physical, instinctual self has been superseded by the higher self and they're in conflict. There is a rivalry between them. The spiritual dimension is above, the physical dimension is below, and the conscious element, which they are both trying to influence, is caught in the middle.

You see this hierarchy very clearly in the two stories we were just discussing. Heaven is above, Hell is below, and the Garden of Eden is in the middle. Mount Olympus is above, Tartarus is below, and the Earth is in the middle. The physical and spiritual sides of our natures are in conflict and our conscious selves are caught in the middle.

You see this relationship in the movie *Ghost*. The conscious world is the real world, and when the good die, they leave the real world and rise up to the spiritual light. When the evil ones die, they are dragged down below into the dark underworld. Light, by the way, is a metaphor for consciousness. Bright or white light is associated with spiritual or higher consciousness, and darkness belongs to the lower, instinctual consciousness. The powers of darkness.

In stories, the most frequent manifestation of the rivalry between the light and dark sides of our nature is the struggle between good and evil. These are all very persistent patterns in story with which I'm sure everyone is familiar.

What I've just described is the basic equation and dominant pattern that is found in almost every story: the struggle between good and evil. The higher, spiritual forces and the lower, instinctual forces are trying to influence the conscious forces, which are caught in the middle, in order to control the destiny of some entity that's being transformed.

CHAPTER 13

THE EGO/HERO ARCHETYPE

I call the ego's participation in the cycles of transformation a "passage," and the hero's participation in these cycles his or her "journey" or "adventure." These cycles and passages have a positive and negative side, an upside and a downside. I illustrate this in our model as arrows going counter-clockwise around the Golden Paradigm.

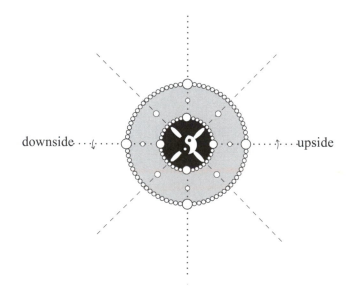

To function properly as the center of consciousness, the ego has to be initiated and strengthened at every step. The actions of the hero show the ego the way through this initiation process.

As Joseph Campbell explains: "The standard path of the mythological adventure of the hero is a magnification of the formula represented in the rites of passage: *separation – initiation – return* which might be named the nuclear unit of the monomyth."

What Jung and Campbell discovered that was so remarkable was a connection between certain patterns in myths and dreams and the rites of passage of primitive tribes, the common purpose being to guide the initiate to higher states of maturity and awareness, i.e. to a greater share of consciousness. The separation-initiation-return pattern is, in fact, innate. Great stories bring these patterns to consciousness.

In his book *The Origins and History of Consciousness*, Erich Neumann writes:

> Individual consciousness passes through the same archetypal stages of development that marked the history of human consciousness as a whole. The stages begin and end with the symbol of the Uroboros, or tail-eating serpent; the intermediary stages are projected in the universal myths of the World Creation, the Great Mother, the Separation of the World Parents, the Birth of the Hero, the Slaying of the Dragon, the Rescue of the Captive, and the Transformation and Deification of the Hero. The hero throughout this sequence is the evolving ego consciousness.

Like the other major archetypes, the ego/hero has a male and female aspect which can be either positive or negative. I call the positive aspect the nascent ego and the negative aspect, the holdfast. In our story model, I call the nascent ego the hero and the holdfast the antihero. The hero can be either male or female, positive or negative. Indiana Jones is a positive male hero, while Sigourney Weaver in *Alien*, Julie Roberts in *Erin Brockovich*, Jodie Foster in *The Silence of the Lambs*, and Uma Thurman in *Kill Bill* are positive female heroes. Macbeth is a negative, male antihero, Scarlett O'Hara is a negative female antihero. So when I use the term hero or antihero in this book, it can mean either a male or a female.

The Nascent Ego

Nascent means about to be born. The nascent ego is the conscious element on the upside of the cycle that is about to be awakened and transformed into hero consciousness (a mature ego). It is the conscious desire to participate in this consciousness-building process. It is the desire to grow, the desire to do something meaningful with our lives, the desire to make a contribution and reach our full potential. It is the part of us that recognizes problems, accepts responsibility, resists temptation, and shares its good fortune. It is the unselfish, positive side of the ego.

In real life, it's anyone who is about to take part in some meaningful transformation. It's real heroes like Lech Walesa in Poland, Vaclav Havel in Czechoslovakia, Mahatma Gandhi in India, or Martin Luther King in the U.S. when they are about to risk everything and sacrifice everything to bring about positive, meaningful change.

In story, it is the potential hero at the beginning of the story before he has proven himself. It's Frodo in *The Lord of the Rings* before the start of the adventure, Luke Skywalker in *Star Wars* before he meets Obi-Wan Kenobi, Neo at the beginning of *The Matrix*, and Jodie Foster in *The Silence of the Lambs* before she is influenced by Hannibal Lecter.

The audience identifies with the hero and the hero draws them into the experience and guides them through the paradigm. The truer the hero is to the ego archetype, the stronger the identification of the recipient of the story. And if the hero is a role model, someone we want to be like, then the story can have a powerful influence on our lives.

The Holdfast

Psychologically, the holdfast is just the opposite. Whereas the nascent ego is a positive impulse that propels us forward toward positive actions or change, the holdfast is the impulse to "hold on" to what we have and resist change. It is the desire to stay in a safe, comfortable place or keep everything exactly as it is. We experience this aspect of the holdfast first as the infant who doesn't want to give up its mother's breast, or the two-year-old tyrants who throw tantrums when they don't get their way, or the child who doesn't want to grow up. This is the negative, selfish side of the ego, the egotistical side that has given the word "ego" a bad name, as in egotistical or egomaniacal.

Dustin Hoffman in *Kramer vs Kramer* is a holdfast. He doesn't want to grow up. The three men in *Three Men and a Baby* are holdfasts. They don't want to give up their playboy-bachelor lifestyles and take on the responsibilities of a wife and family.

The holdfast is also the part of us that gives in to temptation, the part that seeks to give pleasure to the senses, the part that can be taken over by the dark side. It is the impulse to do something that is essentially self-destructive. This is Adam and Eve, Scarlett O'Hara, Othello, and Macbeth. This is also King David after he meets Bathsheba, Samson after he meets Delilah, and William Hurt after he meets Kathleen Turner in *Body Heat*, or Michael Douglas in *Fatal Attraction* or *Basic Instinct*.

A final characteristic of the holdfast is the will to power and insatiable greed. This is the materialistic, power-hungry, tyrannical side of our natures, the side that wants to possess everything it desires, without limit, and control everything it needs. This is Sauron in *The Lord of the Rings*, Voldemort in *Harry Potter* and the little duke in *Shrek*. This is Johnny Friendly, the Lee J. Cobb character in *On The Waterfront*, the corrupt union boss who will do anything to hold on to his power. This is Captain Bligh in *Mutiny on the Bounty*, Little Caesar, or Macbeth. And this is King Herod in the New Testament. Herod is the classic holdfast. When he hears the prophecy that some recently born child will grow up to replace him as king, he orders all of the infants in his kingdom under two years old to be slaughtered.

In real life, the tyrannical holdfast is one of the easiest archetypes to spot. This is Hitler, Mussolini, Stalin, and Mao Tse-tung. This is Erich Honecker in East Germany, Ferdinand Marcos in the Philippines, Kim Jong Il in North Korea, Omar al-Bashir in Sudan, or Saddam Hussein in Iraq. But it can be any politician, company president, or petty tyrant who would rather abuse power than give it up.

The Central Character, Protagonist, and Hero Compared and Defined

The difference between a central character, protagonist, and hero, as I see it, is this: The central character is the main character of the story. In a film, it is the character who is getting the most screen time. The story is being told from their point of view. Protagonist is a Greek word meaning first actor. In the early Greek plays there were no actors, only the chorus. Then they added a first actor, a protagonist. It has come to mean: the one who initiates the action, and the antagonist is the one who opposes the action. The hero is a protagonist who risks his or her life or sacrifices himself or herself for others. The 9/11 firemen are considered heroes because they risked or sacrificed their lives for others. The airline passengers who overpowered the highjackers on the plane that crashed in Pennsylvania are heroes because they sacrificed themselves to save the lives of others.

Examples

In *Jaws*, Roy Scheider, the sheriff, is the central character. He gets the most screen time. He is also the protagonist. He is the one who initiates the action against the shark. He is also a hero because at some point he is willing to risk his life for the sake of the people of Amity Island.

In "Cinderella," Cinderella is the central character. It is definitely her story. But she is neither a protagonist nor a hero. The protagonist, the one who initiates the action, is the good fairy. She gives Cinderella the incentive and the means to go to the ball. The hero, if it's anybody, is the prince. He's the one who goes on the quest with the glass slipper. Cinderella is, in fact, the victim in the story — and the story is being told from her point of view. She is also an anima figure, the love interest that lures the hero into the adventure. The glass slipper is the marvelous element, the thing that makes it possible for the prince to track down the love interest so he can marry her and solve the larger problem of the kingdom which is short one bride.

In *A Christmas Carol*, Scrooge is the central character. The story is about him. But, here again, he is neither a hero nor a protagonist. The protagonists are Marley and the three Christmas ghosts. They are the ones who initiate the action that brings about Scrooge's transformation. But they're not heroes because they're not risking or sacrificing their lives. They're spirits. They're already dead. They're just doing their job. Scrooge is, in fact, the threat, the cause of the problem. And, as such, the main source of resistance. He goes kicking and screaming into his transformation. He doesn't want to do it. He is also, of course, being transformed into a hero. By the end of that story, he is ready to begin sacrificing his wealth for the sake of others.

Villains and Antiheroes Defined

When the story is being told from the point of view of the hero, then I call the threat (the cause of the problem) a villain. If the story is being told from the point of view of that threat, that's when I call them an antihero (Macbeth). On the upside of the *Star Wars* saga (Episodess IV – VI), Darth Vader (formerly Anakin Skywalker) is the villain, the cause of the problem being solved by the hero, Luke Skywalker. On the downside (Episode III) Anakin Skywalker (soon to be Darth Vader) is an antihero. The story is being told from his point of view.

The Stages of the Passage

I illustrate the passage of the hero and antihero in our model by naming the spikes. The stages on the upside are *separation, initiation, integration,* and *rebirth.*

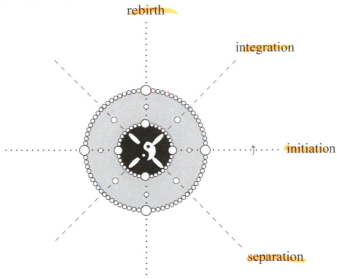

After the ego/hero completes the upside of the passage, he or she will be drawn into the downside and transformed into a holdfast/antihero. Having achieved a great success, the hero will become increasingly reluctant to give up or share any of his newly won power. He will become vulnerable to the seductive powers of the lower self, in the same way that the heroes King David, Samson, and Theseus did.

I call the stages on the downside of the passage: *attachment, regression, alienation,* and *death.*

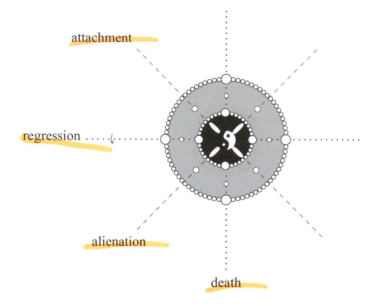

What the upside is to initiation, the downside is to regression. By regression, I mean "reverting back." I mean shutting down the higher self in favor of the demands of the lower, instinctual self. And I see both initiation and regression in this case as being positive — two necessary phases in the process of transformation.

Here is a quote concerning regression from *A Critical Dictionary of Jungian Analysis*:

> Jung's attitude toward regression differed markedly from Freud's. For the latter, regression was almost always a negative phenomenon — something to be fought off and overcome. From 1912 onwards, Jung insisted on the therapeutic and personality enhancing aspects of periods of regression (without denying the harmful nature of prolonged and unproductive regression). Regression may be seen as a period of regeneration prior to subsequent advance.

The ultimate goal of these passages is the creation and expansion of consciousness. The unconscious, according to what we're being told by the archetypal patterns in great stories, is a pool of potential consciousness. We start life, as infants, completely unconscious. The fully realized, ultimate states of mind we hope to achieve reside in the unconscious as conscious potential. The hidden truth revealed by story is all about how these unconscious "potential" energies can be awakened and converted into energies and powers that can be consciously administered and controlled. These unconscious, "potential" energies are, however, extremely powerful and have to be carefully regulated and controlled until the ego has been properly prepared and has proven he or she can handle it. The gauntlet of proof is the passage. To function properly as the center of consciousness, the ego has to be initiated and strengthened at every step. The purpose of story is to guide the ego through these ego-strengthening passages so it can properly administer these powerful, unconscious energies. The actions of the hero in story show the ego the way through this initiation process.

The Garden of Eden story becomes interesting here because it reveals the beginning of the regressive process which results in the higher self being shut down. On the upside of the passage, the hero resists temptation and advances to a higher state. On the downside, the anti-hero, in this case Adam and Eve, give in to temptation and descend to a lower, less desirable state. When the conscious element gives in to the temptations of the lower self, an alienation from the higher self occurs. And that is the basic situation that exists today — the spiritual self is shut down and the serpent brain is gaining the upper hand. The ego doesn't know what's going on but is, nevertheless, in a serious struggle with the lower, physical self, and it's cut off from any real help from above. We see this clearly when we examine all of the physical addictions to sugar, fat, caffeine, nicotine, alcohol, drugs, etc. which we're fighting because our appetites have gone awry. The higher, spiritual power could easily come to our aid and subdue these addictive physical powers but it can't turn on the juice unless the ego can handle it. And the ego can't handle it unless it makes these passages and is strengthened. But it doesn't even know it has to do that because it has lost touch with story, the creative unconscious self, and just about every other source of higher wisdom.

CHAPTER 14

THE MARVELOUS AND TERRIBLE ELEMENTS

In order to complete these passages and reach their respective goals, the nascent ego and holdfast need power; they need the vast, unconscious spiritual, mental, emotional, and physical powers that are waiting to be awakened and released. Psychologically, these are the building blocks of consciousness, the energies without which higher states of being cannot be achieved. They could be extraordinary unrealized creative, healing or intuitive powers, unrealized talent or genius, extraordinary mental, physical or sexual abilities, a profound capacity to love, the power to influence the world (charisma), the power to transcend duality and experience ultimate truth. In real life, they are the money and power necessary to bring about positive and negative changes of fortune. They are the clever schemes necessary to commit crimes, the evidence necessary to prosecute criminals, and the terrible weapons necessary to protect your nation or win hot and cold wars. All things which are difficult to realize but without which the problems cannot be overcome, the tasks cannot be completed and the transformations cannot be realized.

In great stories, we see these extraordinary powers and potentials expressed as these real things or as fabulous treasures like King Solomon's mines, the Fountain of Youth, the ancient Egyptian Book of Thoth, or the Holy Grail. We see them as supernatural powers like invisibility, flying, or X-ray vision — as secret formulas, magic potions, ultimate weapons, or magic objects like the ruby slippers, Aladdin's lamp, a crystal ball, a time machine, or Samson's hair. Or we see them as fantastic places like Camelot, Shangri-La, Eldorado, or the Promised Land; forgotten Paradises like the Garden of Eden; or lost kingdoms like Shambhala, Atlantis, and Utopia.

The hero and the holdfast compete for control of these extraordinary powers. In the hands of the hero, they are Excalibur or the Holy Grail, the building blocks of consciousness. In the hands of the self-destructive antihero, they become voodoo dolls, Svengali's hypnotism, Dracula's addictive fangs. Or they become death stars, doomsday machines, or rings of power, the scourges of mankind.

Joseph Campbell calls these special powers and objects the ultimate boon. Alfred Hitchcock called them the McGuffin, the thing everybody wants. I call them the marvelous or terrible elements.

Bill Moyers asked Joseph Campbell, "What is Heaven?" And Joseph Campbell answered, "Heaven is a symbolic place. Heaven is no place. These are planes of consciousness or fields of experience potential in the human spirit."

CHAPTER 15

THE ARCHETYPES OF THE CREATIVE UNCONSCIOUS SELF

In order to accomplish the actions necessary to release these marvelous and terrible powers, the nascent ego and holdfast have to be motivated and prepared. They cannot perform these tasks alone. The help they need comes from the archetypes of the creative unconscious self. These character archetypes act as the custodians of the miraculous powers and hold the keys to their release. In story, they are the major players, the forces of assistance or resistance — the metaphors that personify these organic energies which are in conflict.

The Physical Archetypes

Carl Jung calls the physical, instinctual archetypes of the lower self the Terrible Mother and the Terrible Father. To me they are the positive and negative physical archetypes. Anatomically it is the R-complex, the reptile brain that controls the lower, physical, animal side of our nature. The lower self is a primordial, earthbound self. It pursues earthly things. And hidden in the matrix of its mysterious and seductive energies are the libido and the id — the source of our most basic instincts, appetites and drives. They are associated with the three lower chakras, the ones that control hunger, sex, aggression, and the will to power. And these are the energies that have been superseded by the energies of our higher brains and they don't like it. So they compete with the higher self for influence over the conscious element, and when the nascent ego attempts one of these passages, they are the principal resisters of all positive change. After the positive ego has been transformed into a holdfast, they are the holdfast's principal supporters, advisers, and guides. They are the negative forces and impulses that seek to control and corrupt us.

In great stories, the metaphors that describe these basic, instinctual energies take a variety of human and animal forms, depending on which aspects of the lower primordial, physical self they are personifying. And like the ego archetype, they can be either masculine or feminine, positive or negative.

In real life, the positive physical archetypes might be represented by a physical therapist, a basketball coach, or any medical doctor who cures physical ills, and the negative physical archetypes by drug dealers and others who are trying to corrupt us.

In story, our wholesome physical appetites might be personified, as they are in the Greek myths, as Eros and Aphrodite, Hecate and Pluto, or Dionysus — the gods of physical love, material wealth, good food and wine. And the negative, aggressive impulses that urge us to seek revenge, seize territory, kill, or go to war might be represented by Ares or Diana, or the Hindu gods Shiva and Kali.

But in our modern society, we have created another snake, a demonic snake, which is the result of the repression of some of these basic, natural instincts. This is a shadow figure, a source of evil — someone or something that has been taken over by the dark side. This is Hannibal Lecter in *The Silence of The Lambs*, Sauron in *The Lord of the Rings*, Voldemort in *Harry Potter*, the Devil in *The Exorcist*, the terrible mother monster in *Aliens*, T-Rex and the velociraptors in *Jurassic Park*, or the shark in *Jaws*. This is Satan, Dracula, the Evil Emperor and Darth Vader in *Star Wars*, the evil behind all evils. And this is Nosferatu, the undead. Dracula is Nosferatu. He's dead but he's immortal. You can't get rid of him. Nosferatu is a perfect metaphor for these repressed psychic elements, which are dead (repressed) but not dead. They come back to haunt us. They are the stuff of horror movies and nightmares.

Psychologically, these repressed elements become the negative energies that inspire lust, hatred, anger and greed, acts of aggression, acts of violence and all of the other deadly sins that can overwhelm us and take away our control. In real life, when people are completely taken over by these dark forces they become serious villains, drug lords, and tyrants. Hitler is still, by far, our best example. But Stalin and Idi Amin are right up there, as are the myriad serial killers and psychopaths that plague our real lives.

Complicating the identification of these shadow figures, in real life and story, is the fact that they will hide their true character. Legitimate antagonists do not hide their negative sides, but the shadow does, and that's why the villain in a whodunit often turns out to be the least likely suspect. He pretends to be all good. A real human being is a complex creature full of contradictions and a mixture of good and bad traits and can easily become a suspect. Real villains will hide all evil traits, so they'll appear to be too good to be true. In real life, we see this all the time. It's how evil operates. Really despicable and corrupt individuals hiding behind virtue or the flag. To advance their political careers, corrupt politicians will conceal all of their negative qualities and say or do anything to get elected. When they get caught, it turns out all they really cared about was money, sex, and power. Honecker in East Germany was apparently such a villain. Tyranny posing as beneficent ruler.

According to Robert McKee, "The worst possible villains are those pretending to be what they despise. Hate posing as love. Vice posing as virtue. Injustice posing as justice."

The neighbors of the Bronx serial killer, Son of Sam, insisted he was the nicest person they ever met. This is how evil operates.

In any event, the shadow has to be resolved first and integrated into our personality before the conscious elements can get back on the right track and proceed with their initiations. The clear message of story is not to repress these natural instincts but to civilize and transform them, to be their master and not their slave.

In *Sleeping Beauty*, the king does not invite a dark witch named Maleficent to the celebration honoring his daughter's birth. She appears anyway and in her anger puts a serious curse on the young princess and the royal court. The important meaningful connection to be made in this story is that we cannot pick and choose which dimensions of our psychic selves we wish to integrate. They all have to be invited to the party. When the negative energies are repressed or left out, they get nasty. And it always leaves the conscious element seriously threatened, somewhat enchanted or beast-like.

The Emotional Archetypes

The R-complex, as we indicated, was superseded by our emotional brain, the limbic system, and this gave rise to the emotional archetypes, which I call the positive and negative emotional father and mother figures.

By emotional self, I mean our social self and our social feelings. Social feelings refer to the things we feel when we interact socially with other people or as part of a group (love, a sense of duty, camaraderie, empathy, compassion, excitement, anxiety, guilt, etc.). The emotional parent figures are concerned about emotional things, about personal relationships, about the role the hero and holdfast/antihero should play in society.

Unlike the spiritual and physical self, the emotional self does not have an agenda, other than to make the social entity, whatever its mores, function as a harmonious or effective whole. A social entity can be a family, a community, a corporation, an invading army, or a mob, and it can give its allegiance to either positive or negative ideals, to a Hitler or a Christ. Its character is determined by its objectives.

In real life, when people play the positive emotional father and mother figure roles, they are guided by the objectives of the higher self. And they are the people who love us, who nurture and protect us and teach us our social responsibilities. They teach us how to get along with others, when to say please and thank you, how to be good parents, how to love, how to give and receive affection and how to cooperate with others and share. They give us advice concerning the professions we should choose. They encourage us to be good citizens and work for the common good, admonish us for being selfish, help us work out our social and emotional problems, and give us the social skills we need to achieve our emotional desires and goals. Psychologically, it's all of the feelings and other inner promptings that inspire and guide us in a similar fashion.

In stories, it's the characters that relate to the hero in this same way. In the movies *Ray* and *Mask*, mothers help their handicapped or disfigured sons make it in the real world. In *Fried Green Tomatoes*, Jessica Tandy uses a story to guide an unhappy housewife back to an understanding of married life. In *Gone with the Wind*, Hattie McDaniel tries unsuccessfully to put Scarlett O'Hara on the right track. In *The Verdict*, Jack Warden helps rehabilitate Paul Newman, an emotionally bankrupt ambulance chaser and alcoholic. In *Class Action*, Gene Hackman is a father who is trying to teach his corporate defending daughter her social responsibility. But it could be any friend, colleague, relative, or stranger that fills that emotional role.

The negative emotional father and mother figures are just the opposite. They are guided by the objectives of the lower self, teach us prejudice and hatred and intolerance, and criticize all our efforts to develop a genuine social conscience. They believe human beings are basically evil and have to be dominated by the proper iron fist or they will run amok. It's a dog-eat-dog world and we have to accept that. We should be ambitious and ruthless and use any means to become king of the hill. If you fail to reach the top, you will be nothing.

In real life, they are the social forces that helped create Hitler and Charles Manson. They teach us how to lie, how to persuade, and how to get power over others. They teach us how to organize a cult or secret neo-Nazi society. They want you to create an elite cadre of paramilitary followers and become like Genghis Khan. They need you to become like Genghis Khan. They need you to achieve that kind of greatness so you can put the masses under your spell. Psychologically, they are the inner impulses and promptings that encourage or drive us in this direction.

In story, this is Livia in *I, Claudius*, a mother who will stop at nothing, including many murders, to see her son, Tiberius, emperor. This is also David Copperfield's black-hearted stepfather and the father who drove his son to suicide in *Dead Poets Society*. It is also Cinderella's wicked stepmother, Mary Tyler Moore in *Ordinary People*, Kate Nelligan in *Prince of Tides* and Henry Fonda in *On Golden Pond*.

The Mental Archetypes

The mental archetypes are the denizens of our thinking brain, the neo-cortex. They are our knowledge, our intelligence, our understanding — our ability to reason, to judge, to think creatively or plot strategies.

Like the emotional self, the mental self doesn't have an agenda. It's neutral, a tool that can serve the objectives of either the higher or the lower self. If you want to save the world, the mind will help you do that, providing you with a strategy and a master plan. On the other hand, if you want to rob a bank or kill someone, it will help you do that as well. It's a tool. Werner von Braun, the father of the German V-2 rocket that nearly destroyed London, became America's leading rocket scientist for thirty years after World War II and was just as comfortable working for the US as he was for Hitler. He was neutral. All he really cared about was making rockets. So, in great stories, the metaphors that reveal these archetypes can serve the interests of either the higher or the lower self.

The positive male and female mental archetypes possess a special knowledge which can help the hero achieve his or her goal. This is Athena in *The Iliad*, Yoda in *Star Wars*, the psychiatrist in *Ordinary People*, Whoopi Goldberg in *Ghost*. In the legends of King Arthur, it's the magician, Merlin. Without the power contained in the invincible sword, Excalibur, Arthur cannot unify England and create Camelot. And without Merlin's help, Arthur cannot possess and control the sword.

In fairy tales, it is frequently an animal like the fox. In *Jungle Book*, it's the panther, Bagheera. In *The Lion King*, it's the shaman baboon, Rifiki. In *Shakespeare in Love*, it's Will's shrink. But it could take the form of a computer or even a wise child, as in the Hindu myth,

"Parade of Ants." In real life, it could be the mentors who influenced Jonas Salk and Albert Einstein, or the advisers who helped the allied leaders win World War II.

The negative mental helpers, the sorcerer and sorceress, can also take the form of witches, traitors, evil geniuses, wizards, computers, or spies. They have the special knowledge and powers that can undermine the hero and guide him to his doom. This is Iago in *Othello* and Mephistopheles in *Faust*, who tempts the ill-fated antihero with the power that will bring about the corruption and damnation of his immortal soul.

In real life, it's Machiavelli, Goebbels, or Adolf Eichmann. They show the holdfast how to be a successful tyrant and fight a *Blitzkrieg* war. They concoct the secret formulas, design the death camps and construct the doomsday machines that will give the holdfast the power to carry out his diabolical schemes.

The Spiritual Archetypes

The spiritual archetypes, which we call the positive or negative spiritual father and mother figures, are the guiding spirits and hidden wisdom of the higher, unbounded, cosmic self. When the nascent ego is ready for its adventure, the energies of the spiritual self are the principal forces trying to bring about that positive change. They are the creative energies that give birth to the psychological impulses that seek to overcome the negative states and achieve the higher states of being. They inspire us to seize the day, to be creative and virtuous, courageous and just, to make sacrifices and to do great things. They are the source of the power that can make or break our lives, and they want us to be liberated and free — to be at one with our selves, our loved ones, our country, our world, our God, and the cosmos. They are the sum and substance of our souls and the guardians of our destiny.

In great stories, as metaphors, these spiritual energies can take many different male and female forms. They can personify all-seeing, all-powerful gods and goddesses like Hera and Zeus, Isis and Osiris, or they can take a mortal form like Obi-wan Kenobi in *Star Wars*,

Gandalf in *The Lord of the Rings*, Dumbledore in *Harry Potter*, Mufasa in *The Lion King*, Marlon Brando in *Superman I*, the wizard and the good witch in *The Wizard of Oz*, and the mother in *My Left Foot*, who helps nurture the artistic talents of her paraplegic son. They can, in fact, be any positive father or mother figure whose main concerns are spiritual matters — i.e. they inspire and help the hero to reach or bring about higher, more desirable states of being.

In real life, we experience these archetypes when we play these spiritual roles, when we inspire, challenge, and help others on the path to higher states of being, or when others inspire and guide us to do the same. Priests and gurus make a profession of it. Ideal parents and grandparents do it from a sense of love and duty.

The emotional mother figure would be more concerned with getting along with others and being a good citizen, the spiritual mother figure with accomplishing great things. Frank Lloyd Wright's mother, it is reported, put photographs of the world's great architectural achievements on the walls of his nursery and told him he was going to be the greatest architect that ever lived. Picasso's mother told him he would be one of the greatest painters. This is that mother — the guardian of our destiny.

The spiritual father and mother appear negative when their laws are broken and they show their wrath. This is the God in the Old Testament, Caleb's father in *East of Eden*, or fire and brimstone preachers. When their charges give in to temptation, go stubbornly in the wrong direction, or are on the brink of disaster, they withhold their powers, threaten them with hellfire or kick them out of Paradise. This is also the religious extremists, fanatics or zealots who deny the lower self any legitimate expression, insist on the repression of all sexual energy, and will kill in the name of their god.

The spiritual and physical archetypes do not have equal power. The higher, spiritual powers can easily dominate the lower powers if the ego/hero has been initiated and the higher powers are in force. We see this in *Dracula*. When the cross (a metaphor of spiritual power) appears, Dracula, despite his incredible physical strength, always shrinks back. Zeus can beat up all the other gods. In *Raiders of the Lost Ark*, when the spiritual powers locked in the Ark of the Covenant are suddenly unleashed, an evil army of Nazis is dissolved like melting wax.

The Anima/Animus Archetypes

According to Carl Jung, the anima is the inner figure of woman held by a man and the animus is the inner figure of man at work in the woman's psyche. They are subliminal to consciousness and function from within the unconscious psyche. They are of benefit to but can also endanger consciousness, hence their positive and negative sides. They act as guides to the soul and become necessary links with creative possibilities and instruments of individuation, individuation being, as I mentioned, Jung's path to a fully realized individual.

In great stories, the positive anima and animus archetypes are expressed as the positive male and female love interests of the hero. I call the negative anima and animus figures, the temptress and the tempter.

We encounter the positive anima in just about every story that has a male hero. She is the feminine love interest. She helps to lure the hero into the adventure and acts as his guide. She is Beatrice in Dante's *Inferno*, Liv Tyler in *The Lord of the Rings*, Nicole Kidman in *Cold Mountain*, Eva Marie Saint in *On the Waterfront*, Andy McDowell in *Groundhog Day,* and Renee Zellweger in *Cinderella Man.*

Psychologically, she's a man's inner vision of divine beauty and the source of his most productive fantasies. In real life, she's the girl he falls in love with and wants to marry, the girl he makes promises and commitments to. Her love inspires him and is a major source of positive reinforcement. Under her spell, he longs to be a real hero, a man of honor, a man who acts courageously and meets his obligations. And if his character is flawed, she's the one who can shape him up or pressure him to get out there and make it happen.

The negative anima is the temptress, the young witch, the femme fatale. She uses sex to lure the hero and the antihero to their doom. This is Glenn Close in *Fatal Attraction*, Kathleen Turner in *Body Heat*, and Sharon Stone in *Basic Instinct*. Psychologically, she's the inner seductress who hides in the centerfolds of a man's mind and she is a major ally of the lower self. In real life, she is a party girl, a slut, a bimbo, or a real fatal attraction.

The positive animus (male love interest) is the ideal husband and lover to the feminine hero. He protects, rescues, and guides. He is her contact to the soul. He is Amor to Psyche, Superman to Lois Lane, the general's son to Mulan, and Leonardo DiCaprio to Kate Winslet in *Titanic*, the one who guides her away from suicide, a disastrous marriage, and a frigid death.

Patrick Swayze in *Ghost* would be a perfect animus figure, guiding Demi Moore from the other side, if Demi Moore's character wasn't so passive. As it is, Swayze is both the animus figure and the hero. It is his adventure. If he were a true animus figure (i.e. if she were the real hero), he would be a perfect metaphor for this male psychological component which does, in fact, try to influence and guide the feminine ego from the other side of consciousness.

The negative animus (tempter) is the negative male counterpart at work in the woman's psyche. Like the temptress, he is a major ally of the lower self, so he tries to sexually seduce, undermine and enslave the feminine ego, but he can also be experienced psychologically as a highly critical inner voice. In real life and story, men taken over by this archetype can be a real bastard, a brutal husband or lover, or a dictatorial male chauvinist pig. He locks his women in a pumpkin shell, a tower, a kitchen, a psychological or real dungeon. He ridicules her ideas, criticizes her appearance, is insanely jealous, and tries to squash any desires she may have for independence. If she's susceptible to substance abuse, he may help her get hooked. If they run short of cash, he may turn her into a prostitute and even become her pimp. In a milder, more romantic form, it's Count Varonsky in *Anna Karenina*. In a less manly, more unpleasant mode, it's the boyfriend in *Tess*. In its most virulent strain, it's Bluebeard, or Terence Stamp in a movie called *The Collector*. It's Julia Robert's husband in *Sleeping with the Enemy* or all the male characters in *Thelma and Louise*.

The Trickster

The function of the tricksters is to stir up trouble and bring about change or progress in any way that they can. They are an essential psychological, fail-safe tool designed to help get us restarted when we're stuck.

Joseph Campbell talks about Edshu an important trickster character of the Yoruba tribe in West Africa. Edshu walks through a village wearing a hat with four sides and each side is a different color. After he's gone, someone will say: "Hey, did you see that god in the red hat that just walked by?" And someone else will counter: "What do you mean? He was wearing a blue hat." An argument breaks out, the village is polarized, and that brings about important change.

The guy who sold Jack the magic beans is a trickster character and so is Marley's ghost in *A Christmas Carol*. Coyote and Raven are important trickster figures in Native American mythology.

Joseph Wiseman in *Viva Zapata* is a negative trickster. He's an anarchist who keeps switching sides and stirring up trouble, first to get a revolution going, then a counter-revolution.

In real life, when we play the trickster role, we might be a relative or a friend goading a couch potato child or comrade to action. Psychologically, it's anything from slips of the tongue to personal accidents that get us into trouble or concern us so much that we're forced to change. A disaster or catastrophe in the real world that brings about reforms is a kind of trickster.

The Threshold Guardians

When we try to make these journeys, the threshold guardians are certain positive and negative obstacles and barriers that stand in our way. They are there to test our resolve and question our preparedness or prevent, thwart, or stall our forward motion.

Psychologically, it can be our doubts and our fears — doubts that we're sufficiently prepared or the fear of criticism, rejection, or failure that prevent us from moving forward courageously. In real life, it's the phone call we're afraid to make to ask for a date or a job. Or it's the people who tell us we're not ready or that something we want to do can't be done and if we attempt it, we will fail. But they're there to test our preparedness. When we're ready to do what we really need to do, then we have to push through these barriers.

One of Joseph Campbell's favorite examples is a ferocious demon guardian that stands in front of a Japanese temple. The demon's authoritative right hand is held out in an intimidating gesture that says: "Don't you dare go beyond this point," while its left hand signals from below with a gentler gesture which encourages you to come in, if you are ready. In stories, the negative threshold guardians manifest themselves as doormen, henchmen or bureaucrats that try to block the hero's path. Or it's the dragon that guards the treasure or the doberman pinschers that guard the villain's estate. In *Harry Potter and the Sorcerer's Stone* it's Fluffy, the three-headed mastiff who guards the trap door. In fact, it's anyone or anything that tries to discourage, frighten, head off, slow down, or otherwise stop the hero's progress. Positive threshold guardians are well-meaning people (or other beings) who stand in the hero's way to make sure that the hero is sufficiently prepared to meet the dangers he or she will have to face.

One of the best examples in recent times is the subway ghost in the movie *Ghost*. Patrick Swayze has to get downtown to see a psychic helper, but a belligerent, aggressive ghost he runs into on the subway scares him off. In a later attempt, he stands up to the ghost and the ghost is transformed into a helper.

CHAPTER 16

SOME SPECIAL QUALITIES OF METAPHOR

Relativity

The first special quality of metaphor is relativity. What this means is that inside the magic circle of a story everything is relative; the same symbol can represent different things in different stories depending on its context. The meaning of a metaphor is determined by its relation to the whole.

If the entity is a kingdom and the prince is in the ego/hero position, then his father, the king, or his mother, the queen, would make excellent metaphors for the positive creative unconscious or higher self. But what if the story is about the king, and he is in the ego/hero position? Then if you wanted to include the higher self, you would have to shop around for something higher, like an emperor or empress, to personify the higher self and complete the equation. And if the emperor is in the ego/hero position, then you might have to bring in the Pope to play the higher role. And if the Pope is the hero, then God himself might have to make an appearance. What a symbol represents depends on its position relative to the conscious center (the ego/hero position) and the whole. So it isn't always easy to know what archetype a metaphor represents, if it's out of context of a story.

Another example of relativity is this. Superman can be the hero and Lois Lane the anima love interest or Lois Lane can be in the ego/hero position with Superman as her animus/love interest and guide. It's all relative. Dracula can be the shadow-like antagonist threat (negative male physical archetype) to a young girl hero or he can be the antihero himself in a story focused on the downside of the wheel. Hannibal Lecter can be a positive/negative male mental archetype to Clarise in *The Silence of the Lambs* or he can be a villain or an antihero in *Hannibal* and *Red Dragon*. It's all relative. In other words, the same character can play different archetypal roles in different stories.

The same is true in real life and that is what this important pattern reveals. Which archetypal role we are playing (i.e. spiritual or mental father and mother figures, negative or positive lovers, helper, holdfast, hero or trickster, etc.) is relative to the situation we happen to be in at the moment and who we're dealing with. It depends on the equation.

The One and the Many

The next special quality is the one and the many. This means that the major archetypes can be divided into any number of other characters. You can have one spiritual God, as in the Old Testament, or hundreds of gods, like the Hindus and ancient Greeks. You can have one villain and one hero or an army of villains and heroes – one goddess of the arts or nine separate muses, one for each of the arts. Or these archetypal elements can be combined. The one God of the Old Testament actually represents all of the major archetypes, positive and negative, in one majestic godhead. Mary Tyler Moore in *Ordinary People* is both the positive and negative, mental and emotional mother. Queen Elizabeth in *Shakespeare in Love* is both the positive and negative spiritual parent archetype. The goddesses Kali, Isis, and Hera are also composites of positive and negative qualities. Lee J. Cobb in *On the Waterfront* is both the holdfast and Mr. Big. In *Star Wars* you have separate characters, Darth Vader and the Evil Emperor, playing those two roles. If there is only one character, then all the different dimensions are contained in that one metaphor. If hundreds of different characters are used, then each one represents a different aspect or dimension of the underlying archetype. A house with one room or a palace with a hundred rooms can be a metaphor of the psyche. It all depends on how much detail you want to go into. In *The Longest Day*, a film about the invasion of Normandy in World War II, the whole allied army is in the ego/hero (anti-threat) position — i.e. they're all there to solve the problem. Each different character featured in that invading force represents a different aspect of that archetype. The same is true of *The Iliad*. The whole Greek army is acting like a collective hero. In the movie *The Dirty Dozen*, you have twelve commandos carrying out the same mission. In *Armageddon*, you have a team of ten or more heroes trying to divert the asteroid. In *Shakespeare in Love*, you have an entire theatrical company trying to create a successful play. Each member of the team represents a different aspect of consciousness. In fairy tales, the king often has three sons, all of whom are in the ego/hero position. The first two will bungle the king's task and the third will do it right. In "Hansel and Gretel," you have two different aspects of the ego consciousness (one male, the other female) tackling the same problem.

What all of this reflects is that each of these major psychic dimensions has many separate functions (in psychology they're called complexes), and each of these separate functions can be expressed separately or combined. Then the major archetypes themselves can operate on their own or in concert with the other major players. They are, in fact, very much like the primary colors. They can be appreciated in their own right or combined to form white (one God), or separated and mixed together to create a thousand different color combinations (the Greek and Hindu pantheons).

The Hero's Profession

Because of the divisibility of these archetypes, the hero can have any profession you can name. The specialties of the different professions are all functions of the ego, and each of these special functions can be isolated and personified as a different hero. We can easily see these different functions operating psychologically when we're in difficulty. When we're sick, our ego-doctor has to handle it and decide if the illness is serious. Will it cure itself or should we call the doctor? Then after we've been to the doctor, we have to decide whether we trust him and his treatment, and so on. When we're being sued or trying to figure out some mystery, then the ego-lawyer or ego-detective has to step in and handle those problems. In real life, it's the real doctors, lawyers, detectives, and priests who are specializing in these different functions that handle these specialized problems. The judge specializes in making judgments, the artist specializes in his creativity, the detective in solving crimes. Whatever career you choose, you are specializing in that conscious function. It's what division of labor is all about, different people specializing in different psychic functions.

In a story, we see this revealed by the different professions of the hero, each different profession being a metaphor for that particular conscious function. The detective represents that part of our conscious self that solves mysteries, the investigative reporter the part which seeks out the truth. Some of the other more prevalent contemporary heroes are the cop, the private detective, the superhero crime fighters, the adventurer, the soldier (warrior), the spy, the lawyer, the doctor, the athlete, the archeologist, the explorer, the teacher, the astronaut, and the judge. Each of these professions or occupations expresses a different function of the conscious self. By far the most popular of these story professions is the crime fighter. And perhaps their popularity stems from the fact that these conscious functions are at the cutting edge of the real world's rather desperate struggle against injustice. The society we live in is rife with serious crime — mass murders, serial killings, terrorist bombings, drugs, the kidnap, rape, abuse, and murder of our women and children, criminal neglect and corruption on the part of government officials, organized crime, corrupt corporations, corrupt doctors, lawyers and judges. The crime fighters in our society are at the leading edge of the fight to bring these evils under control, and many of them, unfortunately, are corrupt themselves. In truth, we are in a life and death struggle with the dark side of our nature. Psychologically, we are all trying to come to terms with these impulses and tendencies in our own psyches.

The Dominant Trait

What is true of the different conscious functions (or professional specialties) is also true of a person's dominant trait, which can also be isolated and personified. Sherlock Holmes' profession is a detective, his dominant quality or trait is deductive reasoning. Ben Affleck's dominant quality in *Shakespeare in Love* is vanity. Othello's dominant trait is jealousy, as is the wicked queen's in *Snow White*. King Midas is greed. Ebenezer Scrooge is miserliness. Charlie Chaplin's tramp is perseverance. Don Juan is lust. Russell Crowe in *Cinderella Man* is fortitude, a courage that permits him to patiently endure great misfortune and pain. Fred Astaire's dominant trait is charm. Woody Allen's dominant trait in his earlier, good movies was neurosis or more specifically hypochondria. Achilles' dominant trait is anger. Macbeth shows us the ins and outs of guilt. Sir Lancelot and Sir Galahad are icons of chivalry. Jiminy Cricket is Pinocchio's conscience. Jack Nicholson's dominant trait in *Terms of Endearment* and the *Witches of Eastwick* is lechery. All of which are significant revelations of character.

The dominant trait is a factor in real life as well. The mind has many facets and qualities. At different times we're dominated by different traits. Anger when we're angry, loyalty when we're loyal, patience when we're being tolerant, and so on. Again, for clarity sake, story likes to isolate and examine one of these traits, explore it in great detail, and show how it operates.

Shapeshifting

The final special quality is shapeshifting. Psychologically, shapeshifting means that the powerful, positive, and negative archetypal energies of the psyche can take on a variety of metaphorical forms and attitudes when they interact with consciousness. They can be mild mannered like Clark Kent or all powerful like Superman. They can be charming and cordial like Jack Nicholson at the beginning of *The Witches of Eastwick* or ferocious and deadly like the demon he is transformed into at the end. Generally speaking, these powerful unconscious energies hold back their real power and true identities in order to protect consciousness. This is especially true in dreams where they will take a variety of innocuous forms to facilitate communication. The really heavy-hitter metaphors like Shiva, Krishna, and Zeus rarely, if ever, reveal their true forms to mortals for this very reason. It could endanger or destroy them. Zeus reluctantly revealed his true self to an ex-lover and she was burnt to a crisp. In *Oh, God!*, John Denver asked George Burns (God) why he appeared to him as an old man. And God explained that he took the form of an old man because it was something that John Denver could easily relate to and not feel threatened by.

On the other hand, our conscious selves, when confronting the outside world, are like wizards and masters of disguise. We have the ability to change our personalities and our personas to suit a variety of situations. We can be vastly different things to different people. This is revealed in story by a character's ability to change form or utilize a disguise. The disguise is a perfect metaphor for the way we change our personas, which is why audiences take such delight in them.

We can also be psychologically transformed. We can do things that compromise or restore our personalities. This is revealed in story by enchantments or transformations — i.e. a prince is turned into a frog or a beast, an old hag is transformed into a princess, a wooden puppet is changed into a real boy. When Billy Batson says the magic word "Shazam," he is transformed into Captain Marvel, a superhero.

Also, when we are taken over by an emotion, it changes who we are for the moment, and a character like Hades, in Disney's *Hercules*, whose hair bursts into flame when he's overcome by a strong, negative emotion or the Hulk, who changes from an ordinary man into an enormous green bruiser when he's angry, tell us a lot about those transformations.

All of these intriguing metaphors have something important to say about the talents and versatility possessed by the human psyche. Its ability to adjust its character and transform itself into a thousand different operating modes as easily as a chameleon changes color is nothing short of phenomenal. All of the wonders of a great story are, in fact, just easy tricks for the human mind.

CHAPTER 17

GROUP PHENOMENA AND THE ENTITY BEING TRANSFORMED

The reason we experience these archetypes in real life is because the groups that we form to help pursue the values we seek tend to organize themselves in similar ways as the psyche, as they are the result of the same fundamental forces. The individual is an expression of the cell, and the tribes, corporations, governments, and all the other groups that we form are expressions of the individual. They were molded by the same evolutionary forces so they tend to be analogous — to reflect the same types of organization and psychology as the individual and the same archetypes.

So, if you compare the president of a country or corporation, the chief of a tribe, the captain of a ship, a governor or a king to the ego, you'll discover that they all have the same function in relation to the whole. They are all, like the ego, decision-making, judgment-oriented, task-creating administrators. The ego functions as the governor, the king, the president of our entire being.

Then if you compare the Congress, the board of directors, the elders of the tribe, or the admiralty to the higher self, you'll find that they also have the same function in relation to the whole. They are all policy makers, lawgivers, overseers, and guides. They are really the ones who control the flow of money (energy) and dispense the power. Similarly, if you compare the role of the governed, the workers, the tribesmen, and the ship's crew to the physical body, you'll find that they also have the same relation to the whole. They obey the laws created and administered by the higher bodies and do the work necessary to make the group function.

Then if you add the struggle for power which exists always in every group, and divide the total population or leadership into rival political factions, and analyze the objectives of the different factions, an identical model will begin to emerge. The same struggle between our higher and lower natures to influence and control the seats of power that we see in ourselves and in story, you will see in the real world. You will see good opposed by evil. Criminals opposed by the police, Democrats against Republicans, liberals against conservatives, Fascists against Communists, tyrannies opposed by democracies, and so on. Wherever there are human beings organized in groups there will be holdfasts overthrowing governments or taking over corporations or unions. And there will be negative emotional parent figures encouraging them, spiritual parent figures trying to reform them, and real heroes opposing them.

Because the human group shares these similarities in organization and function with the human psyche, the human group is an excellent metaphor for the human psyche. You can see this important pattern operating in many great stories and successful films. And this is the phenomenon I call the Entity Being Transformed.

In *Star Wars*, the entity being transformed is a galaxy. The galaxy has an archetypal structure (the forces of good are opposed by the forces of evil and Luke Skywalker is caught in the middle) and it acts as a metaphor of the psyche. And furthermore, the fate of the galaxy is linked to the destiny of the hero. The ego is part of a greater whole and acts on behalf of the whole psyche, and the fate of the psyche depends on the ego's success. The hero is part of a greater whole and acts on behalf of the whole entity, and the fate of the entity depends on the hero's success. By linking the hero and his destiny to the destiny of some group that has this archetypal structure, you create a metaphor of the psyche — and that means a story with extraordinary power.

In the James Bond movies, *Armageddon,* and *The Matrix* the entity that has this archetypal structure is the world. It acts as a metaphor of the psyche. And the fate of the world is linked to the actions of the hero. In *Gladiator,* the entity that has this archetypal structure is the

Roman Empire. And the fate of the empire is linked to the destiny of the hero. In *King Arthur, Mulan,* and *Braveheart* it's a country. In Harry Potter, it's the Wizard World. In *The Lord of the Rings,* it's Middle Earth. In *Batman, Superman, A Christmas Carol* and *The Sixth Sense,* it's a city. In *Erin Brockovich,* it's a town. In the movie, *Hospital,* the entity is a hospital. In *Air Force One,* it's an airplane. In *Animal House,* it's a college. In *On the Waterfront,* it's the waterfront. In *Ordinary People,* it's a family.

In all of these entities you can identify the archetypal structure — metaphors of higher forces opposed by metaphors of lower forces and the fate of the entity is linked to the destiny of the hero who is caught in the middle. If you study hundreds of great stories and films, you will see this phenomenon at work. It is one of the more important patterns.

CHAPTER 18

THE DYNAMIC CYCLE

Now each of these entities in the real world, whether a country, city, corporation, or individual, is going through the same passages, but at vastly different time scales. The larger the group, the slower their progress. The dynamic that drives these transformations is, as we've indicated, the rivalry between the higher, spiritual forces and the lower, instinctual forces to control the destiny of the entity. The success or failure of the rivals depends on their ability to influence and control the conscious elements that are operating in or near the center (i.e. the nascent ego and the holdfast) and to motivate and guide these conscious elements (whether willing or unwilling) through both sides of these consciousness-building passages.

The dynamic works because the higher and lower selves have two very different but complementary agendas. The object of the lower self is to take possession of an entity and redirect it toward goals that fulfill its own desires and needs, which is to accumulate, control, and enjoy everything it needs to satisfy its insatiable cravings for sense objects, security, wealth, and territory. In modern terms, we're talking about money, sex, and power. Whenever the opportunity arises, the lower self will try to shut down the influence of the higher self and take control of the entity by capturing the conscious element and transforming it into a holdfast. Psychologically, this is the appetites and desires of the lower self taking possession of the conscious self and redirecting its goals.

In real life, it's the same thing. Some aspect of the lower self gets control of Saddam Hussein, Stalin, Hitler, or Idi Amin, and they go after the entity. The tyrant becomes the dictator of the entity and the holdfast (negative ego) becomes the tyrant of the mind. When the ego dominates the mind or the tyrant dominates an entity, they attack everything that threatens their dominance and are attracted to anything that can extend their power.

If you wanted to illustrate this phenomena in story, how would you do that? You would show the villains (the metaphors of the lower self) using the holdfast/antiheroes (the conscious self) to take possession of some entity (the psyche) in order to control its destiny. In *Star Wars*, it's the evil empire taking possession of the galaxy. In *Gladiator*, it's Commodus taking possession of the Roman Empire. In *Harry Potter*, it's Voldemort trying to take possession of the Wizard World. In *The Lord of the Rings*, it's Sauron trying to take possession of Middle Earth. In *Erin Brockovich*, it's evil executives taking possession of the electric company and poisoning the environment. At WorldCom and Enron, it's evil executives taking possession of large corporations for personal gain. In *On the Waterfront*, a mobster has taken control of a union. In *The Exorcist* and *Dracula*, the Devil and the count take possession of young girls. In *The Matrix*, alien machines have taken possession of the world. In *Being John Malkovich*, John Cusack takes possession of John Malkovich. This idea of evil taking "possession" is a major factor in great stories and another extremely important pattern.

The energies the lower self controls are extremely powerful and seductive, and, under the right circumstances, they can easily retake possession of the conscious element. The Devil, as they say, has all the best tunes. When they succeed in this, they pull the conscious element (the holdfast/antihero) into their camp and that creates the downside of the cycle, and serious problems for the entity as a whole. In our model, as I've indicated in several places, these serious problems are called states of misfortune.

In real life, we experience these states of misfortune as the great miseries of the world, as the poverty, crime, pollution, tyranny, famine, injustice, slavery, economic depression, disease, and war that periodically haunt our entity. Psychologically, we experience these negative states when we suffer the effects of these real calamities or as our personal miseries — anxiety, depression, fear, the loss of power, the loss of faith, the loss of self, a poverty of spirit, the threat of death, a sense of hopelessness and despair.

In a story, the state of misfortune is the state of misery (or little bit of hell) that exists, or is being created, within the entity. It is the problem of the story that needs to be solved. It can be expressed either as real states of misery and injustice or, in fantasy, as states of enchantment, alien invasions, dragon problems, or exaggerated shark attacks. A bigger-than-life shark attacking tourists at an island resort is an excellent way of expressing metaphorically the negative states of being that occur when we are being overwhelmed by negative, unconscious energies. In *Oedipus Rex* the state of misfortune is a plague. In *Exodus* it's slavery. In *The Iliad* it's a state of dishonor. In *The Lord of the Rings*, it's the threat of tyranny. In *Armageddon* it's the threat of death. In *The Silence of the Lambs*, it's a string of brutal murders. In *Groundhog Day*, it's an enchantment. Bill Murray is stuck in the worst day of his life.

The need for higher consciousness springs from the need to resolve these inner and outer states of misfortune. The goal of the higher self is to liberate the entity from the tyranny and corruption which caused the state of misfortune and to create a new unified and perfectly balanced whole. As with the holdfast and the lower self, the higher self cannot succeed without the cooperation of a new nascent ego, i.e. a new conscious impulse to take the actions necessary to turn things around. The powers controlled by the higher self are also extremely appealing, but even so, the sometimes timid and reluctant nascent ego frequently has to be lured or pushed into the process.

In a story, we see this as the hero getting involved in the adventure and solving the problem. In *Star Wars*, Luke Skywalker takes on the evil empire and liberates the galaxy. In *The Lord of the Rings*, Frodo and his fellowship set out to destroy the Ring of Power. In *The Matrix*, Keanu Reeves finds his superhuman powers and takes on the aliens. Sigourney Weaver, in *Aliens*, locates and destroys the Terrible Mother creature. In *On the Waterfront*, Marlon Brando stands up to the mob and liberates the waterfront. In *Erin Brockovich*, Julia Roberts takes on the electric company and saves the town. In *The Silence of the Lambs*,

Jodie Foster tracks down and rids the world of a fiendish serial killer. In *The Exorcist* and *Dracula*, a priest and a young man with a wooden stake liberate the young girls. These are perfect metaphors for what we experience psychologically when we have been overcome by a negative unconscious state and then are suddenly liberated.

When the higher self and the ego/hero succeed, however, it creates a new prosperity and a new positive state of being (state of good fortune) which, in turn, creates new opportunities for the lower self to influence and regain control of the ego. This creates a new downside and new problems for the entity, which create the need for more positive actions and new, bigger solutions which require new states of awareness and higher consciousness. This is a continuous cycle all the way up and down the wheel. The old cycle ends with a new state of misfortune. The new cycle begins with another impulse to bring about positive change. With each new state of misfortune, a new and different conscious impulse (or hero) is required. The higher self guides the nascent ego and hero through the upside, then the lower forces guide the trans-formed holdfast and antihero through the downside. Each time a new hero makes a pass, they go up a notch to new levels of exaltation and consciousness.

All of this is revealed in story.

In the *Star Wars* saga, Anakin Skywalker starts out as a Jedi, a young hero aligned with the Force, but then he defects to the darkside, becomes a holdfast and an antihero (Darth Vader) and helps bring about the state of tyranny. Later, with the dawning of a new upside, a new hero, Luke Skywalker, guided by the Force, emerges to oppose him. This is a revelation of our own psychology.

In real life, Mikhail Gorbachev starts out as a hero, reforming the Soviet Union. Then he becomes a holdfast, clinging to his power. Boris Yeltsin comes along as the new hero and unseats him. Then Yeltsin becomes another serious holdfast and a new hero has to emerge to undo him. And now the new hero, Putin, is hurling himself into the downside. In France, in 1789, a revolution overthrows an unjust monarchy. The well-intentioned revolutionaries regress into

Robespierre and the Reign of Terror. Napoleon, the new hero, helps to put an end to that phase but then crowns himself emperor and creates another devastating downside.

In real life, we can also see these cycles very clearly when the solution to one problem helps to create another even more serious problem which requires another even better solution, i.e. a scarcity of food in our early history led to the development of agriculture, which resulted in more food and a sedentary life, and that resulted in the even bigger problem of overpopulation, which we still haven't solved. Nuclear reactors helped solve a major energy problem, then created the even bigger problem of toxic waste.

These alternating change of fortune cycles are the engines that drive this whole process. It's a vicious cycle but the net result is higher consciousness. The miracle of our evolution apparently grew out of the need to get out of increasingly more difficult and serious tight spots.

CHAPTER 19

THE HERO'S AND THE ANTIHERO'S JOURNEY

The next set of patterns reveals the passage, which is one complete cycle of the Golden Paradigm. I have divided the passage into eight sections. The four sections on the downside show the passage of the holdfast/antihero while the problem and the state of misfortune are being created — the four sections on the upside show the passage of the ego/hero while the problem is being resolved and the state of good fortune regained. In our story model I call this passage the *whole story* or the big story. Others may refer to it as the backstory or the frame story. But a big difference between this and other story models is the fact that this *whole story* or backstory has a structure that is just as important as the structures of the smaller, more familiar foreground story I will describe in the story focus. Be that as it may, these are the archetypal actions and tasks which are necessary to awaken and release the powers that are necessary to bring about the changes of fortune. Psychologically, it's how consciousness is built up and higher states of being are achieved.

The four sections on the upside of the passage are:

I How the Hero Gets Involved in the Passage (or Adventure)
II How the Hero is Initiated
III How the Hero is Humbled
IV How the Hero is Rewarded — with a little bit of Paradise

The four sections on the downside of the passage are:

V How the Hero Becomes a Holdfast (and an Antihero)
VI How the Antihero Regresses
VII How the Antihero becomes a Tyrant
VIII How the Antihero is Rewarded — with a little bit of Hell

On the upside, good is aggressive, evil is on the defensive, the problem is being resolved and a state of good fortune is being regained. On the downside, it's the reverse — evil is aggressive, good is on the defensive, and a problem and a state of misfortune are being created. The upside officially begins when the hero (the anti-threat, the one who opposes the threat and solves the problem) takes action.

On the downside, the antihero performs an abominable, selfish act that awakens terrible energies that have to be dealt with and transformed. On the upside, the hero performs an unselfish, heroic act that awakens new positive energies which help to defeat or transform the negative energies that were unleashed on the downside.

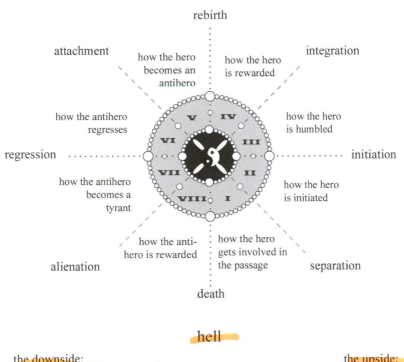

When you are creating or analyzing a story, a good question to ask yourself at any given point is: Is a problem being created or is a problem being resolved? And who is initiating the action that is driving the story? Is it the hero or the antihero? In *Othello*, Iago, Othello's evil servant, is initiating the action which is making that story happen. In *The Last of the Mohicans*, it is the Native American, Magua. His lust for revenge is driving that story. If you know who is initiating the action and which side of the problem you are on, you should not have any difficulty orienting yourself or understanding the events. These are important and worthwhile distinctions.

To review a whole cycle, we'll use *On the Waterfront*, an important 1950s film starring Marlon Brando. And for argument's sake, we'll pretend that Johnny Friendly, the Lee J. Cobb character, started out as a union hero and only became a holdfast and a criminal later on to keep his power. The story would go something like this:

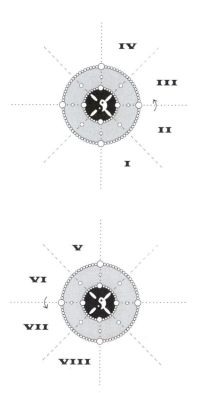

The young and idealistic Friendly rises up through the union ranks (I), opposes and defeats some prior, mildly crooked and dictatorial union boss (II-III), and gets his reward, the union presidency, his bit of paradise (IV). And for awhile everything is jake. He institutes reforms; he is revered by the membership; he loves his job.

But then it looks like he's not going to be reelected and he doesn't want to give up his power. There's a great deal of inner conflict at first, but gradually the evil influences take hold (V). Negative parent figures become his allies and encourage him in his folly. He suppresses dissent, rifles the pension fund and takes bribes. He's alienated from the fatherly board and eventually gets rid of them completely (VI). He becomes a tyrant, a new state of misfortune is created, and the union members become serious victims (VII). His compassion is lost; his humanity is lost; all is lost. He will do anything to keep his power (VIII).

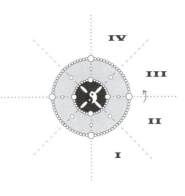

Then a new hero, Marlon Brando, is lured into the process by Eva Marie Saint (positive anima figure) and Karl Malden, a priest (positive spiritual father figure) (I). Then Brando goes through a similar initiation and transformation. He brings Johnny Friendly down (II), helps to create a new state of good fortune (III), and becomes the new head of the union (IV). Later, when it's his turn to step aside, he too may be reluctant to give up the power and become vulnerable. Then another hero will have to be found to oppose him.

These cycles are a major factor in all of our lives, both psychologically and in the real world. If you analyzed the progress or charted the rise and fall of the criminal executives who took possession of Enron and the electric company in *Erin Brockovich*, a union boss like Jimmy Hoffa, J. Edgar Hoover's tenure at the FBI, or a tyrant like Saddam Hussein taking possession of a country, you will see this same pattern. The plots and metaphors contained in great stories are all about these cycles of possession and liberation, regression and initiation, death and rebirth.

The Details of the Whole Story Passage *

I. How the Hero Gets Involved in the Adventure

At this point in the cycle, a serious state of misfortune exists within the entity and action has to be taken. In Joseph Campbell's schema, this is *The Call To Adventure*.

---

* The steps of this whole story passage were built up by information revealed in hundreds of stories and shouldn't be confused with the story structure I will describe in the story focus. Each great story reveals a different aspect of this hidden truth.

Psychologically, this is the moment when we realize that something is wrong and that function of the ego which is responsible (i.e. the ego-doctor, ego-lawyer, ego-detective) has to take it on. In real life, Dian Fossey is coming to terms with the plight of the gorillas in Rwanda. Jonas Salk's attention is being focused on the polio virus. Lech Walesa is reacting to the evil actions perpetuated by the Polish government. Nelson Mandela is considering a strategy to oppose the apartheid government of South Africa. And Martin Luther King contemplates the horrors being brought about by prejudice and bigotry in the United States.

In story, this is the moment when the love interest or spiritual father figure enters the hero's world and solicits his help. In *The Silence of the Lambs*, Jodie Foster is asked to develop a profile of the serial killer. In *The Lord of the Rings*, the responsibility to destroy the Ring of Power is given to Frodo. In *Armageddon*, Billy Bob Thornton asks Bruce Willis to help stop the asteroid. In *The Verdict*, Jack Warden offers a malpractice case to Paul Newman.

Preparedness

Whatever the hero is being called upon to do, it is a potentially dangerous task. We may be ready, like Harry Potter, Indiana Jones, or Superman, and willingly take it on as part of our duties. Or we may be reluctant, like Sigourney Weaver in *Alien*, Tom Cruise in *The Firm*, or Keanu Reeves in *The Matrix*, and have to be lured or pushed into the process. Or we may refuse altogether, like Willie Loman in *Death of a Salesman*, and have to pay the consequences. In great stories, ninety-nine out of a hundred heroes take up the challenge. In real life, the vast majority refuse. To refuse the call means to let the problems slide and not become part of the solution. The world remains in trouble and we remain stuck.

If we are reluctant to get involved, there are good reasons for it. We have a natural, built-in fear of the forces responsible for these states of misfortune. Correcting the ills of the world or confronting inner demons means opposing the forces responsible for these states of misery. That can mean putting our conscious elements at considerable risk. Taking on these forces means facing real dangers, real enemies and very unpleasant truths. These negative forces can make real trouble for us, and we sense that. Unconsciously, we know that behind all of these inner and outer states of misery are forces worth fearing. This creates a fear barrier we are reluctant to cross. We see a good example of this fear in *The Firm*.

Inauthentic State

A second major problem is that we are severely handicapped. We are in an inauthentic state. The society we were brought up in is itself in real trouble and we are a product of that society. It is going through one of these passages itself and is deep into the downside in an age of alienation and discord, an age of corruption and economic stress in which people have lost touch with their values, each other and themselves. This is the society to which we have to conform so this is where we get stuck. The inauthentic state is the measure of our stuckness. It is who we are at the beginning of the passage when we're being asked to get involved.

Rick's inauthentic state in *Casablanca* is that he is a disillusioned patriot. Paul Newman in *The Verdict* is an ambulance chaser and alcoholic. Shakespeare in *Shakespeare in Love* has lost his muse. Al Pacino in *Scent of a Woman* is blind. Scrooge is a miser. Pinocchio is a puppet. Julia Roberts in *Pretty Woman* is a prostitute. Uma Thurman in *Kill Bill* is in a coma. Russell Crowe in *Gladiator* is a slave; in *A Beautiful Mind*, he's delusional. The beast in Disney's *Beauty and the Beast* is an enchanted prince. Psychologically, these metaphors are incredibly valid, indicating the stultified condition of our conscious selves. Compared to what we could be, we are all like ambulance chasers, drunkards, and prostitutes. We are all like Robert DeNiro in *Awakenings*, Bruce Willis in *The Sixth Sense*, Dustin Hoffman in *Rain Man* or the paralyzed hero in *Princess Bride*. We are all like little boys and princes that have been turned into puppets, frogs, and beasts or were left *Home Alone*. And going from where we are to where we could be is like going from a puppet to a real boy, or a frog to a prince.

The mind easily accepts all of these inauthentic states as metaphors of our present condition and identifies with them. Then the great stories show us how to become real people again, how to resolve these inauthentic states and become who we were really meant to be. But in order to do that, we have to get involved in the problem and become part of the solution. The clear message of story is: If you want to reach your full potential, then you have to get involved. You have to find your way through the fear barriers and resolve these inauthentic states. You have to identify, oppose and confront the inner and outer ogres, dragons, giants, and villains that are creating these negative states of being. And you have to overpower, tame, and transform them into something positive. Getting involved in the passage means taking up arms against these inner and outer ills. It means linking your destiny to the fate of an entity that's threatened. It means living and acting like a hero. It means doing what a hero does.

Incentives

But if we are reluctant to get involved because we are full of fear or we are in an inauthentic state, what is going to get us involved? Obviously, there have to be incentives. The most obvious incentive is the need to save your own skin. In *The Firm*, Tom Cruise is doing it to save his own life and the lives of his family. That's a big incentive. Also, there may be consequences for not acting. If it's technically our responsibility, we can be shamed. Or there can be the promise of positive rewards. In *Star Wars*, the spiritual mentor offers the hero a chance to become a Jedi. No small thing in a galaxy taken over by evil. In *Armageddon*, it's a variety of amusing things plus never having to pay taxes again. Beyond that, it has to fit in with some dream or vision. You have to see it as an opportunity. In *Rain Man*, Tom Cruise sees taking control of his autistic brother as a chance to get rich. Frequently it's the desire to become famous or to get the girl. In the beginning it's okay to be motivated, as we all are sometimes, by shallow self-interest because we're in an inauthentic state. Later, we will be transformed into real heroes and those strictly selfish interests will fall away. The journey is a hero-making process. If the hero is attracted to the love interest, that just makes the love interest's job a lot easier. In real life, as in story, love is the great motivator. The promise of romance is the surest way to lure the hero and ourselves into the adventure.

Fantasies and Illusions

Linked closely to the incentives are the fantasies and illusions. If the desire for the incentives is strong enough and the fear not too extreme, there's a natural tendency to deceive ourselves or be vulnerable to deception. We, or those trying to get us involved, will begin to minimize the difficulties and exaggerate the potential rewards.

When I began the search for the meaning of story, I thought it would take me no more than six months to complete. That was an illusion. After many years on the same journey, I still felt the next great revelation, which would finally complete the process, was only months away. And that same carrot lured me forward the entire way until the journey was finally completed. That's self-deception.

In an issue of *Psychology Today*, the cover shows a man wearing rose-colored glasses, and the caption reads: "A Little Self-deception May Be Necessary." And it is. If we knew the real truth up front, we would go the other way. Psychologically, we are being deceived all the time by our unconscious selves. But without this natural tendency, no one would ever put aside practical necessities to pursue knowledge or explore the cosmos.

In a story, we often see this little bit of self-deception expressed as the love interest, the guide to the soul, not telling the hero the whole truth at first. The dangers he or she will have to face may be too great to reveal (*Chinatown*). When the love interest isn't being forthright, this is extremely true to our own psychology, reflecting that self-deception that is necessary to foster the fantasies and illusions that will help to get us involved. And because of its validity, this little bit of deception on the part of the love interest is psychologically very appealing to an audience (*The Maltese Falcon*, *Shakespeare in Love*), since we are all, in effect, constantly deceiving ourselves.

Commitment

Having been deceived and highly motivated, the hero is ready to make a commitment. This is the item that seals our fate. Once we make a commitment, once we give our word, sign a contract or take an oath, there's no turning back, we're obligated to deliver. The commitment is the critical factor. Without the commitment, in matters as serious and consequential as these, the follow through cannot be guaranteed.

Helpers

When the hero makes a commitment, then the helpers appear. This is another of those significant, archetypal patterns which reflect an important psychological truth. When we make a definite commitment to ourselves, then the helpers appear, as unexpected insights and ideas or as real helpers in the real world. As long as we're just sitting on the fence, uncommitted and undecided, the helpers don't appear. But the moment we make a definite commitment about something, then the people around us are suddenly full of helpful advice — there's a friend you should talk to, a school you should attend, a book you should read, and so on. The relationship of the helpers to the hero in a story reveals that psychological connection.

Plans and Preparations

After the commitment is made, the hero sketches out a plan and prepares for action. The first objective will be to determine the extent and cause of the problem, who is responsible, and the thing without which the problem cannot be solved (the marvelous element). If some kind of special training is required, then one of the helpers (spiritual, mental, or emotional parent figures) will provide it. In *Star Wars*, Obi-Wan Kenobi has to teach Luke how to use the light saber and how to get in touch with the Force. In *Mulan*, the young girl has to learn how to develop her masculine side as well as be a warrior. In *Armageddon*, Bruce Willis and his crew have to learn how to survive in space. In *The Matrix*, Keanu Reeves has to be brought up to speed in every possible way. In real life, every passage requires special training. If you're going to be a doctor, a lawyer, a soldier, or an entrepreneur, then you have to have a special education before you take on the problems in those fields.

Self-Reliance

The helpers can provide the guidance and instruction we need, the letters of transit and the amulets to ward off evil, but we have to accomplish the difficult task ourselves. If the helpers do it for us, we will derive very little benefit from the action.

Apprehensions

Other people's lives are affected by the hero's decision. The negative parent figures and negative siblings try to talk us out of it. But we can't be dissuaded. We've made a commitment and our eyes are on the prize. Psychologically, these are the niggling doubts that are always with us but are easy to push aside.

High Hopes and Enthusiasm

The end of this phase is often marked by high hopes and enthusiasm — a genuine conviction that we are going to succeed. In Broadway musicals, it's frequently a big, optimistic musical number at the end of the first act (*Les Miserables*).

II. HOW THE HERO IS INITIATED

The First Reality is Faced

The hero begins his or her journey. In Joseph Campbell's schema, this is *The Road of Trials and Difficult Tasks*. In Aristotle's model, it's the complication phase of the classical structure.

In real life, this is the moment when you take your first step toward the solution to the problem. If you're an investigative reporter, you're out looking for the truth behind the story. If you're Jonas Salk, you're seeking a cure for polio. If you're Lech Walesa, Gandhi, or Martin Luther King, you're taking your revolution into the open. In story, a hero entering an unknown territory or traveling uncharted waters is a perfect way to express what we experience when we enter the world of the problem or probe our unconscious minds seeking a solution.

Problems and Complications

Once involved in the problem, the first thing you will discover is that the situation is much more complicated and difficult than you were led to believe (*The Verdict*, *The Lord of the Rings*). No matter what heroic or non-heroic enterprise or action you undertake, the reality will always be a shock (*The Silence of the Lambs*). The unforeseen and unexpected things that are always out there will invariably make the task more complicated and risky than you supposed (*Armageddon*).

Warnings

The hero's forward motion triggers resistance. And again, no matter what inner or outer state of misfortune you try to reverse, you will be stepping on somebody's toes and you will encounter resistance. Which is positive because, if you're doing this part right, you're bringing the complexity and the unconscious cause of the problem to the surface. But the negative energies want nothing to be found out, so they'll do anything to stop you. But usually they won't do more than is necessary to control or scare you off. If they show more opposition than is necessary, they will give away more of their secrets and that can bring them down. Their first line of defense is a warning. Psychologically, it's the archetypes that give us cautionary feelings.

In real life, it's the adversaries who warned Gandhi, Malcolm X and Martin Luther King to go no further. These are threshold guardians. In a story, the threshold guardian is often a dupe like the police captain in *Dirty Harry* who warns Clint Eastwood to back off.

The hero continues his forward motion and because of his persistence and courage, new helpers appear. If you make the right choices and decisions and take the right actions, you advance, you get more help or information. When we act courageously or do things right, we get assistance. But the more we learn, the more we realize how complex and dangerous things really are.

Temptations

The warnings didn't work so now the villains make their second move. They put the temptress on the hero and offer him a bribe of sex, money, power, or a chance to stay alive. They would still rather own him than kill him.

In real life, the politicians and public officials who have given in to this phase are too numerous to mention. In story, the tempter is an unbelievable sex object or an attaché case filled with cash. Satan offered Jesus a chance to rule the world. Hollywood has gotten this one thing right. They know how to personify the seductive inner voices and sensations that are daring us to switch sides and play the other game. If we give in to these temptations, it's the end of the road. We slip back to the downside.

The commitment keeps us moving in a forward direction, but the stakes are being raised and a second fear barrier is being created. Unconsciously, we know that all of the negative forces we're opposing are secretly connected. Behind a problem like poverty or prejudice or even a man-eating shark, there may lurk a deadly lower self motivated corruption or neglect (the mayor in *Jaws*).

Serious Threats

When the hero resists the temptation, the villains get really nasty. When you take on a negative energy in yourself or in others, never underestimate its vehemence or determination to defeat you.

In real life, if you're a politician they may start calling you a Communist or the "L" word and spread vicious rumors about your sex life. If you're up against the Mafia, they'll send you death threats or put a bomb in your car. If you're Lech Walesa, they may throw you in prison on trumped-up charges. If you were a dissident writer in the old Soviet Union, they put you in a mental institution. This reality is in the background of all of our lives. This is the world we live in and it's happening every day in every entity. If you are opposing the real villains in our society, whether corrupt politicians or outright criminals, the threats and dangers will be very real. In story, an attempt on the hero's life is the way this step is usually described.

In any case, this is the moment when you realize how serious things really are. The negative energies you're opposing are much more powerful, organized and deadly than you were led to believe. You were definitely deceived about that. You've put yourself in real jeopardy and an extremely disastrous outcome is highly probable. The second fear barrier is complete and it's much more terrifying than the first. Your heart sinks and your forward motion is temporarily stopped. In *Casablanca*, this is the moment when Rick becomes disillusioned and drops out of the fight.

The Confrontation

The hero confronts the love interest, the mentor, or the people who have deliberately deceived him (*Chinatown*, *The Silence of the Lambs*, *The Maltese Falcon*). If they don't level with him now, he's going to walk away. Psychologically, this is an inner conflict. You confront your feelings and try to fathom the truth. When the love interest and the other positive archetypes realize the hero is serious, they show him the victims.

The Victims

The victims are the principal sufferers of the misfortune, the individual victims of poverty, injustice, bigotry, slavery, tyranny, dishonor, ignorance and disease; the victims of the Holocaust, the Apocalypse, the plague; the victims of murder and abuse, crack cocaine, the tobacco industry, and environmentally caused genetic disease. Psychologically, it's that part of our psyches that has been cut off, abducted, murdered, repressed, injured, or abused. We may have been aware of the victims before but our empathy was superficial, now we are identifying with the real horror of their plight.

When the hero sees the victims, his compassion and humanity are awakened. This brings about a change of motive and a change of character. Psychologically, this is the moment when we face the full extent of the damage that has been done and are deeply moved. If our compassion is not triggered, we will not be transformed. We will remain out of the fight. The passage will end here and the new conscious element will drift to the downside, but not as a holdfast, which is a converted, fully realized hero, but as a negative anima or animus. When the images of children in pain or innocent people suffering starvation leave us cold then we're not ready for transformation.

In story, this is when Joseph Cotten discovers Orson Welles' bogus penicillin victims in *The Third Man*, Wilhem Dafoe witnesses a My Lai type massacre of women and children in *Platoon*, Paul Newman comes face to face with the malpractice victim in *The Verdict*, and Jodie Foster sees the mutilated body of a young girl in *The Silence of the Lambs*. Their humanity is jolted awake and they are all transformed. All of these examples are perfect metaphors revealing the forces that bring about this radical change in our feelings.

The hero has proved himself and is told the truth. There really is a conspiracy, and powerful and deadly forces like the holdfast are involved. They couldn't tell him the truth before, it would've put all of their lives in jeopardy.

In real life, this is where we learn about death camps, death squads, and secret police — or about corruption and cover-ups and unscrupulous people making obscene profits — or that the tobacco companies not only knew that cigarettes caused death, they processed the nicotine to make them more addictive, and then lied to Congress. Or that J. Edgar Hoover, the head of the FBI, the man who was supposed to be protecting us, was a vicious blackmailer, a friend to organized crime and perhaps far worse. Psychologically, if you confront your inner conflicts, shatter an illusion of self-deception and face reality, you will see the truth.

The truth triggers the hero's sense of outrage. Our compassion brought about a change of character (*The Verdict*), now our outrage triggers a sense of duty that overrides personal considerations and fear of consequences (*The Insider*, *Platoon*). It gives us the ammunition we need to push through the second fear barrier. It is a major turning point.

In real life, it's the moment when a doctor or lawyer, who has developed a real concern for the interests of his patients or clients, is suddenly ready to risk something on their behalf. Or it's the moment when you suddenly become politically active because of your outrage over the environment, the abuse of women and children, or corruption in government. This is also the moment when you realize that as a citizen it is your responsibility and you have to do something about it. In a story, the hero becoming ready, despite the threats of personal harm, to risk everything for the sake of the victims perfectly describes this experience (*Erin Brockovich, On the Waterfront, The Verdict, Platoon, The Silence of the Lambs, Mulan*).

Changes of character have to do with resolving our inauthentic states and reconnecting us to our fellow man. This reconnection helps to transform us from someone who is self centered and selfish into a real hero (*Rain Man*). Without this change of character most changes of fortune couldn't occur, since we wouldn't take the risks necessary to complete the task. The key to achieving higher states of consciousness comes from our being able to now do something for others rather than just ourselves. Our motives can be selfish to begin with (that's sometimes necessary to get us involved) but then they change. And ultimately we do something that benefits the world. Without this reconnection, the rest of the passage isn't going to take place — and this is where most of us remain stuck.

The Trap

In Joseph Campbell's schema this is *The Supreme Ordeal*. In Aristotle's classical structure, it's the reversal and the crisis.

The hero and the love interest devise a brilliant plan and, seeking that without which the problem cannot be solved (the marvelous element), they enter the antagonist's domain. They enter his cave, his castle, his kingdom, or they cross the frontier into his territory. Their presence is detected and something completely unexpected happens. The real force of evil, the dragon or Mr. Big and his enormous power, which they totally underestimated, is suddenly unleashed. It could be Satan (*The Exorcist*), a dozen guys with automatic weapons (*Die Hard*), an army of Orcs (*The Lord of the Rings*) or a hydra with seven heads (*Hercules*). Their little plan falls apart and they are completely overwhelmed. The love interest is taken prisoner and the hero may be taken prisoner as well. They've accomplished the opposite of what they intended and they're in a terrible fix.

Psychologically, the conscious element will always underestimate the reserve power of the negative unconscious, and when it surfaces antagonistically, it's always a shock and completely disorienting. A twenty-five foot shark bursting out of the water and smashing a tiny boat is another excellent metaphor for this experience.

In real life, this is a moment when you see the face of evil, when you discover the true extent of the evil and corruption that exists and get a terrifying glimpse of what you're really up against. The negative energy that created Hitler and Stalin really does exist, and you are overwhelmed by it. For your own protection, this truth about the negative energies and their power, which can be active in yourself and in your adversaries when you face the real world, are carefully and deliberately concealed. If we knew how dangerous these forces really were, before we were prepared to deal with them, we would never venture forth, no matter what the incentives.

The Crisis

The crisis is the second part of *The Supreme Ordeal* and the final stage of the initiation. It is the turning point, the trigger mechanism and, figuratively speaking, the true middle of the principal action on the upside of the passage. The outcome of this event will determine whether good or bad consequences will follow.

Despair

The hero is in an impossible position. All is apparently lost. The evil power he saw revealed was truly terrifying and undefeatable. He sinks into a black despair.

You will know when you have reached this moment in the real passage when you are facing something you totally fear. Your confidence is shattered, you feel trapped and powerless, you have lost all hope and you fall into a deep despair. The hero tied up in a dungeon or in a deserted warehouse is a perfect way to illustrate this state of mind.

Sacrifice

But the hero cannot dwell on his despair. Our child is in a burning building. Hitler is invading our homeland. A cloud of lethal gas is drifting into our neighborhood. Action has to be taken. We must go forward. We have absolutely no choice. If we run away at this stage, we will have a very hard time living with ourselves.

When my children were still young, Diane and I took them to Yosemite National Park for a weekend of camping out. We arrived at ten o'clock at night, and eager for our adventure to begin, we dropped our belongings in the tent we rented and headed into the woods. Fifty yards from the campsite, a huge black bear crashed out of the woods and came charging toward us. My children screamed and ran with their mother back toward the campsite. The bear kept coming and I had no choice but to stand my ground and shine the flashlight I was holding in his charging eyes. He brushed my leg as he ran past me, veered to the left, burst into a picnic area and slapped a garbage can with his paw, which sent it sprawling. Apparently, he wasn't attacking us, but it seemed like a real danger. If I had panicked and left my wife and children unprotected, I couldn't have lived with myself.

So regardless of the risk to ourselves, we can only move in one direction, toward the abominable power, toward our greatest fears. We have to sacrifice ourselves and we have to do it immediately. But to succeed we need to switch to another brain. We need superhuman courage and strength. We need instinctual power. We need a magic sword. The mechanism that triggers this power is our determination to succeed regardless of the cost to ourselves. The moment we make the commitment to sacrifice ourselves, we feel a surge of superhuman power. And that may be accompanied by a revelation or insight that shows us the solution to the problem.

In his book *The Hero with a Thousand Faces*, Joseph Campbell writes:

> The gods and goddesses (unconscious archetypes) then are to be understood as embodiments and custodians of The Elixir of Imperishable Being (the unmanifest form of the vast potential) but not themselves the Ultimate in its primary state. What the hero seeks through his intercourse with them is therefore not finally themselves, but their grace, i.e., the power of their sustaining substance. This miraculous energy-substance and this alone is the Imperishable; the names and forms of the deities who everywhere

embody, dispense, and represent it come and go. This is the m
lous energy of the thunderbolts of Zeus, Yahweh, and the Sup
Buddha, the fertility of the rain of Viracocha, the virtue announ
by the bell rung in the mass at the consecration, and the light of
the ultimate illumination of the saint and sage. Its guardians dare
release it only to the truly proven.

These powerful energies cannot be released willy-nilly. There have to
be safeguards and controls, a trigger mechanism that is reliable and
safe. The commitment to sacrifice is the trigger mechanism which
brings about the release of the hero's remarkable powers. You turn
on the spiritual power by demonstrating that you have the required
strength of character and that reserve power is given to you.

We were helped through the first fear barrier by fantasies and illusions, through the second by compassion and outrage and through
the third and final fear threshold by a foolproof trap with only one
way out — self-sacrifice. We make the commitment, pass the test and
get the thunderbolt — and you can use that power to tame the lower
physical forces.

The Final Assault (the Climax)

The hero goes into battle with the principal opponent (the threat, the
cause of the problem), and the principal opponent is completely and
utterly destroyed. This is the climax of the initiation and the defeat of
all of the forces of resistance that opposed the action.

In ancient Greece it was the three hundred Greek warriors that held off
the entire Persian army at Thermopylae. In the Crimean War it was the
charge of the Light Brigade. In World War I, it was Sergeant York, who
single-handedly captured four hundred well-armed German soldiers.
In World War II, it was Stalingrad, the extraordinary victories of the
RAF over England and, later, the string of allied victories in Europe
from Normandy to the Battle of the Bulge. In the Montreal Olympics
it was the amateur U. S. hockey team defeating Russia's world champion professionals. In the 1990s it was Boris Yeltsin and Lech Walesa
who helped bring down Gorbachev and the Soviet Union. In story,
it is Daniel Day Lewis in *The Last of the Mohicans*, the young girl

in *Mulan*, Indiana Jones in *The Temple of Doom*, Bruce Willis in *Die Hard* taking on a dozen villains one at a time, and Samson killing ten thousand Philistines with the jawbone of an ass.

The hero getting or turning on some miraculous power and easily defeating the villain is a perfect metaphor for that function. The gods releasing a magic sword, an ultimate weapon or a superhuman strength is a perfect metaphor for that reserve power. We have seen the hero in this situation a thousand times, achieving an easy victory despite overwhelming odds. Even when it seems implausible, we accept it because psychologically, when we are in this mode and the higher powers are vanquishing the lower powers, we are truly undefeatable and invincible. But these powers, as I said, can only be turned on when the ego has been initiated (strengthened). When we regress on the downside, they have to be shut down again. The energies of the spirit cannot be turned over to a faltering ego or antihero that's been taken over by the dark side without catastrophic and delusional results.

The final obstacle the hero has to overcome is a metaphor of some powerful negative energy that has to be tamed. In *Dracula*, it's the potentially addictive sex and drugs that can seduce young people in puberty. In *The Iliad* it's anger. In *Snow White* it's jealousy. In James Bond it's power and greed. In *Jaws* and *Jurassic Park*, it's naked aggression. In real life, every uncontrolled release of anger, lust, or aggression is a sign of crisis which requires a change of attitude to control or transform that negative energy.

When the hero defeats the villain with the help of the higher power, it means that he has become master of some aspect of the lower self. The terrible destructive power conjured on the downside has now been transformed and tamed. The hero defeats the villain. The ego subjugates the lower, instinctual energies. Each accomplishment of the ego on the upside tames more and more of this instinctual power.

Assimilation

Having defeated the enemy, the hero strips off his armor or tastes the dragon's blood.

When we face the negative energy that assaults us, we tame and assimilate it — and it empowers us. When you harness or tame these lower powers, you consciously assimilate them and bring them under conscious control. The hero tasting the blood of the dragon he has just slain is a perfect metaphor for our assimilation of these energies. When Marlon Brando endures the beating of the villains at the end of *On the Waterfront*, he defeats them and gains their power. And that's another excellent way of illustrating this same thing.

III. HOW THE HERO IS HUMBLED

The Marvelous Element

The forces of resistance have been vanquished and the marvelous element which can reverse the state of misfortune is recovered. The synthesis of the newly awakened spiritual power and the assimilation of the lower power creates this new marvelous power — the hidden talent, the ultimate boon, the bright ideas, philosophy, charisma that can positively change the world. These are the miraculous powers we cannot acquire without initiation and they are the building blocks of higher consciousness. In a great story, how would you represent these special energies except as the chalice that possesses Christ consciousness, a crystal that can cure disease, a missing father who can restore wholeness, a lost treasure that can abolish poverty or restore a kingdom, a miraculous fountain that can restore youth, a magic potion that can produce love, a secret weapon or a magic sword that can save the world? These are all excellent metaphors for those potential energies, which are out there, or rather in there somewhere, waiting to be manifest in the right people, at the right time, in the right place.

Sexual Union

The hero and the love interest fall into each other's arms. The hero has done his work well and the guiding feminine soul gives him his reward. This is a moment of ecstasy. It could be something you imagine or something you actually experience during sexual activity. Sex is never better than after some great achievement or success. It is another taste of paradise.

Inflation

The love interest, the power, the heroic deeds, the victory, the love making, the success — it's all too much for the hero and it goes to his head. In real life, you've just had a significant success and you feel elated, bathed in light, significantly above the common sort or invincible. And you suddenly believe you're the greatest writer, the greatest filmmaker, lawyer, statesmen, or warrior that has ever lived. You're a genius, a child of destiny, the true Messiah, the one chosen to save or rule the world (Napoleon, Odysseus, the god Indra in "Parade of Ants").

Surge of Power II

The hero acts on the inflation and this triggers another surge of power.

Before it was a hydra or Mr. Big, but this time it is a truly awesome display of unconscious power by the gods which humbles the hero or forces him to flee (magic flight). He barely escapes with his life and has to be rescued (symbolic rebirth).

In World War II spy movies or Indiana Jones, after the hero has defeated forty German guards and retrieved the secret formula or the lost ark, the awesome power appears as the whole German army and he has to run for his life. In *King Solomon's Mines*, it's an earthquake. In James Bond or *Lethal Weapon* movies, it's the villain's hideout or some building that is about to blow up. In Pinocchio, it's the final attack of the whale. In the Hindu myth, "Parade of Ants," it's an ego-shattering reality.

On this point, the message of great stories is very clear, if you act on that inflation, you will, like Napoleon, be slapped down. You will learn in a very unpleasant way that, despite your success, you are not the world's greatest writer or the new Messiah and you're not invincible. Countless other people have had similar ideas and dreams and far greater success. Kublai Khan, for instance. But don't fret, you still have an important role to play.

All of this was well known to ancient Chinese sages. In a cosmos filled with galaxies, they reasoned, the role human beings were meant to play can't be very significant. Knowing this has a very sobering and humbling effect. Knowing this, you can accept your fate and, like Indra, go forward happily playing out the hand you were dealt.

Symbolic Death

The hero is washed up on the beach.

The ego-shattering reality is followed by a depression, which is followed by an acceptance which leads to a rebirth. With respect to the lower power the ego has to be strong; with respect to the higher power, the ego has to be humble. First we have to earn the power, then we have to learn how to use it wisely.

In any event, the hero falling overboard in a storm and being rescued or washed up on the beach like Odysseus or Pinocchio in a symbolic death is a perfect metaphor for what we experience when we are brought back down to earth.

IV. HOW THE HERO IS REWARDED

The Return

Now, strengthened on the one hand and humbled on the other, the hero is truly centered. He is reborn. He returns with his boon and the state of misfortune is reversed. In real life, this is when you put your special talents and gifts to work for mankind, when you become a benefit to the world. If you're Jonas Salk, you put your cure for polio on the market. If you're Ted Turner, you give a billion dollars to charity. If you're William Shakespeare, you write the world's greatest plays.

In a story, this is the resolution — the villains are brought to justice, the galaxy is liberated, or the sheriff of Amity Island returns with proof that the shark is dead. In *The Verdict*, Paul Newman's victory in court helps mankind by discouraging malpractice. In *The Temple of Doom*, Indiana Jones helps the villagers by returning the sacred crystal and the children. In *The Fiery Waters of Tubertynte* the hero uses the healing waters to cure the Queen of Erin. In *The Lord of the Rings*, peace is restored to Middle Earth. In *Gladiator*, the Roman Empire will once again be a republic.

Transcendence

This leads to a rise in the hero's status, to his ascendency. He becomes a knight, a prince, or a king, or he ascends into Heaven and is deified. In real life, our standing is raised because of our courage and accomplishments and we are honored and rewarded. Psychologically, this is the moment when you transcend, when there is an atonement and you become one with some aspect of the self and that aspect is deified (Bruce Willis at the end of *Armageddon*, the heroes of *The Lord of the Rings*). A saint or the son of God rising into Heaven is a perfect metaphor for how that experience feels.

Mystical Marriage

When you become a boon to mankind and your status is raised (i.e. you have transcended) then the anima or animus comes to you and there is a synthesis, a symbolic marriage, a union of opposites. When you start doing it right, the love interest comes to you. You become irresistible to him or her. This is true in all the realms.

Celebration

There is an incredible celebration. What else would be appropriate?

New Home

Then the hero and his bride occupy their new home, their little bit of paradise. Psychologically, you experience a new, elevated state of mind and feel the joy, the rapture, ecstasy and the bliss you previously only had tastes of. This is the end of the journey, the symbolic returning home. In real life, if you reach this summit, what can I say, you feel great.

THE DOWNSIDE

V. How The Hero Becomes an Antihero (Holdfast)
VI. How the Antihero Regresses
VII. How the Antihero Becomes a Tyrant
VIII. How the Antihero is Rewarded

The downside is the exact opposite of the upside. Having achieved a great success, we will, like Adam and Eve, Samson, King David, and Theseus become vulnerable, an easy target for temptation. The greater our success, the greater our vulnerability. This is so true, it's a cliché. Despite all of their virtues, many of our greatest modern heroes have been transformed into holdfasts and been corrupted or become womanizers.

Having tasted real power, we may be reluctant to give it up. In fact, we may develop an insatiable thirst for more and more power, and that will make us even more vulnerable. Plus there are other problems and pressures that can affect this process. A renewed, general prosperity can lead to decadence as it did in Germany before World War II and in the Roman Empire. Or the threat of outside enemies can put pressure on the entity to concentrate power in its leaders. Then there can be impatience on the part of the new leader with democratic processes or with others in authority. "Why can't these puny minds see the importance of my Napoleonic visions. For the sake of the people I've got to do away with them." And so on. All of this can contribute to our vulnerability.

In any case, we are drawn into the downside and new dark powers will be awakened which will transform the current state of good fortune into new states of misfortune and a new hero or new conscious element will have to be found to oppose them. The forces of assistance now become the forces of resistance and the forces of resistance become the forces guiding and aiding the antihero toward his doom. Where there was initiation there is now regression; where there was integration there is now alienation; where there was strength there is now weakness; where there was love there is now lust; where there was unity there is now polarity; where there was light there is now darkness; where there was a prince there is now a tyrant; where there was a superhero there is now a Wolfman or a Mr. Hyde; and where the hero's humanity was being awakened, the antihero's humanity is being shut down. His generosity has become uncontrolled greed, his compassion, hatred and loathing. Where there were celebrations there are now orgies; and where there was a paradise there is now a living hell.

The demise of the antihero is more often than not connected to his overreach, his uncontrolled greed. Even with $15 billion, Pablo Escobar, Ferdinand Marcos, and Saddam Hussein can't stop themselves. They have to keep accumulating. The misery they create finally becomes unbearable and they have to be destroyed. A new hero with a vision, a new Gandhi or Lech Walesa takes up the cause and goes after them. Each time around there's a gain. It is three steps forward and two steps back.

In story, Adam and Eve, Samson, King David, Theseus, *Oedipus Rex*, *Medea, Faust, Othello, Macbeth, Dr. Jekyll and Mr. Hyde, Little Caesar, The Grapes of Wrath, The Wolfman, Gone with the Wind, Snow White, Citizen Kane, Body Heat, Basic Instinct, Raging Bull, The Godfather, Chicago, Jurassic Park, Ocean's Eleven, The Italian Job*, and *Catch Me If You Can*, to name just a few, help to outline and illuminate this path.

Psychologically, what this means is that we grow in stages. Consciousness is built up bit by bit by this process. Nascent egos are continually being born. They mature and regress. They become old egos reluctant to step aside and have to be deposed by strong new impulses to change. If the old, holdfast ego is too strong and the new nascent ego too weak (and the mentors and helpers are not in place) then we get stuck, which is what is happening to most people today.

So these are the structures of the whole story, and actually it's a continuous cycle through all of the entities until all of the opposites are reconciled and some great value like justice or health is achieved for all.

CHAPTER 20

THE STORY FOCUS

We encounter this same passage, as I indicated, in every entity and in all the major passages of our lives. We are also experiencing many of these cycles at once as we simultaneously seek wealth, wisdom, love, health, freedom, justice, and other important values for ourselves, our families, our clients, our country, or the world.

Every problem we face and every action we undertake is related to one or another of these *whole story* cycles and values, and in the course of a single day we may experience dozens of these different passages. We may be on the upside of some of these passages, the downside of others; the initiation stage of one cycle, the regression stage of another, the inflation stage of yet another. We may be heroic in some passages and holdfasts or completely stuck in others. Our ego-doctor could be handling one problem successfully, but our ego-lawyer is getting us into serious legal trouble. Our business can be doing well while our love lives are a catastrophe. Then our love lives improve and our company goes belly up. Our health is on the upside but our house is being destroyed by an earthquake or a flood. Crime is down in our neighborhood but our country is going to war. Each of these events belongs to a different *whole story* cycle and a different value system.

We are also involved in the cycles of other people in which we are playing a variety of archetypal roles. We participate in the cycles of our children, as parental forces of assistance and resistance, when they are experiencing the tyranny of the terrible two's, puberty, or other periodic downsides. We participate in the cycles of our friends or other family members, as threshold guardians and guides, when they're getting hooked on alcohol, cigarettes, and drugs, or when they're being liberated from these substances. In fact, everyone we know that we are involved with is managing the same cluster of cycles and we are participating in them on all different levels, playing many different roles. We are also participating in the up and down cycles of our communities, our cities, our states and nations. And in this respect we carry a similar profile as the President, the conscious, decision-making center of the country, who has to deal with a multiplicity of personal problems and cycles while simultaneously waging war on the nation's poverty, injustice, bigotry, ignorance, terrorism, crime, and disease. Each of which is part of a different cycle. And all of which we may somehow be involved in. Each time we recycle a bit of plastic or pick litter up off the street we are participating in, and having an effect on, the larger war on pollution, which is part of a very serious downside and being fought worldwide. Every political action we take, in fact, including just casting a vote for a candidate who has promised to act like a hero, is a participation in one of these cycles.

We can manage all of this because our extraordinary brains can divide the dozen or so whole cycles we're experiencing simultaneously into a sequence of smaller, manageable events or problems, block out what might distract us and focus on one thing at a time. Then we can shift our attention from one cycle to another and solve one of these smaller problems as necessity dictates. One problem solved or partly solved, then we switch back to some other new or partly solved problem in one of the other cycles.

We don't notice that each of these individual problems is part of a structured cycle because we are experiencing the different cycles in a seemingly random fashion and are constantly shifting our attention from one cycle to another, which makes us think we're experiencing a completely random shift of thoughts and moods. But we aren't. We're experiencing an extraordinary and complex web of interrelated cycles and passages which are governed by the pursuit of some important value like life, health, wealth, freedom, justice, etc. and by the avoidance of their opposites – death, disease, poverty, slavery, injustice, and so on.

All of this is revealed in story, which, as I mentioned, likes to isolate these value cycles, focus on one aspect, and examine it in great detail.

The Trojan War

In *The Iliad*, for instance, the aspect of the whole passage being explored in detail (i.e. the focus of the story) has to do with Achilles' anger. Achilles and Agamemnon have an argument over a girl who was given to Achilles as a prize. Agamemnon takes the girl back, Achilles feels dishonored, gets angry and drops out of the fight. The Greek army falls apart without him and is almost destroyed. The story ends when Achilles lets go of his anger and returns to the fight. But this incident, which encompasses the entire book of *The Iliad*, is only a very small part of the larger, *whole story*, the structures of which we just described.

This larger, *whole story*, which reveals the passage, began, as I mentioned earlier, at the wedding of King Peleus and the sea goddess, Thetis, and has to do with the wrath of two goddesses, Hera and Athena, who despise the Trojan, Paris, because, in the rigged contest to determine the fairest goddess, he chose Aphrodite over them. They are so put out by this affront, they plot the downfall of Paris and his native city, Troy. After Aphrodite rewards Paris by helping him seduce Helen (the downside), the offended goddesses help her husband, King Menelaos, raise the army he needs to attack Troy and get her back (the upside). They're nine years into the war when the tragic incident between Agamemnon and Achilles occurs, and the *whole story* is revealed through the exposition contained in that one extremely narrow focus. The episode involving the Trojan horse, which is the real climax of the larger *whole story* passage, doesn't occur until a year after *The Iliad* ends and isn't even mentioned in that story.

The Odyssey is another focus on that same *whole story* and reveals other details of the passage, including the episode involving the Trojan horse. It begins a long time after the fall of Troy and is all about Odysseus' ten year struggle to return home. You could create a hundred other stories, each focusing on a different aspect of that one passage. And that is, in fact, what Euripides and many other Greek dramatists did (*Iphigenia, Trojan Women, Orestes*, etc.)

The way the *whole story* and the story focus are structured and related to each other is the metaphor that illustrates with great clarity how the mind isolates one cycle and focuses on one aspect at a time.

The Iliad - -The Whole Story

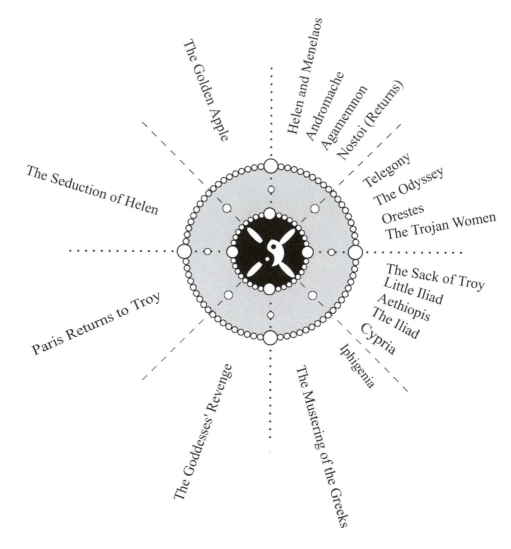

The value being pursued in the *whole story* of *The Iliad* is honor (and the avoidance of its opposite, dishonor) and every facet of the *whole story* is an exploration of that subject. Each individual story (or story focus) reveals a different aspect of the larger *whole story*. No single story could begin to reveal everything contained in the passage which is far too vast and complex and technically has no end. Most stories created today are about lawlessness and are focused on the upside in sections I and II. They begin with the hero getting involved in an adventure and end with a climactic battle with the villain. This could reflect our preoccupation with the problems of inauthenticity and crime — and the serious need we have to gain control over our negative energies.

World War II

Using World War II as another *whole story* which reveals the passage, you can see a similar example in modern times. Hitler takes over Europe (the downside) and the Allies ban together to destroy him and liberate the continent (the upside). The value being pursued is freedom, the scourge being avoided is tyranny and the slavery and death which that implies. *The Longest Day*, a focus on that whole story, is all about D-Day and the taking of the beaches of Normandy by the allied forces. Like *The Iliad* the entire story is focused on that one battle, but the *whole story*, WWII, is very much in the background. In *Saving Private Ryan*, Spielberg isolates a dilemma of justice and humanity surrounding one individual soldier who is caught up in that same invasion. In *Schindler's List*, another story in the larger context of that same war, Jews employed in a factory are rescued from the Holocaust by one enterprising German businessman. In *The Great Escape*, we see a spectacular escape of allied soldiers from a German prison camp. The entire story is focused on this one event which took place sometime during the crisis phase of the whole passage between the time when the Allied forces invaded Europe and the climax of the *whole story*, the Battle of the Bulge. In *Patton*, the character of the general who engineered this string of victories is thoroughly explored. In *Casablanca*, a former patriot and freedom fighter named Rick has become disillusioned and, like Achilles, dropped out of the fight. The principal action of the story focuses on how Rick is brought back into the fight. And, here again, World War II and the larger questions of tyranny and freedom are ever present in the background.

World War II -- The Whole Story

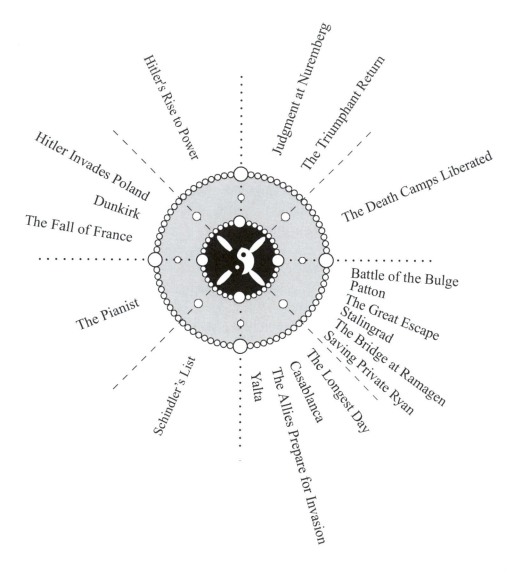

The real war, which started in 1939, ended in 1945 with the occupation of Berlin. The allied victory was the result of the coordinated efforts of millions of people, all of which were essential to a positive outcome. There is no way you can assess or organize and study all of those details which are extremely complex and very hard to analyze and draw concrete lessons from. So we need story to help us understand this event. By dividing the war into stories, you isolate essentials that make it possible for us to see inside this complex web of interrelated events and examine the structures and dimensions we can't ordinarily see because of the confusion of details. Each of the stories mentioned above reveals a different facet of the *whole story* passage of World War II, and that larger story is always referenced in the background. That is how the mind looks at big events and fathoms their complexity. Story is, in fact, the ideal way to communicate the pieces of the puzzle. It is a magnifying glass which permits the examination of the parts without losing sight of the whole. And when you artistically treat these stories, you ferret out a hidden truth that can tell us a lot about our own psychology and the real causes of the war. All of which make story a very useful tool.

King Arthur

The myriad legends of King Arthur sketch out three complete *whole story* cycles. The first upside cycle begins with Arthur's father, King Uther Pendragon, unifying the country. On the downside of the first cycle, Pendragon is taken over by lust and the unification falls apart. The second upside cycle involves the young King Arthur who, with

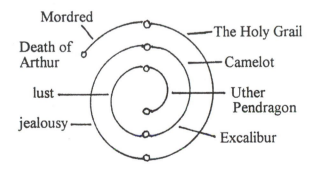

the help of Merlin and the miraculous sword, Excalibur, reunifies the country and creates Camelot. This renewed state of good fortune then falls completely apart because of jealousy, creating another downside. The only thing that can save the kingdom after that is the Holy Grail and that sparks the upside of a third cycle, wherein Sir Galahad and the other most virtuous knights pursue the quest for the Holy Grail. This is eventually achieved, but then the whole thing falls apart again with the rise of Mordred, the evil, illegitimate son of Arthur, who ultimately brings about his father's death.

Each different adventure of all of the different knights illuminates some other dimension of the whole, and if you take the time to analyze all of the stories associated with all of these cycles, you will see how they overlap, how one story takes up where another leaves off. If you do this with enough stories and piece them together, the much larger, coherent structure of the passage will be revealed. That is how the structures of the Golden Paradigm and Storywheel were discovered. If you build your story model, only using the things all great stories have in common, you will miss the structures created by their differences.

Types of Story Focus

In real life, when we are involved in one of these cycles and some action has to be taken, the types of things we focus on are similar to those outlined in the eight stages of the passage and, consequently, there are several different types of critical action that a story will focus on.

The first type takes place in section I of the passage. It is focused on the character of the hero and has to do with getting the hero to join or return to the fight. In these stories, the hero is in an inauthentic state. He or she has gotten off the track and is not dealing with the larger problem, and the story is focusing on his or her problem rather than some other important action. They are either incapacitated (*Kill Bill, Princess Bride*), enchanted (*Beauty and the Beast, Pinocchio, Groundhog Day*), on the wrong side (*Gone with the Wind, Catch Me If You Can, On the Waterfront, A Christmas Carol, The Verdict*), reluctant to get involved (*Alexander Nevsky, High Noon*), or they have dropped out of the fight entirely (*The Iliad, Casablanca*). These stories are about the transformation of the hero's character and show the hero being brought back to a heroic frame of mind and returning to the fight. The *whole story*, of course, is always referenced in the background.

In this type of story on the downside, the story is focused on the corruption rather than the rehabilitation of some antihero. *Othello*, *Macbeth*, *Body Heat*, *Basic Instinct*, *The Godfather*, *Chicago*, and *Faust* are all focused on the downside. John Milton's *Paradise Lost* begins after the *whole story's* great battle between God and Satan and is all about Satan's efforts to corrupt Adam and Eve. *Macbeth*, which begins on the upside after the climactic battle with the former Thane of Cordor, is focused on the downside and is all about Macbeth's corruption and guilt. *Othello* is focused on jealousy and is all about the destruction of the Moor by his servant, Iago.

Another type of story is focused in the Initiation Stage (II). The hero has been brought into the fight and the focus shifts toward the major and minor direct actions the hero has to perform — i.e., the battles that must be fought to solve the problem (*Erin Brockovich*, *The Silence of the Lambs*), liberate the entity (*The Lord of the Rings*, *Star Wars*, *Jaws*, *The Longest Day*), or the power that has to be gained to win those battles (*The Holy Grail*, *Excalibur*). In stories of direct action, the hero's character is not in question. He is in an authentic, heroic state. He realizes his place in the scheme, accepts his responsibility, takes action and accepts his fate. He is in the fight and on track, discovering, pursuing and defeating the cause of the problem and evolving to a higher state of consciousness. The story is focused around some decisive action and illustrates how that is done. It could be the main action of the initiation (*Star Wars*) or a single battle, as in *The Longest Day*.

Similar stories on the downside focus on the antihero's efforts to secure his or her objectives and the resistance they encounter before succeeding (Anakin Skywalker in *Star Wars III*, Livia in *I, Claudius*, and Hitler in the mini-series *The Rise of Evil*).

Other types of story are focused on the events that take place in sections III and IV, after the conclusion of the initiation. Those in section III focus on the hero's inflation or on his encounter and escape from the final surge of hidden power. The return of Odysseus in *The Odyssey* is one example, the Hindu myth, "Parade of Ants," another. "Parade" begins after the climax of the *whole story's* great battle, which is alluded to in the exposition, and is all about the inflation and humbling of the god Indra. Those in section IV focus on the resolution of the problem, the transcendence of the hero, the wedding or the celebration, and they give us a glimpse of paradise. In *Father of the Bride*, the entire story focuses on a single incident, the wedding, and the *whole story* is revealed in the context of that one event. In *My Dinner With Andre*, the entire two-hour film covers a single dinner conversation between two men. This remarkable and very entertaining film, which takes place somewhere in IV after the hero's return, works because one of the participants acts as a storyteller and reveals the *whole story* through his personal adventure from disillusioned artist to reborn spiritual man.

These very important patterns make us aware of the types of situations we will encounter in the passage and the things we may need to focus on.

The Structures and Dynamics of the Story Focus

Wherever your story is focused on the wheel, you not only have to be aware of the problem and the solution of the focus, you have to know how the actions relate to the big picture and how they will affect the future. The structures of the story focus illuminates this:

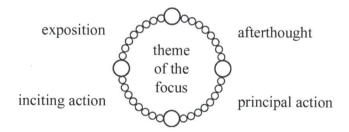

The thematic element — the anger, inflation, etc., that is being focused on — is in the center. Developing the focus explores the relation of that thematic element to the value of the *whole story*. In *Casablanca*, the subject of the *whole story* on the downside is tyranny. The value being pursued on the upside is freedom. The theme of the focus is patriotism. The story reveals how patriotism relates to tyranny and freedom, i.e., you can't defeat tyranny and regain freedom without it.

Just as in the larger, *whole story*, the inciting action of the focus is the downside action that describes how the problem of the focus was created and the principal action is an upside action which shows us how this particular problem is resolved. The two subordinate structures of the focus are the exposition and the afterthought. They relate the focus to the whole passage. The exposition links it to past and present events and the afterthought links it to the future. This structure is a perfect illustration of how our minds are functioning when we're focusing on a problem that's related to one of these passages.

The *whole story* behind Casablanca, as I mentioned, is World War II, and the focus of that *whole story* is the transformation of one individual, an ex-patriot named Rick, who has dropped out of the fight. But the *whole story* is always very much in the background. That comes to us from the exposition. The inciting action tells us how Rick became disillusioned in Paris and lost his patriotism and the principal action shows us how Rick gets that patriotism back. The afterthought is everything we know will happen after Rick and Claude Rains disappear into the fog: that Rick is now back in the fight and will play an important role in the war.

The Principal Action

The most important of these structures is the principal action because that is the action that solves the problem and brings about the change of fortune. In real life, a problem-solving, principal action is interrupted by problems from other cycles and it's hard to know where one experience begins and the others end. In story, these problem-solving, principal actions are separated from all the other problems and cycles, treated artistically, and reconstructed into an unbroken unity that can be studied when we're motivated to look beyond the sugar coat of the story at what's hidden inside.

In real life, after we've analyzed the problem, we create a theory and a plan which will continually be adjusted until the problem is solved. The principal action is the main objective of that plan. It is the central, unifying action that leads to the defeat of Hitler, the tracking down of a serial killer or the victory over some injustice. In a great story, it's these things plus the actions necessary to solve a dragon or alien problem. In *The Exorcist*, it's casting out the Devil. In *Raiders of the Lost Ark*, it's finding the lost ark. In *The Lord of the Rings*, it's the destruction of the Ring of Power. In "Parade of Ants," it's the actions that lead to the humbling of Indra. In *A Christmas Carol*, it's the transformation of Scrooge.

This central action holds these stories together and gives them a unity of action. According to Aristotle: "The imitation (of a story) is one when the object imitated is one. So the plot, being an imitation of an action, must imitate one action, and the whole of that (one action)."

The principal action in story is also, as it is in life, the line of action that causes all of the antagonism and resistance and is the source of the greatest tension and suspense. The real key to understanding story and problem-solving actions in real life is the understanding of the structures hidden in this principal action. It is also the action that brings about the change of fortune.

Great stories are all about changes of fortune and the principal actions that bring them about. In real life, every action we take as heroes brings about a change of fortune. It is an extremely important pattern and they are two of the most important and useful things a storymaker can know about story and a human being can know about life.

The Structures of the Principal Action

The principal action has four structures: the solution formula, the genre structure, the universal structure, and the classical structure.

The Solution Formula

In real life, we automatically divide the principal action into a number of other important actions which are necessary to carry out our plan and bring about the solution. These larger actions can in turn be divided up again into other even smaller subordinate actions, and the right combination of these smaller actions will create a solution formula. In short, it's all the little problems that have to be solved in order to accomplish the larger mission.

In a story, it is the hero's theory or plan which will constantly be revised. The methods the heroes use to solve their problems reveal these solution formulas and, in a great story, these actions can, and should, actually teach us how to catch a serial killer, solve a shark problem, transform a miser, or unseat a tyrant. The more elegant the solution, the more hidden truth the action contains.

The Genre Structure

The second structure of the principal action is the genre structure. Each of the separate large and small actions of the solution formula has either a mental, emotional, physical, or spiritual character. And when you sort these out, they become the plots and subplots of your story. The dominant action or plot will give the story its genre. You can recognize which is which by how the actions end.

Mental story actions (plots) end in solutions or enigmas. When this plot is dominant it's called a mystery. The dominant plot of a Sherlock Holmes whodunit is mental. It's a mystery. The identity of the killer has to be figured out with the mind. *Ordinary People* is a psychological mystery. The dominant plot is the solution to the mystery of the boy's suicidal tendencies.

Emotional story actions (plots) end in separation or reunion. When this action is dominant it's a love story. *Casablanca* is a love story. The dominant plot is emotional, and it ends in the separation of the lovers. The most important thread that has to be worked out is Rick's relationship with Ilsa. He has to understand why she didn't show up at the railway station in Paris. All of this is emotional. The mystery surrounding Rick's neutrality, the transcendental powers of the letters of transit and the physical struggle with the Germans and the Vichy government are minor by comparison. That is why it is thought of as a love story. The emotional element is dominant. *Shakespeare in Love* is the same. The emotional plot is the dominant plot and it ends in separation.

And it doesn't have to be boy–girl. The dominant plot of *Oliver Twist* is emotional. It ends with the reunion of the boy, Oliver, with his rightful guardian. The dominant plot of *The Champ* is also emotional. It ends, when the father dies, with the separation of the boy from his father. In *Finding Nemo*, the emotional, dominant plot ends with the reunion of Nemo and his father.

Physical story actions end in victory or defeat. When this action is dominant, I call it a war story. The dominant plot of *Jaws* is physical, a war with a shark, and it will end in either victory or defeat. The dominant plot of *Gladiator* is also physical — a war between Russell Crowe (Maximus) and Joaquin Phoenix (Commodus), and it ends in victory or defeat. *Rocky* and *Chariots of Fire* are also physical. The dominant plots are resolved by a physical action and they will end with a victory or defeat.

Spiritual story actions end in transcendence or descendence. When this action is dominant, I call the story transcendental. When you transcend you achieve a higher plane, you gain a little bit of Paradise. When you descend, you slip to a lower plane, you gain a little bit of Hell. Like *Ghost*, the dominant plot of *The Sixth Sense* is transcendental. It ends with the central character, Bruce Willis, transcending to a higher plane. In *The Passion of the Christ,* the story of Jesus' death and resurrection is transcendental. *Gladiator* also ends with Russell Crowe achieving a higher plane. He rejoins his wife and son in Elysium, the Roman Paradise, but it's not the dominant plot.

These structures are interrelated and interdependent. In order to do something physical, you have to accomplish something mental; in order to accomplish something mental, you have to achieve something emotional, and so on. Every problem-solving action we take will have these four dimensions working in concert. One of those four elements will be dominant and that dominant element will give the problem its emotional, mental, physical, or spiritual character and the other dimensions will be subordinate. If the problem we are trying to solve is physical, then emotional and mental factors have to be involved if the main problem is to be resolved. If the problems are emotional, then mental and physical factors have to be worked out as well. In other words, to perform one of these necessary actions you need the coordinated efforts of the mind, the body, the heart, and the soul. You can't solve a problem of one of these dimensions without the involvement of the other dimensions.

So, if you want to create a better living space in your garage, which is to say, transcend to a place of greater comfort for yourself, that's spiritual, i.e. you want to get a little closer to what you believe is Paradise. In order to do that, though, you will need a plan, which is a mental activity. Then you have to get the cooperation of your significant other or any helpers you might need (emotional). And finally you will have to do a lot of physical work (physical).

All of this is revealed in story. In *Jaws* and in *Rocky*, the dominant plot (principal action) is physical (a war with a shark and a prize fighter's war with his own body) and the emotional and mental elements, which are subordinate, also have to be worked out in order to succeed. In *Jaws*, to restore Amity Island to its former tranquility (spiritual), Roy Scheider has to physically confront and destroy the shark (physical). To accomplish that he needs to understand the nature of the beast (mental), and to do that he needs to get the cooperation of the experts, Richard Dreyfuss and Robert Shaw (emotional). In *Rocky*, to succeed as a fighter (physical), Sylvester Stallone has to work out relationships with Talia Shire and her brother (emotional), and solve the mystery of his own fears, *Rocky*, and the loss of his courage, *Rocky II* and *III* (mental). These are the plots and subplots that are showing us how real life and the mind work when we try to solve problems.

The Universal Structure

The third structure is the universal structure. Sometimes in real life when you carry out one of these necessary actions, you will get the desired result. Other times you will not and you will need the universal structure to complete the task. This universal structure is

——— ential unit of action that can be described by the problem-solving formula: Trial plus Error plus Reflection plus Perseverance equals the Desired Result — $T + E + R + P = DR$. We take an action (trial), the result is different than we anticipated (error). There is, as John Howard Lawson describes it, a gap between expectation and result. We reassess the results, adjust our theory, revise our plan (reflection), and take another action – and we keep doing this (perseverance) until the problem is solved (desired result).

You will find this process in everything you do — from trying to find the right screw in a jar filled with different sized screws, searching the house for your lost keys or landing a man on the moon. You try something and if that doesn't work, you think about it and try something else. There is almost no other way to solve a problem.

In *Groundhog Day*, to break his enchantment Bill Murray has to repeat this universal action hundreds of times until he finally gets it right. Usually, the hero only has to do it two or three times. The climactic actions of *Alien* and *Terminator* are other good examples of this very important pattern. The heroes have to repeat their monster-destroying actions three times before they get the desired result.

The Classical Structure

More often than not this trial and error process will lead you through the phases of the final and most important structure of action which is the classical structure. Its components are: complications, reversal, crisis, discovery, climax, and resolution, all of which were outlined in the initiation phase of the passage. I introduced you to complications, crisis, climax, and resolution when I spoke about the Essence of Story, which is the structure you will see in all large and small problem-solving actions that encounter resistance. Now, we'll add reversal and discovery to our discussion. I did not mention them before because they are not essential. You can, according to Aristotle, have a story without reversal or discovery but you cannot have a story without complications, crisis, climax and resolution. So reversal and discovery are not essential but they do have properties which can delight an audience.

So — armed with our theory, our plan, and the trial and error process, we set out to accomplish a task and encounter resistance, which results in complications. These complications frequently lead to a reversal (i.e., we are achieving the opposite of what we intended). The reversal leads to a crisis (the apparent defeat of our best efforts), and the crisis leads to a discovery (an insight that can lead to a solution). All of this leads to the climactic actions necessary to resolve the crisis and bring about a solution (climax), and the climax leads to a resolution (a transformation back to a state of good fortune).

This classical structure is critical because this is the structure that brings to the surface the negative energies which caused the problem and sets them up for transformation. No matter what problem-solving action we undertake, we will encounter and need these components. This, too, is revealed in story.

In *Jaws*, a shark starts eating tourists at the height of the season (state of misfortune). The sheriff, Roy Scheider, and two shark experts set out to track him down (principal action). Their boat, it turns out, isn't big enough and one of the shark experts is off his rocker (complications). The shark gets the upper hand and smashes their boat (reversal, i.e. they're not destroying the shark, the shark is destroying them) and their boat is sinking (crisis). As the disaster progresses, Scheider realizes the shark will swallow anything, including a tank of explosive gas (discovery). He jams the tank into the shark's mouth, shoots it, and blows the shark to oblivion (climax). The shark dead, peace and prosperity are restored to Amity Island (resolution). The state of misfortune has been changed back to a state of good fortune.

You will see this structure in important minor actions in real life and story as well. If the hero is breaking into the villain's office, he may have trouble picking the lock (complications), then the night watchman is heard coming down the hall (reversal – crisis). The hero quickens his efforts and realizes he's been using the wrong tool (discovery); he finds the right tool and opens the door (climax) and gets safely inside (resolution). Our lives, in fact, are defined by these elements. Whether we're trying to hunt and gather, create a story, repair a damaged relationship, build a pyramid, or defeat Hitler, we will encounter this structure.

The most important element in the classical story structure is the crisis. It's the most important thing we need to master in order to survive. The Chinese word for crisis means danger and opportunity, which is to say: you're in an emergency, immediate action has to be taken, and you have only two options. If you make the right choice, you will avoid catastrophe and things will get better. But if you make the wrong decision, things will get a lot worse. In story, this is the event that forces the hero to make the sacrifice (or decision) that frees the power (or the knowledge) that provides the means to overcome the difficulty and climax the action. So — beyond revealing the secrets of life, this is the great mission of story, to teach us how to manage crises.

This classical story structure (along with the problem and the change of fortune) has been a major factor in human affairs and in stories created in the oral tradition, for tens, if not hundreds, of thousands of years. It has been a major factor in stories written by individual authors since Aristotle first described it 2400 years ago. The early Greek dramatists who evolved this dramatic structure, which Aristotle observed, had tapped into these dimensions of real life. The principles of dramatic action are, in fact, the laws of action in real life artistically treated.

This is important because it means that classical story structure is linked to both the structures of action in real life and the very essence of story — that without which there would be no story. And if it involves the essence of story, it must be very important indeed. Stories, after all, hide the secrets of life, so the essence of story must, of necessity, hide one of its deepest secrets, and so it does. It is in fact the action that took the human mind up the evolutionary path. Pursuing life, food, health, security, happiness, wisdom, freedom, and justice, we confronted problems, sought solutions, and encountered the resistance which created the complications, crises, climactic actions and resolutions of the classical structure. We tried this and we tried that. The unforeseen created the complications, and persistence provoked the negative energies and triggered an unexpected response. We thought it over, revised our theories and our plans, took another action and passed through the classical structure. And this ordeal gave us the information we needed to solve the problem and reach a resolution. This is how problems were solved then and this is how problems are solved now. That is how the negative energies of the lower self are brought into the open and transformed and this is how consciousness is built up bit by bit. It is the key to the passage, the key to higher consciousness, the key to everything.

Story-wise, however, there are still some vital ingredients missing. A story can have a principal action with a classical structure and still not make any sense, if it's not in the context of some larger *whole story*. If you rely on classical structure as your understanding of story, you can get into serious trouble. You can struggle with that model all of your life and still not have a story come out right. In real life, if you are pursuing these actions without knowing they are connected to a greater whole, they will come to nothing. That is why Joseph Campbell's work is so important. His monomyth, the hero's journey, connects story to the real purpose of story and gives significance to the types of actions which need to be selected. It also begins to reveal the transcendental structures that can guide the hero and us to higher states of being. The Golden Paradigm then tries to take things a step further and demonstrates why the classical story structure and the hero's journey need to be connected to the larger, *whole story* passage if it is to have real power and meaning. Only then do we see clearly that the real structures of a great story are a mirror of the human mind in transformation.

Wisdom

Every action in real life contains a lesson and this is how we learn. We depend on this to build our experience. Each time you take an action and get an unexpected or disappointing result, you learn something. Each time you take an action and discover the cause of a problem, you learn something. If the lesson is strong enough, then the incident is worth repeating and you can retell it as a story and share that lesson.

In great stories, this is revealed by the main bit of wisdom the action contains. Each great story acts out an important general truth that can be applied to many different situations. The actions of the story demonstrate that wisdom. It is the lesson of the action. If the bit of wisdom conveyed by the story is *crime doesn't pay*, then the action of the story will act that out. The criminal will come to some terrible end and the audience will come to that conclusion.

In *Casablanca*, the wisdom is: *When it comes to matters of the heart, don't make assumptions. Things are never what they seem.* When Ilsa didn't show up at the railroad station in Paris, Rick assumed it meant she had lied to him about her feelings — and if that love was false, it makes everything else, including the war, pointless. He becomes disillusioned and drops out of the fight. Later, he discovers the truth. She had a good reason for not showing up. His assumptions were incorrect. That being resolved, he gets back into the fight.

The wisdom of *The Iliad*, according to Ben Jonson, is: *United we stand, divided we fall.* This is clearly demonstrated by the action, which is a treatise on the devastating effects of anger. After the argument with Agamemnon, the angry Achilles and his army drop out of the fight and the Greeks are being overrun and ravaged by the Trojans. Later, when unity is restored, Achilles gets back into the fight, the tide changes back in favor of the Greeks, and they eventually sack Troy.

The wisdom in *Jurassic Park,* like the wisdom in *Frankenstein* and the debacle of our own nuclear energy wastes, is clearly advising us to think twice before playing God.

The wisdom in *Groundhog Day* is also very profound. If you are tired of reliving the same horrible day, it shows you exactly what you have to do to break that enchantment — namely, make yourself both capable of love and worthy of love. It's that simple (or that difficult). But if you can manage it, you will wake up in a whole new and magical world.

In a great story, the wisdom is never obvious. It is hidden for later discovery. If the wisdom in a story is too obvious, it becomes a moral tale, or, worse yet, a story with a message, which is something for the intellect and not the heart.

The Scene

The most important unit of action in a story film is the scene. In real life, certain actions and ideas are more essential to a solution than others. In story, we see this revealed by the structure of the scenes, which isolate the essential steps (the core elements) and illuminate them. This core element becomes the center or fascination of the scene. It is what the scene is about. It links the scene to the passage and story focus and governs the actions around which the scene is built. And in a great story the scene will often only have this one objective. When this is true, then everything in that scene — the actions, the characters, the atmosphere, the mood, the setting, etc. — can serve that one objective and create a powerful artistic statement.

In Zeffirelli's *Romeo and Juliet,* the balcony scene is all about one thing, the declaration of love, and everything in that scene, the setting, the mood, the music supports that one idea. Besides helping to make it artistically powerful, limiting the scene to one objective greatly increases the clarity and helps to focus the feelings of the audience. They sink right into the essential feeling. In Dickens' *A Christmas Carol* the whole beginning has only one objective: to establish that Ebenezer Scrooge is a miser. We see this in the setting and the mood but also in the action. Scrooge is counting his money. Cratchit is cold but is allowed to use only one piece of coal. Good Samaritans arrive trying to raise funds for the poor and Scrooge turns them away. *The Godfather* is made up of sixty or so short filmic scenes which are made potent and clear by their simplicity. In *Snow White* there are eighteen or so fully illuminated and enriched scenes making up the entire film, which is another reason why these films are so effective. The simpler the scenes are, the richer they are — the clearer their meaning and the stronger their impact emotionally.

CHAPTER 21

THE SUGAR COAT

The sugar coat is the entertainment dimension, which are the pleasant sensations the audience feels when they experience your story. In real life, they are the jumble of feelings we experience as we jump from cycle to cycle. In a great story, they are one set of these feelings isolated and purified so they can be experienced together in a meaningful sequence. The promise of these feelings helps to lure the audience into the experience and the fulfillment of that promise gives them pleasure and a sense of having been entertained. They are produced by the same metaphors and actions that reveal the hidden truth and the closer you get to the hidden truth, the more powerful the feelings. The more powerful the feelings, the more our interest is heightened and our excitement aroused.

These entertainment dimensions are also created by isolation. When you isolate a story element, you focus attention on that element, heighten the interest and the emotional involvement. And when you artistically treat that story element, you purify and intensify the hidden truth it contains. That purified, intensified truth is highly charged with the emotional values we experience as entertainment.

The most important of these feelings are those associated with the actions of the genre structures. When you isolate the plots and subplots of these genre structures, you isolate the feelings associated with them — the feelings associated with a romance, a thriller, a mystery, an adventure, etc. Each of these different genres will take the audience on a different emotional journey. The most noteworthy of these feelings are laughter and tears, passion, suspense, excitement, magic, love, hate, fear, terror, awe, horror, hope, despair, desire, disgust, enchantment, sympathy, attraction, lust, anger, and surprise. These are the feelings the audience experiences when the characters guide them through the paradigm. These feelings are like flags that mark the way, and the sequence of these feelings will help the audience identify the experience when they're ready to make a meaningful connection. They only need to ask themselves what caused those feelings and they will begin to see the hidden patterns.

The emotional values that make up the sugar coat are enhanced by a number of factors. The first is make-believe. Make-believe separates the intriguing aspects and mechanics of a given situation from the fear of the consequences we might experience in real life. In real life, nothing could be less entertaining or enlightening than a real serial killer stalking your neighborhood. Your only concern would be to get rid of him as soon as possible. In a story, where you can eliminate the fear of consequences, you are left with the pleasant sensations associated with the hunt, and you can study the mechanics of that experience objectively. Using this separation, a story can artistically treat and translate even the most horrible real crimes into an intriguing entertainment that conceals an important truth in a powerful metaphor.

Another factor is structure. Separated from the fear of consequences, the archetypal rivalry which can be so deadly in real life becomes a game in story. The same structures, in fact, that make a game fun make a story fun –the fact that it involves opposing sides, boundaries, important things at stake, a marvelous element, possible victories or defeats, and a ticking clock. The only difference between an ordinary game like football and the story game is the size of the playing field, which in story can be as big as a galaxy (*Star Wars*). And that is to say, as big as the human mind.

Another factor augmenting the sugar coat is real life. Audiences are fascinated and delighted by successful imitations of real life — real human gestures, expressions, moods, and conversation. When a great story artistically treats real life to create a metaphor, it retains that fascination and becomes a primary interest holder. It rivets the attention. Without that dimension, *Fatal Attraction*, *The Exorcist*, and *The Silence of the Lambs* would be ordinary horror movies. Not nearly as entertaining and not nearly as successful.

Two final factors are the technical and aesthetic dimensions. The aesthetic dimensions — clarity, beauty, elegance, harmony, rhythm, grace — are the pleasing effects that are created by the skillful and artistic use of the technical dimensions, i.e. variety, contrast, proportion, timing, symmetry, tempo, etc. Proportion and symmetry are major factors in the creation of beauty. And perfect proportion, like beauty itself, is a noble torment of the mind.

Contrast is a major factor in creating clarity. When you contrast such things as good and evil, spiritual and physical, rich and poor, light and dark, silence and sounds, you heighten the effect of both and greatly increase the clarity.

Rhythm is the key to elegance and grace. Perfect rhythm is the ideal combination of repetition and variety (similarity and change). A story has a certain rhythm. Every different type of story has a different rhythm. This is true of tempo and pace as well. Real life has its own special tempo and pace, and every different type of story (i.e. mystery, love story, action adventure, etc.) has its own characteristic tempo and pace. While obscure and almost forgotten, *Das Boot*, *The Lifeguard*, and *The Culpepper Cattle Company* are worth tracking down to study in this regard. Their pace seems synchronized with some internal, organic tempo and pace.

All of the hundred or so powerful metaphors and dimensions that create a great story have an impact on the sugar coat, on the entertainment values of the story, and the more dimensions (truth) the story contains the greater the emotional impact on the audience. The good news here being that great stories not only contain the secrets of life, these hidden secrets make them super powerful and extremely entertaining. And those two ingredients — power and entertainment — are the keys to a great success. *Groundhog Day* would be a good example. It is not only profound but extremely entertaining.

CHAPTER 22

THE STORYWHEEL REVISITED

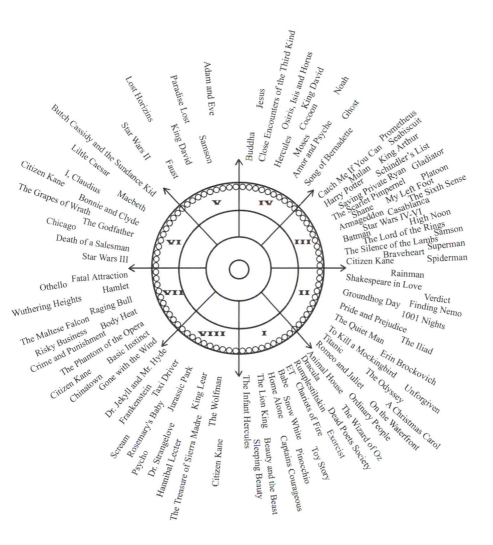

When I was seven years old, I wanted to be Captain Marvel, a super-hero like Superman. In everyday life, Marvel was a crippled newsboy named Billy Batson. But when he needed to become Captain Marvel to fight evil or protect the innocent, he cried out "Shazam!" and was hit by a lightning bolt, and that lightning bolt transformed him into the superhero.

On Thanksgiving of that year, when my whole family gathered at my Aunt Marie's for our traditional Thanksgiving dinner, I snuck into one of the empty bedrooms and spent three hours alone in that room praying to God to make me Captain Marvel. And with tears in my eyes and all the sincerity I could muster (at that age it was my domi-nant trait), I promised to use the power only to do good.

After three hours, I stood before the mirror on the dresser, trembling with a sense of destiny and having absolutely no doubt that I was about to be transformed into the most powerful force for good on earth, I cried out "Shazam," and braced myself for the megavolts. But nothing happened. I repeated the gist of my vows, clenched my fist and shouted the magic word two more times. Still it was in vain. I was stunned and very disappointed. It severely damaged my relations with the Supreme Being.

Thirty years later I realized that the storywheel is Shazam. The great story is Shazam. That is how we transform ourselves from crippled, inauthentic newsboys into human marvels, by following that path. The great story uses its imagery to stimulate our imaginations and give us little tastes of paradise which trigger fantasies that lead us to desires for positive actions in the real world. Then as we pursue these goals, the stories guide us through the passages using meaningful connec-tions, each story revealing a little bit more of the truth. And piece by piece, bit by bit, drop by drop, the whole truth is gradually revealed. And, despite ourselves, we find our selves, realize our dreams, and, like Captain Marvel, Hercules, Psyche, and King Shahryar we reach our full potential. The creative unconscious self is the source of that wisdom and that power. The great story is the guardian of that wisdom and that power. And if you unravel their mysteries and fathom their secrets you can participate in your own creation.

PART FOUR

THE ART OF STORYMAKING

"The way to defend art is to produce it."
Edward Cerny

CHAPTER 23

THE CREATIVE PROCESS
AND THE NEW
ARTIST-STORYMAKER

To create something means to bring something forth, to bring something into being, to fashion or produce something that didn't previously exist, in this case a story. Earlier I talked about the natural storymaking process in which the creative unconscious self used the oral tradition to help transform an incident worth repeating into a story that contained the secrets of life. This process was cut off, in part because of the written word, leaving billions of people without this vital, life-giving information. The new artist-storymakers perceive this need and have a desire to fulfill it. Armed with a fluency in the language of metaphor and a sophisticated story model, we insert ourselves into this process. We enter into a partnership with the creative unconscious self and use the creative process to construct great stories that will benefit and entertain those who experience them.

The key to all of this is our feelings. Feelings are at the threshold between the conscious and unconscious worlds and are without a doubt a communication from our unconscious to our conscious selves. This link is obvious with physical or spiritual feelings. When we feel physical pain we know something is physically wrong, that it's a communication. Similarly, when we experience strong spiritual feelings, we sense they are a message or reward of some kind. But this communication is less obvious with feelings associated with mental or emotional creative processes. While playing with your creative ideas, the positive and negative intuitive feelings you are experiencing are important messages from your creative unconscious self. If you learn how to read these feelings, then playing with your creative ideas becomes a direct means of contact. Every experience of feeling is an attempt to bring unconscious content and influence to consciousness. Getting in touch with your feelings is getting in touch with your self. Getting in touch with your self through your feelings is the heart and soul of the creative process.

Four other important resources participate in this collaboration: your *imagination*, your *technique*, your *knowledge*, and your *experience*.

Your imagination is the "image" making function. It is the staging area, the place where creative activity takes place, and it is the process that transforms the raw energy of the unconscious into visual images, into metaphors. It is your ability to create new images and ideas by combining previous experiences. The stored memories of real or imaginary things are the raw clay. The curious tendencies of the mind are the artistic tools that help to recombine and shape that raw clay into new creative ideas. The process functions freely and automatically and is largely unconscious.

Technique is the conscious function, the method of working which helps you achieve the desired result. The imagination brings the raw, unconscious material to the surface and the conscious technique helps to fashion that raw material into a powerful metaphor that contains the hidden truth.

The knowledge is the special understanding you possess of your art. It's what you know about story. It's what you need to know to become a master storymaker. The special knowledge I teach in this book has to do with the Golden Paradigm, which is our story model. Without this, or some other special knowledge, as a point of reference, it is difficult to get effective unconscious cooperation and support. And without unconscious cooperation and support, you can't get the hidden truth programmed into your stories and they won't have any real power or meaning. The better your story model, the better your story because the more of this vital information you can access.

As for experience — there is just no substitute for it. The more you work with these processes, the better you are going to get.

CHAPTER 24

IMITATIONS OF REAL LIFE

What the metaphor is to hidden truth, imitations of real life are to art. It is the artistic dimension, the one that holds the mirror up to nature, and if you aspire to real greatness, this is the dimension you should be most interested in. The writers who master this dimension win Pulitzer and Nobel prizes, filmmakers who master it win Academy Awards.

If the artist-storymaker sets out, not just to entertain, but to explore life and discover truth, you can feel it in their work. It makes a powerful impression. And I'm not just talking about the works of Shakespeare, Dickens, Milton, and Dostoyevski, I'm talking about motion pictures like *The Godfather, The Pianist, A Beautiful Mind, Schindler's List, Ordinary People, Witness, Raging Bull,* and *Babette's Feast*. From the very first instant, you realize you're dealing with something of substance. It doesn't compromise the entertainment, it enhances and intensifies it. A story that is exploring life has a certain very appealing pace and feel to it that draws the audience in and rivets their attention. And, as I indicated earlier, you can really see the power of this dimension if you realize this one quality transformed films like *Fatal Attraction* and *The Silence of the Lambs* from being simple horror movies into highly acclaimed, realistic dramas — and it added a hundred million dollars to their grosses.

Another virtue of this dimension is that it can be used as camouflage. The audience should be so embroiled in the lives of the characters that they don't notice the structure, and one of the best ways to do that is to put everything in the context of real life. In the opening scene of *The Godfather,* the main sensation you have is that you're at a wedding, but there are some very heavy plot elements unfolding in that context. In another part of the film, on his way to execute a family traitor, one of the hitmen stops at a deli to pick up some *cannoli* for his wife. Or the Corleone family is planning a gang war while making spaghetti together — everything is in the context of everyday life.

Mastery of this dimension is achieved by the observation of life, by observing how people really behave, how they relate to each other — how parents relate to their children, how husbands relate to their wives, how people really talk. If you're not a practiced observer, you'll find that people act very differently than you thought, if you haven't consciously been observing them. When you live life, you have a subjective point of view. When you observe life, you detach yourself and acquire an objective point of view, and then the experience of life is very different.

According to Tom Wolfe, "The author should be out in the field the same as the reporter, living, observing, and experiencing life."

This is the storymaker's fieldwork. It is also the actor's fieldwork. Meryl Streep said that the thing she regretted most about being a celebrity was that she could no longer ride the subway watching how people behave.

To become a good observer, you have to learn how to see. If you've ever tried to draw a human face or hand, you know what I mean. It's very difficult. An artist has to learn how to see. So does a story-maker.

When I was still in my early twenties, my wife and I were driving around the outskirts of the UCLA campus. We were with our two daughters and happened to be talking about koala bears. Diane said they only eat the leaves of eucalyptus trees, and she pointed to some examples that we just happened to be passing. I was amazed and asked her how she knew they were eucalyptus trees. (I grew up in New York City and didn't know a tree from a telephone pole). She laughed at my ignorance and explained how easy it was, you simply looked at the shape of the trees and the shape of their leaves. Hmm.

I began doing that and became fascinated by trees. I took some botany courses at UCLA and, in my spare time, began walking around the campus or in the Santa Monica mountains collecting leaf samples and studying their differences. It took awhile but I finally caught on.

My very favorite discovery was a ginkgo tree on the UCLA campus. The ginkgo tree comes from China and has a leaf shaped like this. It has been around for over three hundred thousand years and is the most ancient tree species in the world. It's ancientness and the fact that it came from China gave it a mystical quality like a venerable Chinese sage, and I formed a special bond with that tree. For years I was drawn to it. I loved to sit under it and contemplate the story model, my own problems, or the fate of the world.

Then one spring I returned to New York City and was strolling along the streets of my old neighborhood. Much to my surprise I discovered that the streets where I grew up were lined with ginkgo trees. They were everywhere and had been there since before I was born. I had played with my soldiers under their boughs and never noticed them. It's amazing how much you overlook until you become a practiced observer.

CHAPTER 25

SOURCES OF MATERIAL

What are some good sources of material? To begin with you can do your own version of an already existing myth, legend, or classic, and take it the next evolutionary step, in an otherwise cut-off evolutionary process. The biggest names in literature — Homer, Milton, Sophocles, Shakespeare, and Goethe among others — all did exactly that. They took an existing legend or myth and put their personal stamp on it. If you do that, ninety percent of the work has been done for you by the oral tradition. *The Mists of Avalon* is Mary Zimmer Bradley's version of the King Arthur stories from Morgan Le Fey's point of view. *The Seven Percent Solution* is Nicholas Meyer's take on Sherlock Holmes. *Mary Reilly* is a maid's eye view of *Dr. Jekyll and Mr. Hyde*. *Beauty and the Beast* is how Disney sees that classic, and so on.

A second possibility has to do with taking a real incident worth repeating and creating either a true or fictional story out of that event by finding the archetypes and the model in the true story and artistically treating the subject. *JFK* is Oliver Stone's retelling of the Kennedy assassination. *In Cold Blood* is Truman Capote's recreation of the brutal murder of a Midwestern family. *All the President's Men* is an artistic treatment of the events surrounding the Watergate burglary.

A third way to start would be to analyze the old great stories and discover the precedent structures, which are the underlying core motifs, and redress them in an entirely new costume. If you analyze *Alien*, you will find *Beowulf*. Grendel taking possession of a castle and devouring its knights one by one and an alien monster taking over a space ship and devouring its crew one by one are similar metaphors with similar meanings being made relevant by differences of time and place. If you analyze *The Lion King*, you will find *Hamlet*. An evil uncle murders his brother, steals his kingdom and queen, and tries to prevent his nephew, the rightful heir, from assuming the throne. The change of time and place and a change from human to animal do not affect the meaning of the metaphor. They just make it more accessible to children. If you analyze *Groundhog Day*, you will find *Beauty and the Beast*. To break his enchantment, Bill Murray, an arrogant boor, has to learn how to love and be worthy of love. If you analyze *Cold Mountain*, you will find *The Odyssey*. A soldier who has gone off to war needs to return home to rescue a loved one in jeopardy, but has great difficulty. If you analyze *On the Waterfront*, you will find *Mutiny on the Bounty*. A basically ethical henchman, on the wrong side, is transformed by love and can no longer tolerate injustice. If you analyze *West Side Story* and *Pretty Woman*, you will find *Romeo and Juliet* and *Cinderella*. These precedent structures are adaptable to any age or time, and can be redressed as a hundred different metaphors, depending on the audience you're trying to reach.

A final option is to evolve a completely original idea, starting with a fascination.

CHAPTER 26

SIX CREATIVE TECHNIQUES

Whichever path you choose, the creative process and the creative tools will be the same. You will use the true or imagined material as your starting place (as your fascination) and follow the same creative steps. The creative process I am describing utilizes six creative techniques. The first is probing the fascination.

Probing the Fascination

By fascination I mean any idea or visual image that has strong feelings attached to it. The process begins with a fascination. It could be anything that gets your juices going and inspires you to create a story. It could be a piece of music, a favorite song, a fantasy, a dream, some intriguing character or situation, a scene in your head, a haunting memory, a beautiful face, an incredible atmosphere, and so on.

By probing the fascination I mean working with that fascination creatively. You experience it, explore it, romance it. You plug it into your imagination in ways that create other images and ideas, the same as you do when you elaborate or give details and structure to a fantasy or daydream. You translate feelings into visual images (into metaphors) and use your imagination to bring more raw, unconscious, story-relevant material to the surface.

The important thing is to engage your intuitive feelings because that puts you in touch with your creative unconscious self and the energy behind those images. The stronger the feelings, the stronger the contact. And when you're in touch with your feelings, you're in touch with your self. You use the fascination as a point of contact with your self and you translate feelings into visual images — into metaphors.

Comparing and Selecting

When you probe a fascination, you will generate much more raw material than you need, and the idea here is to keep the ideas that have the strongest positive feelings attached to them and throw away the rest. Get rid of everything you can and continue to work with the few most powerful ideas. It's like panning for gold or separating the wheat from the chaff. There's always a lot of chaff to get rid of. The artistic tools operating here are the tendency to remember what makes a strong impression and to forget what leaves you cold. Using that as a guide, keep the ideas that really haunt you and get rid of everything else. In other words, respect the ideas that have power. The stronger the feelings associated with an idea, the more hidden truth it contains.

Modeling

In the third technique, modeling, you examine the emotionally charged images you've selected and begin identifying and associating them with the archetypes of the story model. You listen to the feelings associated with these images and realize that this is the value being pursued, this is the entity being transformed, this is the threat that caused the problem, this is the state of misfortune, this is the hero, these are the people who lure the hero into the adventure, this is the marvelous element, this event is part of the crisis, and so on.

The model helps to facilitate communication with your creative unconscious self because it was created by the patterns put into great stories by the creative unconscious itself — and when you use the model as a reference, you create metaphors that make a psychological connection and reveal the hidden truth. All of which will be confirmed by your feelings.

If you're dealing with a true story, you are looking for these same archetypal patterns in the real incidents. You are probing the fascinations of that true story and you're identifying and associating the elements with the model. If the story you're creating has to do with Enron, then you examine the emotionally charged characters and incidents related to that scandal, you listen to the feelings associated with these images and ideas and you realize that Ken Lay and his executive cronies are the threat, the cause of the problem. The corporation is the entity being transformed. Justice is the value being pursued. The shareholders, who lost billions, are the victims. The police investigators and the prosecutors are the anti-threats, the ones with the responsibility to solve the problem, and the evidence is the marvelous element, the thing without which the problem can't be solved — and so on.

Conjuring

In the fourth creative technique, you take the emerging metaphors and evolve them into more and more powerful examples of the archetypes. This is called conjuring. When you conjure, you are playing with the developing characters, powers, and events and trying them in a hundred different combinations, like Edison inventing his light bulb. He tried over one hundred and twenty different filaments before he found the right one, tungsten. Here again you are listening to your feelings and trying to discover the most pleasing patterns and potent combinations. You keep rearranging things trying to evolve them into more and more powerful metaphors.

Testing

After you've worked up the whole model, then you test the model by walking through it to see how it feels. You walk through the steps of the *whole story* passage you've sketched out or the scenes of the focus, just to get a sense of how it feels. You take it a beat at a time, being as sensitive as you can to your own responses. If something doesn't feel right, then you work on that problem. You take it apart and try something else. You change the characters, shift scenes around, etc. You replace some of the first ideas and walk through it again.

Problem Solving

Face all the problems and negative feelings directly. If something is wrong, take it apart and try something else. Storymaking is mostly confronting and solving problems. The more problems and negative feelings you confront and resolve, the better your work is going to be. Any problems left unsolved at the end of the day you can sleep on. Let Rumpelstiltskin take over and transform your pile of straw into gold while you sleep. More often than not, the problems will be resolved when you wake up in the morning.

Rollo May, who wrote a book called *The Courage to Create*, describes it this way: "You go through a period of intensive work, confront all the dilemmas, conflicts, and blocks, then put it aside and let the unconscious do its work."

Throughout this process, as I've mentioned, you are working with your intuitive feelings. Your intuitive feelings are helping you make all of the necessary decisions. Everything you do creatively, every change, every thought, every new selection has a feeling connotation. It will either feel good or bad and you will make your decisions accordingly.

The most important feelings to pay attention to are your negative intuitive feelings. These are the unpleasant feelings, which you have to learn to tolerate, that are telling you that something isn't working. These are the feelings that can guide you to greatness. Negative feelings counterbalance positive feelings. If we didn't have negative feelings, we would be easily satisfied with what we have accomplished, so we wouldn't change it and it would stop evolving.

Listening to your feelings is not about being right or wrong or your work being good or bad, it's about being closer to, or farther away from, the truth. It's like the child's game where you're trying to find something and you're being told that you're getting warm or getting cold. Positive intuitive feelings mean you're getting warm (closer to), and negative intuitive feelings that you're getting cold (farther away from) the truth. Listening to your intuitive feelings means being guided to the truth by your self. If it doesn't feel right, it isn't right. Something is wrong. You've got a problem, and you resolve that problem by the trial and error process; you try different things until the feelings change. Ninety-nine percent of the time negative feelings simply mean it needs more work or it has to be placed differently or it's almost right but not quite or it really doesn't work. If it really doesn't work, throw out what you have and redo everything affected by the problem.

You've heard that the artist suffers. This is apparently what that is all about. Artists voluntarily confront and deal with their negative feelings in order to create something and grow. It is a controlled, voluntary suffering for the sake of getting at the truth. Sometimes the feelings and the suffering can get pretty rough. There's usually at least one stage in the process where they get so desperate and unpleasant you lose all hope and are ready to quit.

Some years ago, when I was preparing this material for the seminars I teach, I experienced one of these unpleasant episodes. And during that time I had a dream in which I was standing in the doorway of my kitchen just outside the threshold and looking inside. My wife, a notorious anima figure in my dreams, was standing just inside the doorway to the right, facing one of the kitchen counters. Another extremely beautiful but younger girl with dark hair was standing in front of the stove to my left looking directly into my eyes. Just as this was happening, my wife began to melt (like the witch in *The Wizard of Oz*) until all that remained was one beautiful leg and a puddle of what looked like the vanilla ice cream I'd eaten the night before.

I looked back at the beautiful girl in front of the stove. Her look intensified and became challenging and with her right hand she gestured that I should come to her. Uneasy about doing as she commanded, I stayed outside the doorway. Then I woke up.

I was anxious about the dream and confused by it. Then I suddenly remembered something I had said the day before while preparing the course. When I had reached the place where I say, "And sometimes these feelings get pretty rough…" I was considering saying, "If you can't stand the heat, stay out of the kitchen." And then I understood the dream. In terms of negative feelings (heat), I had reached a crisis point in the work. My usual anima and guide was melting away from the new heat being generated by the emerging anima figure who was standing near the stove. This new anima figure was beckoning me to come closer so I could experience this new heat, but I was staying out of the kitchen. In other words, I was being hypocritical. I was about to tell my students that it gets rough sometimes and if you can't stand the heat stay out of the kitchen — and the dream was telling me that's exactly what I was doing. There were thresholds of creative suffering I was not ready to take. I was staying out of the kitchen myself.

I began working with the "new heat" and I came through it. If you go through it, you come through it. Learn to trust the negative feelings. Negative feelings are, of course, not really negative, but they are unpleasant. Become sensitive, also, to the subtle, micro feelings like the princess in "The Princess and the Pea." Work with them, sail into them, and find out what they're saying. In any event, don't take them personally as a judgment on your work.

CHAPTER 27

CREATING THE WHOLE
STORY PASSAGE

The Fascination

The process begins with a fascination, an intriguing idea you want to turn into a story. The feelings connected to that fascination establish contact with the creative unconscious. The stronger the feelings the stronger the contact.

The inspiration for *Casablanca* may have come from a haunting tune like "La Marseillaise" or "As Time Goes By," or the image of Rick sitting at a bar haunted by memories of a lost love. In *Saving Private Ryan*, it was a true story about a mother who lost three of her four sons in WWII, and the army makes an effort to save her fourth son, who is also in harm's way. Hundreds of other stories have been inspired by WWII, and in years to come there will no doubt be hundreds of stories inspired by the events surrounding the current war on terror.

JK Rowling, the author of the *Harry Potter* books, said in an interview that she was riding on a train when the image of the boy, Harry Potter, came to her full blown, including the lightning scar on his forehead. It struck her like a revelation but that's all she saw. Everything else she had to work out on her own.

When you find something like that, something that really fascinates you, then that becomes your inspiration, your starting point. Then you probe that fascination. You plug it into your imagination and use it like a crystal ball. You work with it and play with it until you've created a bounty of other intriguing ideas and fascinations that can also be probed. Ultimately, every character, action, and scene will have its own fascination at its center. Then you select the strongest images and ideas and begin modeling. Everything you need to construct the model can be found in that fascination. And probing that fascination for your other ideas will create a "feel" that gives a unity to the story in the same way that a musical key gives unity to a musical composition.

In any event, it's important to explore the things in life that really fascinate you — and play with a lot of different possibilities until you find something that really works for you.

The Principal, Unifying Elements

The principal (or unifying) elements necessary to construct the model, which you will discover in that fascination, are the story patterns I listed in Part Three and are now incorporated in the model.

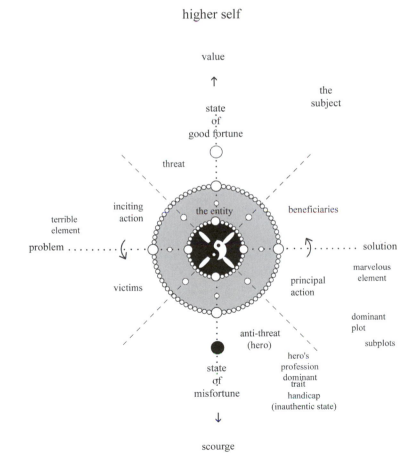

As I indicated earlier, the key to identifying and creating the metaphors of these archetypes is association. You associate the characters and actions you are discovering with the archetypes in the model. You work with your intuitive feelings and realize that this is the threat, this is the temptress, this is the subject, this is the problem, this is the entity being transformed, this is the hero, and so on. You determine the archetypal role the different elements are playing in relation to the whole and bit by bit you construct the paradigm. You identify them like pieces in a picture puzzle and assign a place for them. Then you probe these new elements looking for the ideas and images that surround them. Your feelings are guiding you to that truth and you are using the model as a point of reference. Again, the important thing is to engage your feelings because that puts you in touch with your self. Then you work with those feelings until they guide you to the characters, actions, and events you need in your model.

The Subject

There is no particular sequence you need to follow, but one of the first things you might want to discover in that fascination is the subject you want to explore. To find the subject you probe the feelings associated with the fascination, seeking the source or essence of that fascination. The fascinating subject is the source of those feelings. If, for instance, the fascination involves two people relating to each other romantically, you probe the feelings associated with that fascination and discover those feelings are inspired by, or are about, love, sex, or romance. If you probe the feelings associated with a fascination, you'll discover what it is about the fascination that fascinates you. You locate the feelings in the fascination and let them lead you to a subject that really intrigues you. And you play with this process until you find something really powerful.

So what kind of feelings are being aroused in your fascination? Is it a longing for tenderness and love? Does it involve justice or power? Is it about lust, a longing for excitement or adventure? Does it provoke anger or outrage? Clearly *Erin Brockovich* and *The Insider* were motivated by some kind of outrage on the part of the authors.

So what is your story about? Is it about ghosts, mummies, demonic possession, invisibility, a spy, injustice, tyranny, fascism, an unsolved mystery, a magic lamp? The feelings should lead you to the subject.

Concerning *Harry Potter*, we can imagine JK Rowling probing her fascination, picturing the boy with the lightning scar, probing the feelings associated with those images — and realizing "Ah-ha!" it's about sorcery and magic. The boy is a powerful young wizard. You probe the fascination of your idea and realize that *The Sixth Sense* is about fear, *A Beautiful Mind* is about mental illness, *The Pianist* is about survival, and *Saving Private Ryan* is about sacrifice — the amount of sacrifice one family should be required to make in a time of war. If you did a spy story, you would discover it was about espionage. If you did a story about 9/11, you would discover it was about terrorism. Probing the fascination of *Gladiator*, you discover it's about tyranny and the ultimate combat required to defeat it. And trying this and trying that, you realize it's about gladiators, and you've got a great title, a title that reveals both the subject and the genre.

The Quintessential

Then, if you want to make the subject you have chosen more fascinating, you take it to the quintessential — you evolve it into the best example of that subject. You make *Harry Potter* about the most extraordinary magic the world has ever seen, you make *Gladiator* the most extraordinary example of slavery or ultimate combat imaginable. If you're doing a spy story, you make it about the most extraordinary espionage the world has ever known. If you're doing a story about 9/11, you make it the definitive last word on terrorism.

According to the dictionary, the quintessential is the pure, concentrated essence of anything — it is the ultimate example of something — the most perfect manifestation or embodiment of a quality or thing. It is the ultimate good or bad, best or worst example of something. The world's fastest runner is the quintessential runner. The world's deadliest snake is the quintessential deadly snake. Hitler is the quintessential megalomaniac. Einstein is the essence of mathematical genius. He is symbolic of genius.

If your subject is a marvelous element like a secret chamber, which is fascinating in itself, you can make it even more fascinating by making it the most intriguing secret chamber of all time. If you make the subject the most extraordinary example of something, you will make that idea more intriguing.

How do you do that? By conjuring. You study the best-known secret chambers, analyze their unique qualities, then, while monitoring your feelings, you use the artistic tools and trial and error to slowly evolve that concept into a new ideal secret chamber. Instead of an ordinary prison, you make your prison even more miserable than the Black Hole of Calcutta, reportedly the worst place ever to be incarcerated. Instead of an ordinary murder, you make it a perfect murder. The perfect murder is more fascinating than an ordinary murder and the most perfect murder of all time is more fascinating than your run-of-the-mill perfect murder.

And somewhere in that process *The Perfect Murder* has popped out as a great title. The fascinating subject, in fact, is a good place to look for a great title. You probe the fascination of the subject looking for words, phrases, names, or events associated with that subject.

The reason *Cleopatra's Secret Diaries* fascinated me so much was because the idea of secret diaries (the subject) was taken to the quintessential. Making them Cleopatra's secret diaries takes them to the quintessential because she is one of the most famous lovers in history – which makes her secret diaries about ultimate intimate secrets.

The Problem

Once you find the subject you want to explore, you're ready to attack the problem and its components, which are:

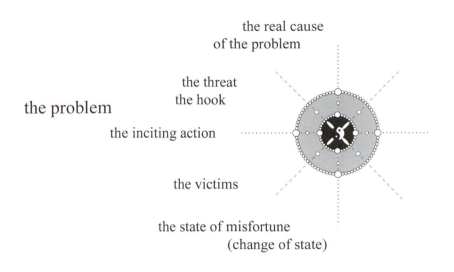

the real cause
of the problem

the threat
the hook

the problem

the inciting action

the victims

the state of misfortune
(change of state)

Note: The subject you selected may have led you directly to the focus of the story (Achilles' anger, Rick's neutrality, Scrooge's greed, a single battle, etc.), but for the purpose of this exercise we will develop the problem of the larger, *whole story* first.

The Threat and the Inciting Action

Next you probe the fascinating subject trying to find the threat you want to work with. The threat, as I've indicated elsewhere, is the agent or perpetrator that causes the problem which brings about the change of fortune. It is also the main source of the resistance that causes the classical story structure to form when someone tries to solve this problem. It is also the heart of the high concept, great idea and may be the very thing that brings the story into being. The inciting action is the action being performed by the threat.

You can find the threat and inciting action by probing the fascinating subject or other fascinations you've discovered. Regarding *Harry Potter*, somewhere in the feelings and images JK Rowling was working with, the image of Voldemort, the dark wizard popped into her head. She tried others, but guided by her feelings, she knew he was the one – and he wants to become the ruler of the Wizard World. And Harry is the only one potentially powerful enough to stand in his way. So Harry must die. In a similar way, J. R. R. Tolkien, the author of *The Lord of the Rings*, has found his ultimate source of evil in Sauron. The authors of *Gladiator* have found the young usurper in Commodus. In *A Beautiful Mind*, it's a mental illness. In *Ordinary People*, it's a mother who hates her son. In *The Pianist*, it's the Nazis who have taken over Poland. In *The Silence of the Lambs*, it's the serial killer. In *Erin Brockovich* and Enron, it's evil executives who have taken possession of their corporations. In *Jaws*, it's the shark. In a story about 9/11, you discover that it's Osama bin Laden and his Al Qaeda terrorist network. In *Casablanca*, in the larger *whole story*, it's the Nazis who have taken over Europe. In *A Christmas Carol*, it's the poverty that's plaguing London. In *The Sixth Sense*, it's the spirits of dead people, who have unfinished emotional business and are haunting the city of Philadelphia — and again, you may already know that you will focus your story on the boy's fear, but now you're working out the larger context.

If the threat you are creating feels right, then it is making a psychological connection. If it doesn't feel right, you keep looking. You keep probing the subject until you find a threat that really fascinates you — a dark force that really intrigues you and then you personify it. Also the cause doesn't have to be a man-made evil. It can be a volcano, a shark, an alien monster, a perfect storm, a tidal wave, an asteroid, or an ice age. When the threat isn't man-made, it will usually result in a polarization of the humans involved, and someone will take a position that directly or indirectly aids the non-human threat. The mayor in *Jaws* is such a character. For all intents and purposes, he is an unindicted co-conspirator. Without his interference, the shark would not have been nearly so successful. Ashe in *Alien* is a similar character. He is on Sigourney Weaver's team but has become part of the problem rather than the solution.

But whether it's Commodus, Voldemort, T-Rex, a volcano, or a shark, these are all personifications of something on the dark side — personifications of some aspect of the lower self, the negative unconscious. Commodus is a personification of that impulse to be an all-powerful tyrant. T-Rex and Jaws are personifications of naked aggression.

These impulses come from the lower self, and they're all variations on the theme of the Devil, who is the personification of the selfish and antisocial impulses that arise from our instinctual primordial selves. And when you create the threat you are creating a metaphor of these negative energies. The threat is the ever-present threat from the lower self, the dark side of our nature.

In any event, you need to feel the force of negative energy in your story — the presence of the threat that creates the problem and keeps the tension alive. And you have to make that threat interesting. In all of the above examples the presence of the threat is very clearly felt. And the problem has to be significant enough to attract our attention and hold our interest, and it has to be intriguing and relevant. Otherwise, it's not fairly representing the negative unconscious (the lower self), which is in reality a serious potential threat to consciousness, until you learn how to manage and transform its energy. And so is anyone in real life who has been taken over by these dark forces. They are a similar, serious potential threat.

Then if you want to make the threat you are creating more fascinating, you take it to the quintessential. You strive to evolve Voldemort or Sauron into the darkest, most powerful and diabolical forces of darkness that have ever existed. You strive to make Commodus the worst tyrant, Hannibal Lecter the worst serial killer, and the dead people the boy is seeing in *The Sixth Sense* the most frightening of specters. Iago in *Othello* is the most treacherous of servants.

The storm in *The Perfect Storm* is the storm of the century. A perfect storm. And there's another good title emerging from the process: *The Perfect Storm*. That title plus the image of a little boat climbing the face of a hundred foot wave is all the information a potential viewer will need to be lured into the theater, if that's their thing.

The Entity Being Transformed

When you find the threat you want to work with, you find the problem. If you find the problem first, you can figure out what the threat is by figuring out what caused the problem. And when you find the problem, you generally find the entity being transformed. You only need to ask yourself, what group is being affected by the problem? Is it a family, a neighborhood, a city, an institution, a country, the world, or an entire galaxy? And even if your story is going to be focused on a small part of that world, it is useful to know who is in control of that larger entity.

In *Saving Private Ryan*, Hitler has taken possession of Europe. He is in control of that larger entity. In *Gladiator*, Commodus has taken possession of the Roman Empire. In *Harry Potter*, Voldemort is trying to take possession of the Wizard World. In *The Lord of the Rings*, Sauron is trying to take possession of Middle Earth. And as I indicated earlier, the idea of taking possession is an extremely important pattern in great stories, and the larger, *whole story* always has this struggle present — the struggle between the higher and lower selves to control the destiny of the entity. So, if your story is on the downside and your central character is a thief, and the entity being affected by the thief's actions is a city, it might be useful to understand the disposition of the mayor of that city. If the mayor is corrupt, the police might also be corrupt, and the corrupt police might be creating a favorable environment for crime.

In any event, consider a lot of different arenas and wait until the fascination guides you to a place or group that really intrigues you, then gradually evolve it into your own world, your own Camelot, Chinatown, or Metropolis. Create a world that people will want to escape to. Fill it with precious objects, a marvelous atmosphere and people you really care about, people whose inner depths you really want to explore. Ross MacDonald created a view of Los Angeles no one had seen before. Dashell Hammett created a San Francisco that belonged to Sam Spade, Sir Arthur Conan Doyle a London that belonged to Sherlock Holmes, William Faulkner a fictional county in Mississippi, and George Lucas a galaxy ruled by the Force and the Dark Side. Creating a world that hasn't been seen before will give a critical freshness and appeal to your ideas.

The Value Being Pursued

When you find the threat, the problem and the entity, you can usually figure out what scourge is being created on the downside — be that death, disease, injustice, slavery, etc. and what value you will want the anti-threat to pursue on the upside, be that life, health, justice, or freedom. In *Armageddon*, the value being pursued is life and the scourge being avoided is death. The life of everyone on earth is threatened. In *The Silence of the Lambs*, it's justice. In *The Pianist*, it's survival. In *A Christmas Carol*, it's the wealth that can cure poverty. In *Mulan*, it's freedom.

The Hook

Next you find the hook, which is the unique aspect of the threat you are exploring. To create the hook you make the threat more alarming and dangerous, or you make it more intriguing and unique.

In *Jaws*, the great white shark is twenty-five feet long, which is much larger and more dangerous than normal. And that's the hook. A one-foot great white shark would not be very scary. Exaggerating the size of the shark makes the threat more alarming and dangerous. In *Saving Private Ryan*, a mother has lost three of her four sons in World War II and the army finally wakes up and realizes that's not right, so they want to remove her fourth son from harm's way. But where is the fourth son? In truth, he may have been safe and sound at Fort Dix in New Jersey, but in the film Spielberg put him in the middle of the worst battle of the war, the invasion of Normandy, and no one knows where he is. In *Indecent Proposal*, a young couple, desperate for money, is offered a million dollars by a friendly tycoon, Robert Redford. But there's a catch. He wants to sleep with the wife, Demi Moore. And that's the hook. The temptation is the threat, because it's a threat to their relationship. The catch is the hook. That's the thing that makes the situation so intriguing, the thing that makes us wonder what we would do in a similar situation. Everyone has their price, as they say, and this movie makes people wonder, if they were in a similar situation, what their price would be. And that makes the idea very intriguing.

So to find the hook, you identify the threat and exaggerate the difficulty, or you increase the danger or the temptation. You ask yourself: what is the most interesting, difficult, or dangerous situation that can surround the problem, the threat? Or what is the absolute worst thing that could happen? If you did a story about 9/11, what is unique about this particular terrorist threat? For one thing it involves suicide bombers, who could be armed with exotic biological weapons like anthrax and smallpox or other weapons of mass destruction. How do you defeat such an enemy? That's a very big hook.

The Victims and the State of Misfortune

Now what is the state of misfortune? Is it tyranny, poverty, slavery, injustice, disease, death, the threat of death, an alien invasion? Again, you want it to be something that really fascinates or concerns you that you want to say something about or explore. Then make the treatment of it interesting and different. Look at the problem from a different angle than we've seen before. And who are the victims? If you find the victims, you find the state of misfortune. Sometimes it's the hero.

In *Gladiator*, it's slavery and everything else that goes with a state of tyranny. Russell Crowe is the victim as well. In *Harry Potter*, it's the threatened death of Harry Potter and everyone else Voldemort needs to kill. That's an ever present danger in all of the books. In *Saving Private Ryan*, it's the threatened death of the fourth son. In *The Silence of the Lambs*, it's the young murder victims that are being mutilated and skinned alive. In *A Thousand and One Nights*, it's the nightly mistresses of the king who are being beheaded, and the hero, Shahrazad, is scheduled to be his next victim. In *The Count of Monte Cristo*, the hero is falsely accused of a crime. In *The Sixth Sense*, the young boy is the victim who is being hounded by the dead people who were, for the most part, the victims of violent crime. In *Ordinary People*, it's a suicidal son. In *A Beautiful Mind*, Russell Crowe is the victim of a mental illness.

You probe the state of misfortune to find the details surrounding their lives. You may come up with dozens of possibilities, then select the ideas that work best. And make the victims or potential victims beings we'll feel sympathy for, beings who can arouse our compassion and our outrage, reawaken our humanity, dissolve our inauthentic states, and make us long to become heroes again.

The Real Cause of the Problem

Then you locate the real cause of the problem. Commodus, Voldemort, the serial killer, the asteroid, the shark are the cause of the problem, but now you want to discover the indirect, real cause that made these calamities possible.

In Italy in 79 AD, the volcano Vesuvius erupted, obliterating two great cities, Herculeneum and Pompeii. Vesuvius is the cause of the problem, obviously. But what is the real cause? The real cause has to do with locating a city at its base. If you find the real cause of the problem, you will find meaning. If you know the real cause of the problem, you can extrapolate meaning. You need to understand the real cause of the problem to get at meaning. So what is the meaning or lesson derived from the Vesuvius example? "It's a bad idea to locate a city at the base of an active volcano."

In *Gladiator*, what is the real cause of Commodus' actions? Commodus was unloved by his father. He is crying out for love. He believes love will come to him automatically if he is emperor. So he kills his father and takes control of the empire. And the meaning? Something like: "Love your children or they will become tyrants or criminals." In *Ordinary People*, a mother secretly hates her son and he becomes suicidal. "If you hate your children they will hate themselves." And so on.

After you've identified the threat, see if you can trace or relate the cause of the problem back to the center of the entity, to the source of the desires, motivations and influences that are the real causes of problems, i.e. the lower self. If the holdfast commanding that position is not a dedicated criminal or tyrant, is there nevertheless a dangerous corruption, complacency, ignorance, or neglect somewhere in the background? We need to know what really caused the problem. We need to identify some of the negative energies that are responsible, bring them out into the open and personify them. Why, after all, were those two cities located at the base of an active volcano? Was it the brainstorm of some greedy developer? Very possibly. In the better gangster movies of the 1940s, they always traced the real cause of criminal behavior back to the society itself.

The Downside

After you understand the problem, sketch out the downside of the cycle. This reveals the details of how the larger problem came about and the negative forces (character archetypes) who helped to create it. And this reveals the archetypal structure of the entity and the identity of the lower self forces who are motivating, influencing, and guiding the holdfast/antihero.

In *Gladiator*, how did Commodus accomplish his ends? What obstacles did he have to overcome? Who are the negative archetypes that encouraged and assisted him? How much resistance did they run into? (The inciting action will also have a classical structure, if it encounters resistance.) How many people does he have to kill or bribe to secure his position? The most significant of these being his father, the Emperor, Russell Crowe and his family. What crisis precipitates the murder of his father? And what is the terrible element, that without which the coup would not have been possible? I think the answer, in this case, might be patronage. You gain the cooperation of those who will benefit from your actions. Without the assistance of Quintus, Russell Crowe's second in command, the coup would not have been possible. In *The Sixth Sense*, how did Philadelphia acquire its ghosts? In *Harry Potter*, how is Lord Voldemort going to take over the Wizard World? In *Ordinary People*, why is the young boy suicidal? In *Star Wars*, how does the Evil Empire get control of the galaxy? In a 9/11 story, what is Al Qaeda's master plan? How do they intend to achieve that plan? What do they hope to accomplish with all their terrorist bombings? In *The Lord of the Rings*, how is Sauron going to take possession of Middle Earth. What is his plan and his strategy? What is the terrible element, the thing without which his dream cannot be accomplished? The Ring of Power, obviously.

You are probing all of the powerful fascinations you've accumulated searching for these elements. And these are some of the questions you're asking yourself. You are monitoring your feelings, trying numerous possibilities, selecting the most powerful, and associating them with the archetypes on the model.

This is where you discover that *Jurassic Park* and *The Godfather* are downside stories. *Jurassic Park* begins on the upside. Richard Attenborough is showing some scientists the island paradise and theme park he is developing as a home for the dinosaurs he's created. By the end of the story, the heroes have fled and the dinosaurs have taken possession of the island. By the end of *The Godfather*, Michael Corleone (Al Pacino), who at the beginning wanted nothing to do with the family business, has been drawn into the downside, killed all of the leaders of the rival crime families and taken possession of their territories. The musical *Chicago* is about two women entertainers getting away with murder. *The Italian Job*, *The Score*, *Matchstick Men*, and *Ocean's Eleven* are also about people getting away with crimes. *Catch Me If You Can* spends 90% of the film on the downside detailing Leonardo DiCaprio's successful career as the world's best con man. In the last 10% of the film, however, there's a brief upside in which Tom Hanks recruits DiCaprio to work for the FBI. You know you're on the downside, if the antihero is being aggressive and victorious and the so-called good guys are on the defensive.

The Archetypes

The archetypes you are creating are expressions of your self. They personify different aspects of your self. Evolving the different archetypes lets you experience the different physical, mental, emotional, and spiritual levels of your self. It puts you in touch with these dimensions, and this is how you create a true self-expression. You ask yourself: how does anger, terrorism, greed, tyranny, or a serial killer come about? What psychological forces are responsible? What are the emotional, spiritual, mental, and physical impulses and influences that bring about these events? Then you monitor your feelings, work with your creative unconscious self, and personify these impulses. And that's how you evolve the other characters. They are personifications of these isolated dimensions.

As in real life, these character archetypes are realized to the extent they are helping or hindering the hero or antihero. Their actions toward the hero and antihero reveal and define their characters. This is true of all of the unconscious archetypes. Find out what role they are playing relative to the hero or the antihero and you will discover their characters. The hero walks past a doorman and the doorman doesn't react. That doorman has no character. He is a supernumerary, an extra. But the moment the doorman steps in front of the hero, puts his hand on his chest, and says: "Hey! Where do you think you're going?" Then he's a character, a threshold guardian, an obstacle the hero has to deal with and overcome.

Also, the heavies don't have to be arch villains, they can be simple antagonists. There are, in fact, three different types of human threat — antagonists, criminals, and psychopaths. Antagonists are legitimate adversaries. They have a legitimate beef. *The West Wing* is a good example. There are a lot of people opposing each other but they aren't really evil. They just have different political agendas. There are also no evil characters in *The Iliad*. They are all ethically pretty much the same. In *Shakespeare in Love* there are plenty of antagonists but only one evil character, the little boy who feeds mice to stray cats and betrays people for money. Criminals are antagonists and antiheroes that have criminal tendencies. They know the difference between right and wrong but they don't play by the rules; they break the law. Commodus is a villain. Killing your father is wrong, and he knows it. Psychopaths, on the other hand, are shadow figures. They personify something that was repressed and has turned nasty, and their behavior is compulsive. They do evil, antisocial things to gain their ends and take pleasure in it. Freddie, Jason, and Hannibal Lecter are psychopaths.

When you probe the fascination looking for these downside elements, be aggressive. Ask yourself direct questions and seek active cooperation from your creative unconscious partner. What is the entity being transformed? Who are the negative emotional or mental archetypes? Who is the temptress? Who are the victims? How is the antihero lured into the adventure? What is the terrible element? And who are the archetypal forces that will resist and try to thwart the antihero's efforts? When you pose a question to your self, you will get an answer. It may not come that instant or even that day, but it will come eventually in the form of an image, a feeling, or an idea; then locate that image or feeling on the model.

Then as the archetypes begin to emerge, act as a medium. Let the energies of these archetypes express themselves through you. Let the feelings of aggression, courage, loyalty, compassion, greed, and lust come forth and personify them. If it's a Nazi, a bigot, a beautiful temptress, a tyrant, a serial killer, a terrorist, a positive father figure, or a T-Rex, get in touch with these dimensions of your self. They're all in there somewhere. Then work with and question them. Find out what they're after and why. Keep doing this until you thoroughly understand who they are and the role they were meant to play relative to the whole. Then as each character is created from another aspect of your self, you will begin to see and feel the psychological entity being created. It's the key to creating great characters and an excellent way of getting in touch with your self.

Stephen King said that the nurse, Kathy Bates, in the movie *Misery*, was a personification of his addiction to drugs, and this is how he worked out his addiction problem — and that's exactly right.

CREATING THE UPSIDE
The Solution to the Problem

What is the solution to the problem? And now you're building the upside, which officially begins when the hero takes action — when someone tries to solve the problem. And the solution should be describable as a single action — the destruction of the shark, the defeat of Hitler, the transformation of Scrooge. In *Harry Potter*, the solution to the problem is the ultimate destruction of Voldemort, and the thwarting of Voldemort's plans in each of the seven books. In *The Lord of the Rings*, it's the destruction of Sauron vis-à-vis the destruction of the Ring of Power. In *Gladiator*, it's the destruction of Commodus. In *The Sixth Sense*, it's giving Philadelphia some relief from its ghosts. In *The Pianist*, it's surviving the war. In *A Beautiful*

Mind, Russell Crowe has to learn to live with his delusions. In *A Thousand and One Nights*, it's the transformation of the king. In *The Silence of the Lambs*, it's catching the serial killer. In a 9/11 story, it's a solution to the terrorist problem that brings about a lasting peace.

Remember you're still just creating the world. The solution is the second half of the big problem or central event of that larger *whole story*. We haven't decided yet where we will focus the story.

The Hero (the Anti-Threat).

Whose responsibility is it to solve the problem? In *Harry Potter*, it's Harry Potter. In *The Lord of the Rings*, it's Frodo and the Fellowship of the Ring. In The Matrix, it's Neo (Keanu Reeves). In *The Sixth Sense*, it's actually the little boy. With Bruce Willis' help, he will be the first person to overcome his fear of his psychic gift and address the real problem that is plaguing Philadelphia. In *A Beautiful Mind*, it's Russell Crowe, who must, in effect, facilitate his own cure. In *Ordinary People*, it's the psychiatrist, Judd Hirch, and the boy's father, Donald Sutherland. In *A Thousand and One Nights*, it's Shahrazad, the vizier's daughter, who has volunteered to be the king's next victim. In *The Silence of the Lambs*, it's Jodie Foster acting for the FBI. In *Gladiator*, it's Maximus, Russell Crowe. In *Casablanca*, in the larger, *whole story*, it's Roosevelt, Churchill, and Stalin. They're the ones responsible for taking care of Hitler. *Seabiscuit* is also an interesting case. The entity being transformed is the country. The big problem is the economic Depression, which has completely demoralized the nation. The solution to the problem is hope. The hero is the horse, Seabiscuit. He is the one who is going to give hope back to the country, because, like so many others who are down on their luck, he is a bony-kneed, unlikely underdog who has to overcome all the odds and become a super champion.

Also, the heroes don't have to be professional doctors, lawyers, or detectives, they can be ordinary citizens carrying out that ego function in an unofficial capacity — the parents in *Lorenzo's Oil* and Ellen Burstyn in *The Exorcist* take over the responsibilities of the defaulting doctors.

Why do the problem first? Do you wake up in the morning and call the fire department just in case? No. You wait until there's a fire. You wait until there's a problem. The hero comes into play when there is a need. So even if you know who the hero is going to be (he or she may be part of your original fascination), it's still best to understand the larger problem as soon as possible.

The Hero as Victim

Sometimes the hero is the victim. Sometimes that's preferable. In *Harry Potter*, Harry is the threatened victim. In every book he is Voldemort's primary target. In *Gladiator*, Russell Crowe is also a victim of the tyranny. His family has been murdered and he's put into slavery. In *A Beautiful Mind*, Russell Crowe is a victim of his own mental illness. In *The Sixth Sense*, Bruce Willis is a victim of one of his patients and the little boy is being haunted by the dead people. In *The Pianist*, Adrien Brody is a fugitive from the Nazis and definitely a victim. In *Ordinary People*, the son is the victim of his own mother's hatred. In *Kill Bill*, Uma Thurman is the ultimate victim. Her husband was gunned down at their wedding and she was critically wounded. She lies in a coma for years, during which time she is repeatedly raped by despicable creeps who are paying an orderly for the privilege. But when she finally wakes up — look out!

In any event, the hero has to be someone we are concerned about — someone we care how things will work out for them. Making them also the victim, the sufferer, helps accomplish that. It intensifies our involvement with them.

The Hero's Profession

Now, what is the hero's profession? The specialties of the different professions are all functions of the ego, and each of these special functions can be personified as a different hero. Harry Potter is a young wizard. Russell Crowe in *Gladiator* is a former Roman general and a gladiator. Bruce Willis in *The Sixth Sense* is a child psychologist and the boy is a young psychic. Tom Hanks in *Saving Private Ryan* is an army captain. Gregory Peck in *To Kill A Mockingbird* is a lawyer.

Spencer Tracy in *Judgment at Nuremberg* is a judge. Sherlock Holmes is a detective. Tom Cruise in *Top Gun* is a fighter pilot. Shakespeare in *Shakespeare in Love* is a playwright.

Get in touch with the ego function your hero will represent — with that part of your conscious self that has that responsibility and work with it creatively. Identify the virtues of that function, artistically treat them, and monitor your feelings. It will teach you what that type of hero (or ego function) really does and give you a little of the special training your hero will need to accomplish his goal. Your hero will then become a psychological role model. That will make an important psychological connection with the audience and add significantly to the power of your work. The truer a hero is to the ego-archetype he or she represents, the greater the impact that hero will have on the audience.

Then if you want to make that character more fascinating, take it to the quintessential. Strive to create a definitive portrait of that professional function, i.e. make the hero, not just an okay spy but a great spy, a great warrior, a great doctor. You make Harry Potter not just an ordinary wizard but the most famous and powerful young wizard of all time, which the author did. You make Russell Crowe not just an ordinary gladiator but the greatest gladiator that ever lived. You make Shakespeare the greatest playwright of all time, which he is. You make Bruce Willis in *The Sixth Sense* a great child psychologist, which he almost is. In *Armageddon*, he's the world's best oil driller. You make Cary Grant in *To Catch a Thief* the world's best cat burglar. You make Leonardo DiCaprio in *Catch Me If You Can* the world's best forger and conman. You make Richard Gere in *Chicago* the greatest shyster, and you make Keanu Reeves in *The Matrix* the most extraordinary "you are the one!"

Great stories, myths, and legends are dominated by quintessential elements. King Arthur is the most chivalrous king. Samson is the strongest man. King Herod is the nastiest tyrant. King Solomon is the wisest king. Don Juan is the greatest lover. Jack the Ripper is the most infamous serial killer. Genghis Khan is the quintessence of barbaric conquest. In *The Iliad*, Zeus is the most powerful god, Helen of Troy is the most beautiful woman, Achilles is the greatest warrior, and Ares is the most treacherous god.

In real life we are obsessed with quintessentials. We want to know who and what are the best and worst in everything. Our evolution was also all about quintessentials. Survival of the fittest is all about being the biggest, the strongest, the swiftest, the most beautiful, the most cunning, the most deadly. And so it is in story. It is a big part of the hidden truth, and this is what truly interests and fascinates people. It's what audiences really want to see.

The Dominant Trait

Then, what is the hero's dominant trait? The dominant trait is the dominant character trait which the character personifies. Every truly great character has a dominant trait.

Sherlock Holmes' profession, as I mentioned, is a detective, his dominant quality or trait is deductive reasoning. Othello's dominant trait is jealousy. King Midas is greed. Don Juan is lust. Macbeth's dominant trait is guilt. Sir Galahad's is chivalry, and so on. They are quintessential personifications of these qualities, and that is the secret of their success. And that is the key to making your characters truly memorable and even merchandisable. You take them to the quintessential.

If you want to create such a character, identify their dominant trait, personify it, conjure it, and evolve it into the quintessence of that quality. Archie Bunker is one of the most memorable characters that ever appeared on TV. Why? He's the quintessential bigot. You take a quality like prejudice, arrogance, conceit, courage, sincerity, generosity, loyalty, jealousy, lust, greed, and so on — learn as much as you can about that quality, personify it, conjure it, and evolve that character into the quintessence of that quality.

The dominant trait should, of course, be in the context of a full human being and largely camouflaged. If you just play the dominant trait and leave out the rest of the human being, you will create a stereotype or a cliché. The more human and colorful the characters are the better.

Siskel and Ebert praised a James Bond villain called Largo (played by Klaus Maria von Brandaur) because he was not just a one-dimensional megalomaniac who wants to rule the world. Real people are full of contradictions, inner conflicts, hopes, dreams, foibles, despairs, combinations of good and bad strengths and weaknesses. In a well-drawn character, we should see all of these qualities, as you do in Satan in Milton's *Paradise Lost*. He is still Satan, the personification of Evil, but he is a very complex, tormented and interesting character, questioning just about everything he has ever done. Audiences love well-rounded, fully realized characters, especially villains. So the dominant trait is a dominant quality, not the only quality.

This is a fact in real life as well. When we are angry, that is our dominant quality for the moment; then we get over our anger and shift to sincerity or compassion then that becomes our dominant. But story likes to isolate these different qualities (threads) and examine them separately, in great detail.

The dominant traits of the characters are revealed by the choices the character makes. Whether the characters are honest or dishonest, loyal or disloyal, generous or greedy, selfish or altruistic is determined by the choices they make. One character refuses a bribe, the other accepts it. Those choices define their characters. Character is built up bit by bit by these choices. Robert McKee says that deep character is revealed by choices made under pressure. By my reckoning, the deep character that will be revealed under pressure on the upside of the passage by the hero and the other positive archetypes will be good and the deep character revealed under pressure on the downside by the antihero and the other negative archetypes will be bad.

Style

Another important dimension that complements the dominant trait of a great character is style. When the dominant traits of two characters are otherwise alike, style sets them apart and further defines their characters. The difference between Sherlock Holmes, Charlie Chan, and Hercule Poirot, all of whom have the same dominant trait (deductive reasoning), is largely a matter of style. Holmes' approach is methodical, Chan is intuitive, Poirot is fastidious. These are interesting and worthwhile distinctions, and we see this reflected in the way they dress, the way they walk, the way they comb their hair. Giving your characters style means understanding them, and yourself, on yet another level.

Creating Charismatic Characters

So how would you go about creating one of these charismatic characters? How would you create a charismatic figure like Napoleon? You work with your emerging character until you become aware of his dominant trait — the trait which expresses itself more forcefully and persistently than his other qualities.

In Napoleon's case, you could choose between inflation, a world vision, or military genius. If you choose inflation, you work with that dimension until you have evolved that character into the quintessence of that quality. It will govern all of your choices, including your selection of the scenes. He had the Pope travel all the way to Paris to preside over his coronation at the cathedral of Notre Dame. Then, as the Pope was about to put the crown on his head, Napoleon took the crown out of his hands, and did something no one else had ever done, he crowned himself. He will still be a military genius, but that won't be the main thing you're focusing on. Then you fill out the rest of his life and give him a certain style — mannerisms and attitudes that express the dominant quality. And you'll create an immortal character.

How would you create a character like Stalin? You take a dominant quality like paranoia and do the same thing. You work with that dimension until you evolve that character into the personification of that trait. He killed twenty million of his own countrymen protecting his position.

How would you create a character like Lucrezia Borgia? You would take a dominant quality like ruthlessness and evolve that character into a personification of that trait.

How would you create an immortal character like Dracula? You take a dominant quality like blood lust and make that character the quintessence of that characteristic. Then you put that in the context of a full human being, as they did with Frank Langella's *Dracula*.

What dominant qualities would you combine and evolve to create a Fred Astaire? Dance and charm. He was the greatest dancer of his time and certainly the most charming of film personalities. He is the quintessence of those qualities.

And how about T-Rex? How would you create an adversary like that? What is his dominant trait? Aggression. You take a quality like aggression and evolve that beast into the biggest, most aggressive carnivore that has ever lived. You make him the very essence of aggression — the ultimate example of aggression. You would do the same with a shark named Jaws. Identical dominant traits, somewhat different styles.

Can a story be about an ordinary person? Of course. But make him or her the most ordinary person that has ever lived, and you will make that character fascinating. What about a dull person? Yes. But make him the dullest person ever. Make him the quintessence of dullness, the best example of dullness. And if you get someone like Bill Murray to play the part, it will be very funny. It will be fascinating. People will flock to see it. In fact, Peter Sellers' character in *Being There* appears to have been just that. He is so dull he is fascinating.

The Inauthentic State

Are the heroes ready or are they in an inauthentic state? The authentic or inauthentic state is the state the hero is in at the beginning of the story. Is he or she ready for the adventure or does some personal problem have to be worked out first? Our authentic state is who we were really meant to be. Our inauthentic state is anything less than that.

Harry Potter, despite his youth, seems psychologically completely prepared. So are Indiana Jones and Superman. They are in an authentic state. Bruce Willis in *Armageddon* is almost prepared, although he's somewhat of a mercenary. Jodie Foster in *The Silence of the Lambs* is also just about ready. She just has to work out that problem with the bleating lambs. In *Titanic*, Leonardo DiCaprio has fallen into the problem and has no choice. But he acts instinctively and is equal to the task.

Simba in *The Lion King*, on the other hand, is totally unprepared, and a good part of the story is about resolving that inauthentic state. Shakespeare in *Shakespeare in Love* has lost his muse. Al Pacino in *Scent of a Woman* is blind. In *Toy Story*, Buzz Lightyear is in a curious state of enchantment. He believes he really is a space warrior and is denying that he's just a toy. Bill Murray in *Groundhog Day* is trapped in the worst day of his life. In *Gladiator*, slavery also acts as Crowe's inauthentic state because it keeps him out of the fight. He has to overcome his slavery, so to speak, before he can have his revenge or fulfill Marcus Aurelius' wish. In *The Sixth Sense*, the boy is paralyzed by fear, and Bruce Willis is dead. He was killed by a former patient who didn't like the results of his treatment, so he has a lot of unfinished emotional business, and while he's passing from here to there in the nether world, he stops to help a boy in trouble, hoping to resolve his own guilt. When the characters are in an inauthentic state, that has to be resolved before they can solve the problem. Psychologically, there's always something to be worked out.

Return to the High Concept

Then, if you like, you can add this dimension to the high concept you're creating by contrasting the inauthentic hero with the problem he or she has to solve.

In *Jaws*, a sheriff who is afraid of the water has to hunt down a giant great white shark in a boat that's too small. In *Armageddon*, to save the planet a mercenary oil driller has to bury a nuclear device on an asteroid hurtling toward the Earth at 22,000 mph. In *A Christmas Carol*, to save Tiny Tim three ghosts have to transform an old miser on Christmas eve. In *The Sixth Sense*, to get out of limbo, a murdered child psychologist has to cure a little boy who has the same problem as the patient who murdered him.

The Marvelous Element

Now, what is the marvelous element, the thing without which the problem can't be solved or the state of misfortune reversed? In *Harry Potter*, it's an encyclopedia of marvelous elements. Harry has the lightning scar which warns him when Voldemort is near, the cloak of invisibility, the fabulous broomstick, and dozens of others, and he's obviously accumulating all of these incredible powers for the big battle with Voldemort in the future. In *The Sixth Sense*, it's the tape of the previous boy's session, where Willis overhears his former patient also talking to dead people. This gives him the understanding he needs to solve the new boy's problem. In *Armageddon*, it's a nuclear device in an eight-hundred-foot shaft drilled into the surface of the asteroid hurtling toward the earth. In *A Thousand And One Nights*, it's a string of hundreds of great stories, each one of which is playing a role in King Shahryar's transformation. In *The Silence of the Lambs*, it's a profile of the serial killer that can help locate and identify him. In *Ordinary People*, it's the secret behind the young boy's suicidal tendencies. In *Titanic*, it's the lifeboats, which, unfortunately, can't hold everybody. In *Gladiator*, it's something rather unusual and, therefore, worth mentioning. What is the thing that acts as Russell Crowe's magic shield and protects him from the Emperor? The love of the crowd. It empowers and protects him and makes it possible for him to get near the Emperor and survive. Without that he would be an easy prey. So the marvelous element doesn't have to be an object like a magic sword. It can be anything. It can be an idea.

In a story about 9/11, what would the marvelous element be — the thing without which the problem can't be solved? Will it be a secret weapon that roots out all terrorists? A solution to the Palestinian problem? A cure for the poverty and injustice that breeds martyrs? Keep working until you find something that really satisfies you.

There are tremendous advantages to having such an element in your story, to have everything hinge on the hero achieving, discovering or retrieving some critical element or extraordinary power which is extremely difficult or dangerous to accomplish or obtain. Like the principal action itself, it can help focus your objectives, unify the action, justify all of the resistance, make clear what everyone is doing, and bring about the transformation. This is definitely a dimension that is worth mastering.

If the power you need is a supernatural good or evil quality, you can create the marvelous or terrible element by associating it with an object. The Holy Grail has power because it is associated with Christ consciousness, the Hope Diamond because it is associated with an evil curse. Evidence, because it is associated with the power to convict a criminal. A dagger that belonged to Genghis Khan, sneakers that belonged to Michael Jordan, glasses that belonged to Hitler, a lucky penny that belonged to John D. Rockefeller would take on the good or bad qualities we associate with those people.

The Upside

Now sketch out the upside of the passage. How does the Hero Get Involved in the Adventure? How is the Hero Initiated? How is the Hero Humbled? How is the Hero Rewarded?

In *The Lord of the Rings*, how does Frodo finally manage to destroy the Ring of Power and defeat Sauron? How does Harry Potter ultimately defeat Voldemort? In *Gladiator*, how does Russell Crowe destroy Commodus and restore the republic? In *A Beautiful Mind*, how does Russell Crowe come to terms with his mental illness? In *Ordinary People*, how is the young boy restored to sound mental health? In *The Sixth Sense*, how does Philadelphia finally resolve its ghost problem? How do the allies ultimately defeat Hitler in the larger whole story that surrounds Rick's story in *Casablanca*? What complications and obstacles do they have to overcome? Who are the positive archetypes that encourage and assist those who are solving the problem? How much resistance do they run into? It doesn't have to be in great detail. It can just be the essential steps. We're still in the first creative stage; we're creating the world. We haven't talked about the story focus yet.

Nor does the hero of the larger story have to experience every stage. Not everyone will be affected by anger and inflation, and so forth. But you need to know how the hero got involved and what the incentives were. And you need to know how the hero was initiated, who the people were that helped and guided him or her, how the problem was solved, what happens after the climax of the initiation and how everything is resolved.

Probe the fascination of the essential steps you already have and that will help you find the steps in between. But don't try to build major structures too early in the process. Structure has power and, once it's in place, you might not want to take it apart, any more than you would want to reframe your house. So don't let the structure jell. Gather as much raw data as you can and work with it, but be flexible and open to change. Keep everything in a fluid state. Let nothing be tied down. Everything is a reference point that can lead to other, better ideas. When it stops evolving, it stops growing. And set the rivalry up like a game and make it fun. Remember the power that is in that rivalry, that game. The best way to teach is to make the learning fun and there is no better example of this in the universe than story.

The Archetypes of the Creative Unconscious

Now probe the fascination and develop the other major players you've discovered. Find out what role the archetypes are playing relative to the hero and you will discover their characters. And don't forget to be aggressive. Ask yourself direct questions: How is the hero lured into the adventure? Who are the love interests and the archetypal forces that will assist the hero and help him or her solve the problem? Who are the archetypal forces that will resist and try to thwart the hero's efforts? And what is the marvelous element? Then mobilize the forces of assistance and resistance. The positive forces motivate, teach, guide, help, test. The negative forces tempt, threaten, oppose, obstruct, thwart, challenge, delay, stop, and their resistance creates the complications, crises, climaxes, and resolutions of the classical structure. On the downside, it is the reverse — the negative forces motivate and guide the antihero and the positive forces resist and create the complications.

Get in touch with these dimensions in your self and slowly sort out which archetypes they are. Are they male or female? Predominantly emotional? mental? physical? spiritual? mentor? anima? animus? threshold guardian? trickster? Is their influence positive or negative? Are they encouraging the central character to do something selfish or unselfish?

Conflict

Not just the main opposing forces but all of the elements both positive and negative should be in conflict. Everyone has their own agenda. They all have needs. Just like the organs of the body which are working together but have their individual chemical and nutritional needs. They all have the same objective but different points of view concerning what the priorities are and how each goal can be achieved.

Those who help may resist getting involved and need to be convinced. Oliver Reed in *Gladiator* is a very reluctant helper, as is the senator played by Derek Jacobi. The hero and the love interest may have different opinions concerning how to solve the problem. They have to learn how to work together. All of the negative forces also have their separate agendas which bring them into conflict. All of this reflects the inner conflicts that are always with us.

In any case, it is always more dramatic when people are at odds than in ready agreement. But it has to be meaningful conflict, not just conflict for the sake of conflict. It has to ring true psychologically. In Hollywood, it is well known that conflict is important, but frequently it is just gratuitous, two people bickering endlessly about everything and anything. The two brothers in a movie called *Backdraft* had this problem. They were constantly at each other's throats, but it was forced and it wasn't advancing the story. So let it be a real conflict of interest stemming from deeply held convictions or important needs. Get in touch with the reasons for conflict and the conflicts within yourself and personify them.

Sometimes characters who start off opposing the hero are transformed along the way. That's good because it expresses the psychological truth that all negatives are transformable into positives. There's also a possible virtue if the good guys and the bad guys know each other. It reflects a personal relationship which is psychologically true. Psychologically, we have an important relationship with the negative forces inside us. They are all related. These forces may appear like strangers at first but later we find out there's a connection. In Charles Dickens' novels, the villain is frequently an evil relative who is trying to cheat the hero out of his fortune or do him harm. *Hamlet* and *The Lion King* are other important examples of that. Also, if it's necessary to utterly destroy the arch villain because he's just too evil, it might be valuable to have dupes or henchmen who can be rehabilitated. That will ring true psychologically, because the negative forces that are hidden beneath the shadow can be transformed into something positive (Valerie Perrine in *Superman*, Ben Jonson in *Shane*).

If you have difficulty working out any of these dimensions, go back to the original fascination, which is now in the context of an entity, and work with that. As always, try a lot of different ideas and listen to your feelings. Your feelings are helping you make all the necessary decisions. Your feelings are guiding you to the truth. Everything you do creatively — every change, every new element, every new idea, every new selection or configuration has a feeling connotation. It will either feel good or bad and you will make your decisions accordingly.

Camouflage

All of the symbolic elements, of course, have to be hidden. There are big points off, if the audience realizes it is watching something symbolic. It becomes an allegory, which is the lowest form of story metaphor and an intellectual rather than an emotional experience. In the film *The Natural*, Darren McGavin has a big glass eye, the evil woman wears black, the good woman wears white and you're saying to yourself "Gee, all of this must mean something." It's very distracting. On the other hand, when you're watching *Dracula* or *Jaws*, you're never deflected by the thought that it means something. You're experiencing the metaphor through your feelings, not your intellect. You encounter the images, respond emotionally, and absorb their meaning unconsciously. You don't have to think about it and it has a profound and lasting affect.

Sometimes authors don't even know that they are creating a metaphor. Herman Melville denied until he died that *Moby Dick* had any symbolic meaning. It was just a story, he insisted. But that's too bad. The equation created by the great white whale, Ahab, the ship and the ocean have a psychological significance whether he likes it or not.

If you work correctly, this could easily happen. In other words, you don't really have to understand what your story metaphor means, only how it feels. If it feels right, it means something, even if you don't understand what that something is. So let it be an adventure of discovery and take comfort in the fact that you are not working alone. The source of those positive and negative intuitive feelings is a serious partner. Be patient and have faith in the process. You're in the business of discovering and revealing the truth.

CHAPTER 28

CREATING THE
STORY FOCUS

The Story Focus

After you've created the world (the *whole story*) and sketched out the big problem, begin thinking about the focus of your story.

You may, of course, already know what the focus of your story will be. It may be the big problem of the *whole story* which you just sketched out or, if it's a smaller focus, it may have been part of your original fascination, the first piece of the picture puzzle you picked up, but still it's important to work out the *whole story* before you make a final decision. You may discover something a lot more interesting than your first choice.

In any case, you can explore any place on the wheel you like, in as much depth as you like, as long as it involves some major or minor problem solving action that is essential to the progress of the whole passage. Explore a number of different possibilities, then select the one you ultimately find the most intriguing and compelling. You can do a full sweep of the big problem of the *whole story* on the upside, from the hero getting involved to the climax of the initiation (I & II), or you can focus on some small piece of that action — the transformation of the hero (I), a single battle (II), some aspect of the aftermath (III), or the return (IV). Or you can focus on the downside and create another *Godfather* or *Macbeth* (V – VIII).

The narrower the focus, the more depth and subtlety. The broader the stroke, the more action, the less depth. And whatever focus you choose, you will then tell the rest of the *whole story* through that vantage point. If you choose a time when everything is coming to a head, the power of the entire circle can be realized through that one focal point. The whole wheel can come rushing through that one point in a powerful and entertaining way — as it does in *The Iliad*, *Casablanca*, and *Death of a Salesman*.

In *Harry Potter and the Sorcerer's Stone*, we have the big story of Voldemort trying to take over the whole wizard world, but we're seeing that story through what focus in part one? Harry's education — his preparation and training as a wizard. The focus of the first book, which is in the context of that larger, whole story, is Harry's efforts to prevent Voldemort from gaining the power of the Sorcerer's Stone. In *Gladiator*, we have the *whole story* of Commodus' usurpation of the Roman Empire, and that big problem is the problem being addressed in the story. But the real focus of the story is Russell Crowe's slavery as a gladiator, which, in effect, takes him out of the fight and acts as a kind of inauthentic state that he has to overcome in order to complete the task. In *The Lord of the Rings*, we are also dealing with the main problem, Sauron's desire to gain control of Middle Earth, and we're focused on Frodo's efforts to destroy the Ring of Power, which will have a direct effect on that big problem. But then that effort is divided into three separate parts. In *Ordinary People*, we are again focused on the main problem, but it is a much smaller entity. In *Saving Private Ryan*, we are not focused on the main problem. We have WW II as the *whole story* context in the background, but the single action we're focusing on is the army's efforts to rescue a family's only surviving son from the middle of the war's worst battle. In *Casablanca*, we have WWII again, but the focus of the story is the transformation of one patriot named Rick who has dropped out of the fight. In *The Pianist*, the story focuses on Adrien Brody, an isolated Jew who is determined to survive that same war. In *The Sixth Sense*, we have the larger story of Philadelphia being disturbed by legions of dead people who have been tragically killed. These miserable souls are stuck in limbo and have unfinished emotional business. The story is focused on a young boy who can see these dead people but is terrified of them, and it tells us all about how his fear came about and how that fear was resolved. In truth, the boy is a nascent ego, a nascent hero who could potentially save Philadelphia from its ghost calamity, if he could overcome his fear. But he hasn't joined the fight because he's afraid of his psychic gift. Later, when he overcomes his fear and has his psychic powers in tact, he uses that boon to seek justice for the sake of one of the haunting spirits, a murdered little girl. In *Star Wars*, you have the larger story of the Evil Empire taking control of the galaxy and then ultimately losing that control. This larger story is told in the context of six different parts, or six separate focuses. The three parts on the downside tell us how Anakin Skywalker was drawn into the dark-side, transformed into Darth Vader, and the role he plays as the Evil Emperor's principal ally. The three parts on the upside tell us how Luke Skywalker is drawn into the fight and how the Evil Empire is ultimately defeated.

In a story about 9/11 we could focus on the big problem — Osama bin Laden and his Al Qaeda terrorist network and our big effort to defeat them, or we could tell that story from the POV of a hundred other possible focuses which are held together by this one extremely large event. The pursuit and capture of one suspected terrorist, for instance. Or you could tell the story of the plane that was forced down in Pennsylvania by heroic passengers. Or you could tell the anthrax story. Or do a full two-hour movie about the efforts to save people trapped in the World Trade Center. Or you could narrow that focus and tell the story of just one person's efforts to escape from some high floor. Or you could focus on the war in Afghanistan or Iraq.

There Can Be More Than One Focus

In Tolstoy's *War and Peace*, you have the big story of Napoleon's invasion of Russia and his ultimate defeat, but that story is told from the point of view of at least four different main characters — Pierre, Natasha, Nicolas Rostov, and Prince Andrew. Each one is a separate focus, which contains its own line of action and character progression. The same is true of the movie, *Traffic*, which also has four separate focuses. In the larger *whole story*, there is the big war on drugs. The person who has the responsibility to solve that problem is Michael Douglas, the newly appointed drug czar. Another focus is the plight of Douglas' daughter, who is a drug addict. Douglas, as her father, ultimately has that responsibility also. The third focus tells us the story of Benecio Del Toro, a narcotics cop in Tijuana who is going up against a local drug lord and a corrupt general who is backed up by a small army. The fourth focus is on Catherine Zeta-Jones, who is being drawn into the downside. Her husband, a big drug dealer, has been arrested and this story is focused on her transformation from an innocent housewife, who can't bear to lose her current life style, into an accomplice in the murder of the key witness against her husband.

Narrative Structure — Point of View

In real life, we can examine a problem not just from our own but from just about any other point of view. The mind can alter its point of view in a given situation and become objective. This is reflected in storymaking by the fact that having set up the whole cycle and the focus, you can tell the story from the point of view of any character, which is to say, any archetype. In Dostoyevski's *Crime and Punishment*, there is a murder and a police investigation (a downside inciting action and an upside principal action). Most stories of this type are told from the point of view of the police investigator. Dostoyevski tells his story from the point of view of the murderer. The police inspector makes only occasional appearances but he's out there somewhere trying to solve the problem. *Cinderella*, as I mentioned earlier, is told from the point of view of the victim and *A Christmas Carol* from the point of view of the threat. *Catch Me If You Can* is another very similar story, which is told from the point of view of Leonardo Di Caprio, a quintessential conman, who is the threat creating the problem. Tom Hanks is the anti-threat, the FBI agent (hero) who is trying to solve the problem. *Dead Poets Society* is told from the point of view of Robin Williams, the mentor of the future heroes. *The Sixth Sense* is also being told from the point of view of the helper, Bruce Willis, *Indiana Jones* from the point of view of the hero, *Macbeth* from the point of view of the antihero. The real hero of *Macbeth* is Macduff. He is the one who ultimately confronts and defeats Macbeth at the end, but he only has a small part. In the first part of *I, Claudius*, the story is told from the point of view of another antihero, Livia, who will stop at nothing, including many murders, to make her son, Tiberius, Emperor. All of these stories have the same basic structure and as long as you can see the *whole story* in the background, you can focus on anyone's point of view that you choose.

The Structures of the Story Focus

Whichever focus you select, it will have these four structures: the inciting action, which will show us how the problem of the focus came about; the principal action, which will show us how the problem of the focus is resolved; the exposition, which will reveal all of the necessary past and present information we need concerning the *whole story*; and the afterthought, which will tell us how the actions of the story will effect the *whole story* after the story ends.

To create these structures, you probe all of the fascinations you've accumulated that are relevant to the focus, select the most powerful results, then determine which actions, characters, and scenes belong to the inciting and principal actions and which actions, characters, and events will be revealed in the exposition and afterthought. If you're focusing on the big problem much of this will already be worked out, but if you're focusing on one of the smaller problems, then the same criteria will apply that applied when you were constructing the larger problem of the *whole story*.

In *The Sixth Sense*, the little boy's problem has already been established when the movie begins. The inciting action — how the little boy acquired his ability to see dead people and was haunted by it — is only revealed through the exposition. The principal action cures the little boy of his fear and liberates Bruce Willis from limbo. In the afterthought, we know that the little boy will no longer be troubled by his fear and, because of his extraordinary gift, may well play a major role in helping Philadelphia resolve its formidable ghost problem. We also know that Bruce Willis will find peace with himself.

In a story about 9/11, if you chose the Pennsylvania plane incident as your focus, then the inciting action will establish all of the actions necessary to bring about this particular hijacking. It will also reveal the intent of the hijackers, which was to crash the plane into the white house, the Capitol, or some other World Trade Center–like target. The principal action would be everything the passengers had to do, including sacrificing themselves, to prevent that action from taking place. The exposition would be everything outside of this action we need to know about 9/11 and the backgrounds of the characters. The afterthought would be any effects this event might have on the future, namely, it might inspire others to act heroically in a similar situation.

Creating the Principal Action

The principal action, as we've discussed, has four structures: the solution formula, the genre structures, the universal structure, and the classical structure. In a downside story focus, these same structures will be encountered by the antihero when he tries to execute his diabolical plans.

Creating the Solution Formula

Having isolated the principal action, you now divide it up into all of the large and small actions the hero will have to take, and all of the obstacles the hero will have to overcome, in order to carry out his or her mandate, which is to identify, locate, evaluate, confront and either destroy, neutralize, or transform the cause of the problem. This is, in effect, the hero's theory or plan which will constantly be revised. It is also your scenario — the sketching out of your scenes and the working out of your plot, and you play with a lot of different ideas until you find the best possible solution.

In *Gladiator*, it's the details of how Russell Crowe will ultimately overcome his slavery and bring about the destruction of Commodus. In *Jaws*, it's how the sheriff, Roy Scheider, is going to gain the cooperation of the two experts and destroy the shark. In *A Beautiful Mind*, it's how Russell Crowe will ultimately learn to cope with his mental illness.

In *The Sixth Sense*, it's how Bruce Willis will help the boy overcome his fear. In *Harry Potter*, it's how Harry is going to ultimately destroy Voldemort in the *whole story* or, in the first book, how Harry is going to avoid death and prevent Voldemort from obtaining the Sorcerer's Stone. In *Saving Private Ryan*, it's how Tom Hanks will locate and rescue Matt Damon, the fourth son. In a story about 9/11, it's the details of how the passengers will overcome all obstacles to regain control of the plane.

Creating the Genre Structure

Next you work out the genre structures, and remember that each of the separate actions of the solution formula has either an emotional (E), physical (P), mental (M) or spiritual (S) character, and when you sort these out, they become the plots and subplots or your story. The dominant action or plot will give the story its genre.

To find the details of these actions, probe the relevant fascinations of these actions to determine which actions belong to which subplots (this will also clue you in to the types of feelings those scenes will arouse). Then if you make the plots and subplots interdependent, you will create a metaphor of the human mind in action and add that power to your story.

In *The Sixth Sense* Bruce Willis is in limbo, and he has unfinished earthly business. He has to spiritually transcend to find peace (S). In order to do that he has to come to terms with his own physical death (P); in order to do that he has to understand why he was shot (M); to do that he has to help a little boy overcome his fear of dead people (E); to do that he has to solve the mystery of the little boy's problem (M); and to do that he needs to develop an emotional relationship with the boy and gain his trust (E). The mystery is the dominant plot.

In *Gladiator*, in order to be reunited with his dead wife and son, Russell Crowe has to transcend to Elysium (S); to do that he has to restore the Republic (which is also spiritual, a republic being a little closer to Paradise than a tyranny); to do that he has to destroy Commodus (P); and that's the dominant physical plot, which will end in victory or defeat. In order to do that, he has to get the cooperation of Oliver Reed, Derek Jacobi, Commodus' sister, and his fellow gladiators (E); to do that he has to have a credible plan (M); to do that he has to win the love of the crowd (E); and to do that he has to become the greatest gladiator (P).

In *Armageddon*, the dominant plot is a war story, a physical battle with an asteroid that will end in either victory or defeat. But in order to succeed in that difficult mission NASA has to have the cooperation of the designated heroes (E), and in order to get their cooperation, they have to come up with some very convincing ideas (M). The other emotional subplots all have to do with the emotional conflicts Harry has with his daughter, Grace, her boyfriend, A.J., the other members of his crew, and the NASA personnel, all of which also have to be worked out if the mission is to succeed. The other mental subplots have to do with the mathematical and astrophysical puzzles that have to be mastered in order to reach the asteroid and survive. The spiritual subplot has to do with the immortalization of Harry. When he sacrifices himself for his daughter and saves the world, he is instantly deified. The crisis of the dominant, physical plot occurs when the nuclear device won't detonate automatically and someone has to stay behind. The climax of the main emotional subplot happens when Harry saves A.J. from death by taking his place.

In the 9/11 story, to regain control of the plane and save the lives of hundreds or even thousands of people (S), the heroic passengers have to physically go to war with and overpower the terrorist hijackers (P). This physical action was probably the dominant plot of the true story and it ended in victory. But in order to do that, the passenger who initiated the action had to have the cooperation of other passengers (E). In order to do that, he had to have critical information (M), which he might have gotten on his cell phone. If he could tell them what already happened at the World Trade Center and what was likely to happen to them, that would no doubt have inspired many to action.

And these are the plots and subplots which are showing us how real life and the mind work when we try to solve problems.

Conflict

To make the story really interesting, you might want to give a lot of thought to the emotional subplots, which is to say you might want to consider making the story depend on the working out of relationships. This is something that audiences really love. In other words, you sketch out the main plot, then concentrate on the relationships that have to be worked out in order to succeed. For instance, you begin with everyone having their own agenda, then to succeed, they have to learn to work together as a team. *The Lord of the Rings, Jaws, Armageddon,* and *Shakespeare in Love* are all really excellent examples of this. The television series *ER* and *West Wing* are other good examples. In *ER,* they start off with a patient in serious trouble. The different doctors have different ideas concerning how the problem should be treated. This leads to competition and personality conflicts among the staff, which have to be worked out before the main problem, the trauma or disease, can be successfully treated.

Creating the Universal Structure

Each of these large and small action threads, from the principal action on down, will be driven by the universal structure, which is the trial and error formula T + E + R + P = DR (page 164). Some actions present no problems. You need Joe's phone number. You call Katie and she gives it to you. But most problem solving actions require a lot of this T + E activity. In *Harry Potter,* Voldemort is trying everything he can think of to kill Harry. In *Gladiator,* Commodus is doing everything he can to gain the love of the people. In *The Sixth Sense,* Willis has to try many different approaches before he hits on the right one. In the 9/11 story, the heroes will have to make several attempts and persevere through many serious setbacks before succeeding.

Creating the Classical Structure

The hero sets out to solve all of these problems by trail and error and his or her forward motion triggers resistance and that creates the classical structure, which is the structure that brings the negative energy to the surface. The closer you get to the cause of the problem, the stronger the resistance.

To discover this structure, you probe the relevant fascinations until you discover which actions are creating the complications, reversals, crises, discoveries, climaxes, and resolutions in each of these plots.

Creating the Complications

The complications are generally created by things that were unforeseen or unanticipated. We take an action and discover things are more complicated than they seemed — and no one ever reacts exactly the way we expect them to. In *The Sixth Sense*, every reaction of the boy is something Bruce Willis didn't anticipate. In *The Lord of the Rings*, Frodo and his Fellowship of the Ring encounter nothing but complications. For one thing, Frodo is stabbed early on by a Wraith whose sword is infected with a fatal illness. Later, the Fellowship discovers the snow and ice-covered mountain range they hoped to cross is impassable and they have to take the even more dangerous passage through the underground world of Moria. In the 9/11 story, the heroic passengers finally take action. The hijackers are better armed than they thought, several passengers are killed in their initial effort, and they have to retreat.

Creating the Reversal and the Crisis

The reversal usually comes about because we underestimate the hidden ferocity of the adversary that's being provoked and we're overwhelmed. We achieve the opposite of what we intended, and we're swept into a crisis, which can be described as a sudden, serious threat to the hero. In real life, when you confront the real cause of the problem, you will get an unexpectedly harsh response.

To discover the main crisis, try a lot of different things until you find something that really works and make it as big as you can. This is the psychological middle of your story and it should be very stressful.

In *Jaws*, the shark smashes their boat and they experience a reversal and a crisis. They came out there to kill the shark, and now the shark is killing them. In *The Perfect Storm*, George Clooney completely underestimates the force of the storm, and he has made a fatal mistake. In *Hercules*, it's a hydra with seven heads that suddenly pops up. In *Harry*

Potter, every time Voldemort or his allies reveal their true selves, Harry is thrown into chaos.

The main crisis is also the true middle or center of the story (not literally, of course, but figuratively). If you track the action, by cause and effect, forward from the beginning, it will take you to the crisis and no further. If you track the action, by cause and effect, backwards from the end, it will also take you to the crisis and no further. That is because the crisis which is caught in the middle contains a major change of direction (turning point). The crisis is, in fact, the only vantage point from which you can comfortably survey the entire story focus. If you imagine yourself at the crisis, you can see in both directions, back to the beginning or forward to the climax.

Creating the Discovery (or Revelation)

The discovery, or revelation, is the event, idea, revelation, or acquisition that empowers your hero. In *The Sixth Sense*, Bruce Willis realizes the dead people want the little boy's help. He encourages the little boy to ask a dead girl who is haunting him what she wants, and the little girl reveals the details of her murder.

Creating the Climax

Probe the relevant fascinations to discover the climactic actions that resolve the crisis. In *The Sixth Sense*, the little boy retrieves a tape from under the bed of the murdered little girl and turns it over to the girl's father. The father views the tape and discovers that his wife had poisoned the little girl. In *The Lord of the Rings*, the Ring of Power is finally destroyed and Sauron's power collapses.

Creating the Resolution

And finally, how is your story resolved? Probe the fascinations and choose something that is really conclusive and satisfying. In *The Sixth Sense*, the little boy has overcome his fear of his psychic power, he settles things with his mom, and has his boon. Bruce Willis makes peace with his wife and himself, and accepts his death. In *Gladiator*, the Republic is restored to Rome and Russell Crowe rejoins his family in Elysium.

The Three-Act Structure

My very strong recommendation is to avoid thinking in act structure terms when creating a story. Act structure is not story structure. You can't find it in nature. The three (four, five, six, seven) act structures are arbitrary divisions of an action into an arbitrary number of parts — a leftover from the theatre and applicable today only to the theatre and television shows with commercial breaks. But that has nothing to do with story. The Greeks had no act structure in their plays. They were one-act plays. The Romans had five acts. It's arbitrary. It appeared in plays because of the need to have intermissions. People can't sit for three hours in a theatre listening to an auditory experience without taking a break or going to the restroom. It appears in television shows because they want to have commercial breaks so they can sell something. None of which has anything to do with story structure. A two-hour feature film shown in a movie theatre is a continuous action. There are no intermissions. It's one continuous act-less event which revolves around a problem.

What use would it be to think in terms of three parts (or acts) when creating a story like *A Beautiful Mind* — which, if you wanted to divide it into parts, clearly has five parts and not three? In the first part, Russell Crowe is a genius mathematician; in the second part, he is a spy; in the third part we discover the first two parts were a delusion and that he is really mentally ill (the problem); in the fourth part, a first effort is made to solve that problem which fails; and in the fifth part, a second effort is made to solve that problem which succeeds. How would it help to impose a three-act structure? It wouldn't.

If you really want to gauge how irrelevant act structure is to a story, try applying it to a novel — *The Da Vinci Code*, for instance. It would make absolutely no sense. You would quickly realize the idea is absurd. It has nothing to do with story. But the screenplay which becomes a story film is a story in the same way that the novel is a story. The spine and structure of both are essentially the same. And as I've said throughout this book, this is true of the great myths, legends, and fairytales, as well as the classics and modern blockbusters. They all have the same basic structure. Story has adopted these problem-solving structures from real life, and the actions that solve these problems in real life do not contain a three-act structure.

So, if you have an idea for a story and you're wondering how to divide it up into three parts — that's artificial. A much better way to look at a story, when you are creating one, is not through any arbitrary division into acts but through the eyes of the problem, which is the central event and the heart of a great story's structure. That problem has an action that creates it and an action that resolves it, and because of the resistance, that problem-solving action has a classical story structure, namely, it has complications, a crisis, the need for a climactic action to resolve the crisis (the climax) and a resolution. Which is, as I've mentioned, the structure of any problem solving action (real or fiction) that encounters resistance.

Aristotle's classical story structure, which is the dominant feature of this structure, can stand alone. All of the structures you might find in the act are already built into this problem-solving action including conflict and turning points — which is a euphemism for crises. From there, the natural thing to do is divide the principal, problem-solving action into scenes, which are the ideal units of action to reveal the larger, essential actions.

After the story is created, of course, you can divide the action into any number of parts that you like, but it's counterproductive to think in those terms at the story's inception. In other words, you shouldn't be using act structure to lay out or create the story.

However, if you need to use the three-act structure because you're pitching an idea to someone who only speaks that language, then follow Aristotle and translate the idea of three acts into a beginning, a middle, and an end and you'll be able to communicate with them. Then, if you're asked: what is the first act? Tell them how the story begins (which is really what they want to know) and make it as intriguing as possible. If asked: what is the second act? Tell them what's happening in the middle of the story (which includes the main crisis of the dominant plot) and make it as stressful as possible. If asked about the third act, tell them what the climax of the story is (and make that as exciting as possible), and finally how the story is resolved — and make that as satisfying as possible.

What I'm basically saying here is that when you're creating a story, you should put aside the archaic notion of three acts and focus on the natural structures surrounding the problem, which is the central event and heart of your story.

The Scene

As I just indicated, the scene is the ideal unit of action to reveal the larger, essential actions of your story, and when you're working out the details of the scenes, consider making them about one thing. If you do that, then everything in that scene can serve that one objective. You can probe the fascination (core element) of that scene and create the ideal atmosphere, mood, and setting to support it, and you can make a powerful artistic statement. This purity greatly increases the power and clarity of these scenes and also helps to focus the feelings of the audience. They sink right into the appropriate feelings. So the simpler the scene is, the richer you can make it. These are limitations that allow for richness of detail. The more complicated a scene is, the less effective it is because it confuses the emotions by jumping from one feeling or idea to another. If your scenes aren't working, the first thing you should check is if they're too complicated. If they are too complicated, then break them into simpler units, find the core element of the new units, probe their fascinations and see if you aren't creating a far more power-ful effect this way. As always, be guided by your feelings and try a lot of different ideas until you find what really works. The better it works, the closer you are getting to the truth.

Real Life

And put everything in the context of real life. This will add a very appealing and pleasant level of authenticity to the mix. In *Harry Potter*, while the plot is advancing, the wizards go on a camping trip or watch a quitich match, or we see Harry experiencing everyday life at the school. In the television series *The West Wing*, the President's car breaks down on his way to an important meeting, and we see him standing on the curb waiting for a tow truck.

Dialogue

Translate everything you can into action, then add as little dialogue as necessary to explain the actions and express the feelings of the characters.

Great dialogue feels and sounds like real conversation, which is fascinating and full of colorful and emotionally charged patterns. It advances the story, reveals character, and is often humorous. On the way to the airport, a New York cab driver said this to me: "When I feel captivated in New York, I think about Florida and try to picturesque it in my mind."

To make dialogue real, listen to how people really talk and creatively adapt it. If the dialogue is genuine to begin with, it will seem real no matter how you exaggerate, shorten or otherwise alter it. The principles of great dialogue are the laws of conversation in real life artistically treated.

A few of the things you might notice when you are observing real conversation is that people only rarely talk about what's really on their minds. They are talking about the weather but they really want to ask for a date or get to know you better (subtext). People rarely discuss things in sequence. They often have several things to say and wait for an opportunity to make their point, regardless of what the other person is saying. People act differently with different people, especially if they've known them for a long time or if they've known them intimately. People rarely give straight answers but talk indirectly (indirection). I overheard this conversation on the UCLA campus. A boy with blond hair approached a second boy who was hanging out in front of the Ackerman Union.

"Are you going to Tony's later?" the newcomer asked.

The second boy looked surprised. "Were you there Friday night?"

"Marty told me."

"Hey, that's great." And they connected with a high-five.

There was not a single direct answer to any of the questions, but the answers were clear from the context. Is the second boy going to Tony's later? Yes. Was the first boy there Friday night? No.

The Narrative Structure

If you lay out all the actions, including past history and afterthought, in chronological order, the incidents can then be presented in almost any order, i.e. having created your story, you can now tell that story in just about any way that you like. You can begin the story in the middle of the crisis or climax and bring everything else in as part of the exposition (*Die Hard*). Or the story can begin a year after the climactic battle ends ("Parade of Ants"). And if you study the editing of films like *Memento*, *Pulp Fiction, Two for the Road*, and *Toto Le Hero* with this in mind, you will quickly realize that after you have established the basic story, you have almost unlimited creative freedom when it comes to how the incidents of that narrative are arranged and revealed.

This is the result of another unique ability of the human mind — namely, that it can hold a lot of different thoughts in the air until it finally has enough information to see the whole picture or get the point. As long as everything you relate belongs to the subject and the central event, you can reveal those details in almost any arrangement. In *Memento*, for instance, the narrative strikes many people as being either very innovative or very strange. Actually, there is nothing really unusual about the basic story — a woman is using a man who has lost his short term memory to commit a murder. But what is unusual is that the story is being told backwards. And we have the ability to retain all of the strange information we're being given until we finally figure that out. It just all has to come out right in the end. All of which implies unlimited creative possibilities.

Good Beginnings

The only real requirement, as far as a good beginning is concerned, is to make clear as soon as possible what the problem of your story is. If *The Odyssey* started with Odysseus' wanderings, which is what most people think the story is about, we wouldn't know that the real problem of the story has to do with the 120 suitors who have, in Odysseus' absence, taken over his palace, and are tormenting his wife and son and squandering his wealth. If *Casablanca* started in Paris, we would view it as an ordinary, boy meets girl/boy loses girl love story and we would have a lot of difficulty understanding what the story was really about, namely, Rick's neutrality. In *Jaws*, the problem is established in the opening scene — a young girl who has wondered into the ocean for a swim is killed by a shark. We do not have to see the shark make its way up the coast from the Great Barrier Reef in Australia or anything else that the shark did on that journey. The one scene is enough to establish the problem. Anything else we need to know about the shark we can learn as we go from the experts as part of the exposition. In *The Sixth Sense*, the little boy's problem (or rather the mystery surrounding his problem) is already well established when the film begins. He already sees dead people, is already known as a freak, and his family is already dysfunctional as a result of his appearing to be seriously disturbed. This helps to make clear what the real problem is — he's afraid of his psychic gift. How that problem came about is revealed, when necessary, as part of the exposition. George Lucas began his *Star Wars* epic with Episode IV, the beginning of the upside. This makes the main problem very clear — the Evil Empire has taken control of the galaxy. Then came Episodes V and VI, the completion of the upside — how that tyranny was resolved. This was followed by Episodes I, II and III which reveal the downside — how that tyranny came about.

All of the units of action you create can be treated artistically in the same way as the visual images. They can be taken apart, shifted around, conjured and reassembled some place else. You can take an ordinary sentence and work with it in this way (artistically) until it becomes a line of great poetry.* You can work in this way with the sentences of a paragraph or the paragraphs of a chapter, shifting things around, substituting this for that, generating new ideas, selecting the most powerful and conjuring until you have evolved the most potent combinations.

---

*Look at the quote from *A Midsummer Night's Dream* at the opening of Part II. Shakespeare is saying what I'm saying but in a far more eloquent way.

This of course is what rewriting is all about. Conjuring until the words are equal to the visual images you are trying to describe.

Emphasis

The emphasis you give an element will depend on its importance relative to the whole. In real life, when you have a problem, you can look at any aspect of the problem in as much detail as you like — and so it is with story. You can develop or give special emphasis to any part of the focus structure you choose. You can concentrate your story at a particular point and intensify it or spread it out as much as necessary. You can make the climax last two minutes or spread it out over fifteen rounds of boxing, as in *Rocky*. As long as it is consistent with the subject you are trying to explore, you can take any part of your story and intensify, deepen, or elongate it as much as you like.

In *The Passion of the Christ*, Mel Gibson put all of his emphasis, not on the whole story of Jesus' life, which begins in Bethlehem, but with the climax and resolution of his life — namely, his arrest, torture, crucifixion, death and transcendence. And *Harry Potter*, in this regard, is a very interesting case. In the *whole story* passage *preparation* is one of the many important steps the hero has to pass through. As stated on page 132, "if special training is required, then the mentor will provide that." In *Star Wars*, Obi-Wan Kenobi has to teach Luke how to use the light saber, and this exercise lasts only a few minutes. In *Harry Potter*, J. K. Rowling has expanded that one step, Harry's training, into seven books. Think of that. You can focus in on one step of the passage and expand it into any number of books that you like, as long as it is connected to, and an integral part of, the larger, *whole story* passage.

As Joseph Campbell expresses it: "The changes rung on the simple scale of the monomyth defy description. Many tales isolate and greatly enlarge upon one or two of the typical elements of the full cycle (test motif, flight motif, abduction of the bride), others string a number of independent cycles into a single series (as in *The Odyssey*). Differing characters or episodes can become fused, or a single element can reduplicate itself and reappear under many changes."

As long as it all comes full circle at the end, there are no set rules.

CHAPTER 29

STORY ALCHEMY

After you've sketched out the scenes and arranged them in their proper order, the final creative stage will gradually take over. This stage is dominated by the last three creative techniques — conjuring, testing, and problem solving — and is designed to help you create and evolve a perfect metaphor of the hidden truth.

The artistic tools at work here are analysis and recombination, exaggeration and miniaturization, idealization and vilification. You are taking things apart and trying this character and scene here and that character and incident there. You are changing the relationships, altering the relative sizes and strengths and making the positive things better and the negative things worse. You keep in constant touch with your intuitive feelings and wait for the creative unconscious to send you insights and signals.

Every creative playing or conjuring is a question to your self. You are in effect asking your self: Is it like this? The feeling response you get is your answer, and you keep playing with the creative ideas until they come out just right, until they really work.

Take Dracula for instance. You're trying to find something your characters can use to repel him. The first thing you try is a prayer book and you're monitoring your feelings. You imagine Dracula coming toward you with an evil intent. You hold up the book to repel him but nothing happens. He pushes it aside and goes for your throat. So you try rosary beads. Again nothing happens. Finally, you try the cross — and, ahhh! you get a chill up your spine and Dracula shrinks back. Something inside you is saying: that's it.

The asteroid in *Armageddon* may have started out as an ordinary meteor only three miles in diameter. That didn't work too well so they tried one the size of the moon. That was too big so they kept at it until it reached its present form, which they knew was right because of the way it felt. In Disney's *Hercules*, Hades may have started out like the usual Satan without the burning hair, which was realized later. The burning hair that changes color with Hades' moods is brilliant and must have felt extremely good when it was discovered.

And what's true for the characters and marvelous elements is true for the scenes and the arrangement of the scenes. You evolve everything to its ultimate, quintessential form. You keep working until you create a brilliant solution to your problem and find the ideal arrangement for your scenes. The more intriguing, fascinating and awe inspiring everything is, the closer you are getting to the truth.

Words on Paper

When you start working with words on paper or a computer screen instead of just images in your head, you continue with this same evolutionary process — revising, editing, rearranging, rewriting. These are all forms of conjuring. It's what the creative process is all about.

The first things you put down on paper may be very disappointing. But don't get discouraged. It's how the creative process works. Visual images and feelings, especially those with real power, are complex, marvelous and mysterious things. So to find just the right words to express them is bound to be difficult, requiring a great deal of effort, a great deal of trial and error, a great deal of conjuring, a long creative dialogue with your creative unconscious self.

In any case, don't just stare at a blank page, put something down. A bad idea on paper is much better than no idea, because a bad idea is an excellent reference point. It can help you find what you're looking for. Put ten bad ideas on the page and you'll know ten things that what you're looking for is not. And if you know ten things it's not, what it should be will soon reveal itself.

Trial and error, as always, is the key. Just keep working and let your intuitive feelings guide you through the process. Until you get to the end, everything is only a temporary reference point to help lead you to other more powerful ideas. You just keep exploring, conjuring, and listening to your feelings, waiting for something really powerful to emerge. Then you start probing these new, more fascinating ideas until even more powerful fascinations emerge. Eventually you'll strike gold.

The proof of all this is that your work will be noticeably better with every evolution. Every change adds energy to the process.

The Mozart Effect

If you've been working correctly, you may reach a point when the flood gates suddenly open and the right ideas are flowing so fast, you will be astounded. You will know by the way you feel that something extraordinary is happening. When this happens, don't stop. Write as fast as you can and don't question the process or think about what's happening until it's over. If it flows for ten minutes, an hour, or a week, just let it happen. If you stop to do something else, the wave will probably have passed when you return. In any case, it doesn't happen very often, but when it does it's exhilarating.

Making Metaphors Modern

To make metaphors modern and relevant, just utilize modern, contemporary elements of today's idiom. Be aware of contemporary interests and preoccupations and start with those real things — contemporary people, actions, situations, artifacts — and treat them artistically. When you artistically treat, recombine, and reassociate these contemporary things, you'll get the same effects and they will be things that modern people can easily relate to. To make metaphors fresh you have to come up with unique combinations, variations we haven't seen before. Your feelings will tell you when you've chosen a metaphor that makes a psychological connection. You know when something is right or not by how you feel about it. The acid test is always "what works," what gets your juices going. The more powerful the feeling, the closer you are getting to the truth.

And that's the Fourth Great Secret. When you're conjuring creative ideas and you make a correspondence with the hidden truth, you will get a confirmation. It will give you goose flesh. When you hit upon the right combinations, it will let you know. If you create a character, an action, or a marvelous element that makes a psychological connection and contains hidden truth, you will get a confirmation, a feeling that it "works." The more conjuring you do, the more writing and rewriting you do, the more confirmations you will experience. The more confirmations you experience, the more hidden truth you will incorporate into your story and the more power it will have. This is how you tease the truth to the surface. And this is how you steal fire from the gods.

Charisma

When the characters, events and dominant traits actually reach these ultimates, make this psychological connection and become metaphors of the hidden truth, they become charismatic, which is to say symbolic. People will be attracted to them and influenced by them even if they don't know what they mean. The strength of the charisma is brought about by the degree of fidelity to the hidden truth behind the archetypes. The more faithfully the metaphors personify this hidden truth, the more powerful and charismatic the affect. The increase in fidelity is brought about by conjuring. It is the key to making your characters truly memorable and even merchandisable. You can put them on a T-shirt and they will have impact and meaning.

If you put Harry Potter, Hannibal Lecter, Shakespeare, Albert Einstein, Beethoven, Mother Theresa, Charles Manson, Richard Nixon or T-Rex on a T-shirt it will mean something. Why? Because they have come to symbolize something. They personify some important human quality. Characters like Scrooge, Aphrodite, Eros, Hercules, and Samson are unforgettable and symbolic because they have a fully realized dominant trait.

Characters that possess this charisma become like deities. Oedipus, Moses, Zeus, Jesus, Achilles, Krishna, Hamlet, Romeo and Juliet, and King Arthur are unforgettable and Chaplin's tramp, Rhett Butler, Dorothy, E.T., Dracula, Mickey Mouse, and Superman are definite steps in the right direction. Put Superman on a little boy's pajamas and it makes him feel stronger. He'll try to fly around the room. Put Nala, the love interest in *The Lion King*, on a little girl's sneakers and it makes her feel frisky and ready for an adventure. Put Einstein on your T-shirt and it will make you feel smarter. Put Genghis Khan on your leather jacket and you're ready for a Harley. That's charisma.

CHAPTER 30

CREATING THE
SUGAR COAT

After you've fleshed everything out, conjured and perfected all of the metaphors, and clearly understand what you want to say, you can begin to fine tune the metaphors and use the six creative techniques to subtly perfect the actions that create the sugar coat.

Each of the hundred or so powerful dimensions of a story has an impact on the sugar coat, on the entertainment values of the story, so the more dimensions you can add and perfect, the greater the emotional impact on the audience. The more substance you can put behind it, the more powerful your story is going to be — the better the audience will like it and the more often they will come back to enjoy it.

When you isolate the genre actions, you isolate the feelings associated with them. And when you conjure those genre elements and perfect them, you reveal more of the hidden truth and intensify the emotional response. The closer you get to the hidden truth, the greater the response, and if you actually reach the hidden truth, the sugar coat will go off scale.

So learn as much as you can about what an audience feels and why and how those feelings are created. Be aware of what works for you, then figure out why it works. What just happened? What caused those emotions or that laughter? And you will quickly develop an instinct for it. If you're being guided by your positive and negative intuitive feelings, all of this will happen naturally. Remember the promise of these emotions lures the audience into the experience, but it also puts them in touch with themselves, with their own feelings.

If you are creating a tragedy or a romance, you are exaggerating the nobility of the characters and putting the audience in touch with their true potential. You are giving them a taste of who they really are.

If you're creating a comedy, the basic situation will still be real, but you are isolating and exaggerating the character's foibles and flaws, the frequency with which errors occur, and the irony experienced by your characters. Woody Allen, in his earlier better pictures, made people laugh by exaggerating his own hypochondria and neurosis. Laurel and Hardy exaggerated the frequency with which mishaps and catastrophes can occur. Charles Dickens exaggerated the ignorance and belligerent slowness of his bureaucrats and the difficulties his heroes had in trying to deal with them. The more laughter you can provoke, the closer you are getting to the truth. Even serious plays like *Hamlet* have, or should have, a great deal of humor. A story without humor is not about human beings.

If you want to make people cry, separate or reunite two characters the audience cares deeply about, and that will put them in touch with the tragedy of separation deep within their own souls.

If you want to increase the love the audience feels toward your central character, let that central character do kind, humane and loving things. Let him or her show courage and be willing to sacrifice for the sake of others. If you want to make the villain more villainous, isolate the negative forces and conjure them until you have thoroughly vilified him. That will intensify the loathing the audience will feel toward him and it will also intensify the rejection they will feel toward similar impulses arising in themselves.

If you want to increase the passion your audience is feeling, fill your characters with deep emotional feelings like passion and love and you will arouse those feelings in your audience. If the characters could care less about each other, the audience will feel the same about them. Passion is our feeling potential. It's how we should be feeling toward one another. Increasing the passion of your characters puts the audience in touch with those feelings and that hidden truth.

Audiences love it when characters show their feelings — especially changes of heart, forgiveness, acts of kindness, and self sacrifice. *Angels with Dirty Faces* is worth seeing just to see the emotionally charged personal sacrifice James Cagney makes at the end.

If you want to increase the excitement, isolate and artistically treat the physical action and intensify it. Raise the stakes, increase the urgency and the danger and quicken the pace — and save the greatest burst of energy for the climax of the dominant plot. The more exciting it becomes, the closer you are getting to the truth underlying that dimension.

If you want to increase the suspense, make us anxious over how things will turn out and delay the result. Excite interest or curiosity, then hold back the resolution. Anything that causes tension and anxiety causes suspense if it's unrelieved. And what causes tension or anxiety? Anything intriguing or threatening that's unresolved.

The more there is at stake, the greater the tension and suspense, and the closer you are getting to that truth. And if everything is at stake and there's no time to lose — the odds are overwhelming, and success is highly unlikely — you will maximize the tension and suspense and create a perfect metaphor of what the conscious element experiences when it confronts the negative unconscious. In real life, everything is always at stake. There really is no time to lose and the outcome is always extremely uncertain. When nothing is at stake, it's not about life and there is very little tension and suspense.

As for the aesthetic and technical dimensions, you only have to realize they are important and they will begin to work for you. The moment you realize that timing and variety are important you will begin to develop an instinct for it, and the more you work with them, the better it will become. All of these dimensions have an optimum potential, an exact, right proportion that can transform something ordinary into something incredible. And you achieve this incredible potential by creating a golden mean, a perfect balance between too little and too much — between too little variety, for instance, and too much variety. You play with your ideas until suddenly everything falls into place and they begin to glow and you create something so extraordinary and fine it is irresistible. As long as you keep everything in a fluid state and keep evolving it, there's no limit to the beauty you can achieve. The closer you get to the truth, the more pleasing the effect.

Finally, you edit out everything you don't need and make everything you do need as short and as marvelous as possible — i.e. you reduce the number of actions to the least information necessary to describe the action, reveal meaning, and relate the parts to the whole. If you select the right highlights and find the most powerful arrangement, the delighted minds of the audience will fill in all the gaps and the effect will be magical.

In summary, there are six ways to add power to a dimension. The first is to create a metaphor. This is accomplished by associating the elements with the archetypes. The second way is to increase the fidelity of the archetype by conjuring, by trying a hundred different combinations and listening to your intuitive feelings until you discover what really works. The pleasant result of this is charisma. The third way is to add more dimensions. Each of the hundred or so dimensions of story impacts the sugar coat, so the more dimensions you can add and perfect, the greater the emotional impact on the audience. The fourth way is to narrow the focus. The less you look at, the richer you can make what you see. The fifth way is to find the center. The fascination is the center of the story; the core element is the center of the scene, and the crisis is the center of the principal action. If you learn to work from the center, you can make a powerful artistic statement. The sixth and final way to add power is the Golden Mean, which expresses the power hidden in the aesthetic and technical dimensions and is another window through which the hidden truth is revealed.

Hopefully, what all of this will make clear is that there is no conflict between art and entertainment. They are two aspects of the same thing. Entertainment is energized by art and purpose. The more purpose and art you can put into the story, the greater will be the entertainment effects. If you approach story solely from the point of view of entertainment, you will only scratch the surface of the entertainment possibilities and leave out all of the nutritional elements the audience desperately needs.

CHAPTER 31

PERSEVERANCE

On the technical side, I recommend that you work with your creative ideas until you can express them as a great idea, which is to say, a high concept or an incident worth repeating, and then field test it. It is important to put your work out there to be tested. You won't know for sure that you're tapping into something powerful and universal until you have that confirmed by outside sources. So you need to develop relationships with knowledgeable people you can trust to give you an honest reaction. That's not easy to do and it takes time, but it needs to be done. You will learn things about your work that way which you could never figure out on your own.

After you've assimilated that feedback, develop your ideas into a twenty-page treatment or oral pitch and get feedback on that. When you've assimilated those results, then write a first draft or extended treatment and put that out there. And keep doing this until it's finished. There's no limit to the number of drafts. It's an evolutionary process and you should take the time to get it right.

And when you're finally finished, then really get your work out there. Once your work is of a professional quality, then perseverance is the key to success. You persevere until you find the allies who will help you find the agents who will help you find the producers or publishers who will help you get your work to the public. People are at different stages of development and have different needs and different tastes, so you have to find the people who share your chemistry and your vision. It takes a lot of time and effort but they're out there.

F. Scott Fitzgerald received 126 pink slips from publishers rejecting his first novel, *This Side of Paradise*. The 127th publisher accepted it and it was an overnight success. So don't start feeling discouraged until you've been rejected at least that many times. And, if you are a novelist, keep in mind that your hardcover book only has to appeal to one in a hundred readers to become a bestseller. That means that ninety-nine out of a hundred potential readers can completely ignore or dislike your work and you can still be a best-selling author. The same is true of agents, producers, or publishers. One in a hundred is enough to launch a career. So persevere.

In any case, the most important thing is a good start, so be sure to pick a project that is truly worthy of your time and talents. Nine out of ten ideas that you try out will be duds and you'll lose interest in them. Keep working until you find something that has real power, something that's really worth your time, that can sustain your interest for a year or so. And don't try to outguess or make the grade in Hollywood. Hollywood is not set up to develop talent, it's set up to exploit success. Explore the things you really want to write about and do those things in such a way that Hollywood and no one else can resist them. Do something really significant and they will hunt you down.

And remember, at any given moment, you are only one great idea away from success.

CHAPTER 32

CONCLUSION

The Second Potato

After the old woman ate the second potato, she left the merchant and reentered the forest, where she lived for many years. And by the end of that extraordinary time, she had recovered her former youth and beauty, she remembered her past lives, could see into the future and perform miracles. She fathomed the secrets of great stories and could speak with the gods.

After her stay in the forest, she returned to the village where she was born. She was known as the storyteller and her fame spread throughout the land. Her stories taught the women how to weave, the men how to plant, and the children how to play wonderful games and sing magical songs. And at night she danced with the moon and the stars.

Pilgrims from every corner of the earth came to sit by her side. They listened to her stories, felt the warmth of her love and were transformed.

One day an angel appeared to her and offered her life everlasting in a place among the gods, but she chose to stay with her people, and the stories that she told them gave hope and meaning to their lives. They filled their hearts with joy and their souls with little tastes of Paradise. She lived to be three hundred years old, and after she died, she lived on for countless eons in a state of absolute bliss.

The mandate of story is very clear. With every action, in every cycle, at every stage, we are being prepared to play an important role in the world. The goal of one of these passages is the initiation of the ego so that it can absorb and manage the unconscious material and the enormous power that goes with it. We begin in an inauthentic state. We're stuck and we have to be lured into the process. To be lured, there have to be incentives, fantasies and illusions, a little self-deception and a promise of romance. There are commitments to be made and tasks to be accomplished. Fear barriers to be crossed and forces of resistance to be overcome. There are risks to be taken and realities to be faced. Relationships to be established and temptations to be avoided. There are feelings to be awakened and sacrifices to be made — and in the end, we have to confront and overcome our biggest fears, and then cope with inflation if our success goes to our head. And the whole thing is set up so that you can only move in one direction. The incentives and commitments drive us forward. The unforeseen and unanticipated events provide the problems and complications. The crisis provides the solution and in the end, we discover we were equal to the task.

The principal elements — the value being pursued, the entity being transformed, the problem, the state of misfortune, the cause and the solution, the principal action, the marvelous element, the change of fortune — these are all things straight out of our lives. We are the entity being transformed, the state of misfortune is our discontents, there is a cause and a solution, the principal action is what we have to do to change our fortunes, and the marvelous element is the most important thing we have to achieve to make that happen. If we make the right commitments and choices, and we link our destiny to the fate of some entity that is being transformed, we will be guided and assisted the whole way. But we have to do it ourselves and there's no turning back. Refusing the call or turning back are the stuff that tragedies and empty lives are made of. So listen to your dreams, make the commitment, and take action.

As Stith Thompson wrote in *The Folktale*:

> The teller of stories has everywhere and always found eager listeners. Whether his tale is the mere report of a recent happening, a legend of long ago, or an elaborately contrived fiction, men and women have hung upon his words and satisfied their yearnings for information or amusement, for incitement to heroic deeds, for religious edification, or for release from the overpowering monotony of their lives. In villages of central Africa, in outrigger boats on the

Pacific, in the Australian bush, and within the shadow of Hawaiian volcanoes, tales of the present and of the mysterious past, of animals and gods and heroes, and of men and women like themselves, hold listeners in their spell or enrich the conversation of daily life. So it is also in Eskimo igloos under the light of seal-oil lamps, in the tropical jungles of Brazil, and by the totem poles of the British Columbian coast. In Japan too, and China and India, the priest and the scholar, the peasant and the artisan all join in their love of a good story and their honor for the person who tells it well.

I began by saying there are over six billion people in the world with a desperate need for real stories which isn't being met. Give the world something it desperately needs and the world will heap treasures and honors upon you beyond your wildest dreams.

So give the world something it desperately needs.

Give it great stories.

EPILOGUE

I take a serious interest in your storymaking futures. Everything I know or come to know, you will know, if you're interested. So let us know who you are. You can write me in care of the publisher or you can seek out our contact information on our website at www.storymaking.com.

If you run across books or ideas we should be aware of, let us know. And if you're interested in our seminars or our story consulting services, or you would like to be on our mailing list, let us know that, too. There's a revolution taking place in the world of storymaking and you could be a part of it.

James Bonnet
Astoria Filmwrights

"THE ONE WHO TELLS THE STORIES
RULES THE WORLD."

HOPI PROVERB

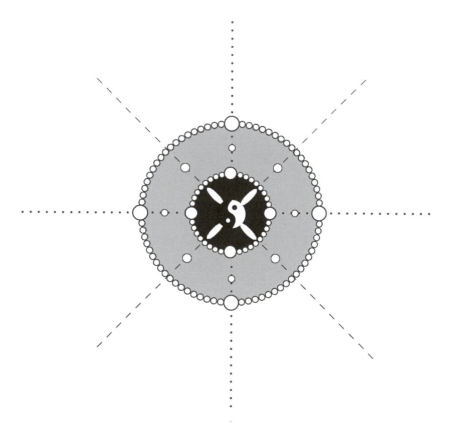

Bibliography

Bettelheim, Bruno. *The Uses of Enchantment.* New York: Alfred A. Knopf, 1976.

Butcher, S. H. *Aristotle's Theory of Poetry and Fine Art.* New York: Dover, 1951.

Campbell, Joseph. *The Hero with a Thousand Faces.* New Jersey: Princeton University Press, 1973.

Edinger, Edward F. *Ego and Archetype.* New York: Putnam, 1974.

Estes, Clarissa Pinkola, Ph.D. *Women Who Run with the Wolves.* New York: Ballantine, 1992.

Raff, Jeffrey. *Jung and the Alchemical Imagination.* Maine: Nicolas Hays, 2000.

Jung, C. G. *The Archetypes and the Collective Unconscious.* New York: Bollingen/Pantheon, 1959.

May, Rollo. *The Courage to Create.* New York: Bantam, 1975.

Neumann, Erich. *Art and the Creative Unconscious.* New York: Bollingen/Pantheon, 1959.

———. *The Origins and History of Consciousness.* New York: Bollingen/Pantheon, 1954.

Samuels, Shorter, and Plaut. *A Critical Dictionary of Jungian Analysis.* London and New York: Routledge & Kegan Paul, 1987.

Thompson, Stith. *The Folktale.* Berkeley: University of California Press, 1977.

Zimmer, Heinrich. *Myths and Symbols in Indian Art and Civilization.* New York: Harper Torchbooks, 1962.

GLOSSARY

Action: The physical activities that make up the incidents of a story.

Aesthetic dimensions: Pleasing effects like clarity, beauty, elegance, harmony, rhythm, and grace that are created by the **technical dimensions**.

Afterthought: One of the structures of the **story focus**, it links the focus to the **whole story** by pointing to events in the future that will effect the *whole story's* outcome.

Alienation: A stage on the **downside** of the **passage** wherein the **holdfast** and the **antihero** take actions which bring about a disintegration of personality. See **integration**.

Anima: An archetype of the **creative unconscious self** which expresses the feminine aspect at work in the man's psyche.

Animus: An archetype of the **creative unconscious self** which expresses the masculine aspect at work in the woman's psyche.

Antagonist: A character who opposes the action initiated by the **protagonist**.

Anti-classic: Stories on the **downside** of the **storywheel** that reveal how the individual is alienated from the society in which he lives. See **classic**.

Anti-fairy tale: Stories on the **downside** of the **storywheel** that reveal how the individual is alienated from himself. See **fairy tale**.

Antihero: The negative, dark side of the hero. The central character in a story that ends tragically on the **downside**.

Antihero's journey: The antihero's progress through the downside of the **passage**.

Anti-legend: Stories on the **downside** of the **storywheel** that reveal how the individual is alienated from the world at large. See **legend**.

Anti-myth: Stories on the downside of the **storywheel** which reveal how the individual is alienated from the spiritual or cosmic self. See **myth**.

Anti-threat: The hero. The one who opposes the threat and solves the problem.

Archetypes: The psychic energies revealed by the recurring patterns (**metaphors**) found in great stories, **myths** and dreams. The model created from these archetypal patterns creates a rough sketch of the **hidden truth**.

Artistic statement: A powerful aesthetic effect that can be created when a scene has only one objective.

Artistic tools of the imagination: Analysis, recombination, exaggeration, miniaturization, idealization, vilification, etc. By altering the relative size, composition, or strength of story elements, the **storymaker** can create **metaphors** that more exactly reveal the **hidden truth**.

Attachment: A stage on the **downside** of the **passage** wherein the **holdfast** and the **antihero** are drawn into the darkside.

Backstory: That part of the story which is off-camera and revealed by the **exposition**. See whole story.

Camouflage: The **imitations of real life**, revelations of **character**, and **entertainment dimensions** that help a great story conceal its **hidden truth**.

Central character: The main character in a story, frequently but not always the hero.

Change of fortune: The cycles of good and bad fortune being created by the **passages** of the **Golden Paradigm**.

Character: A player in a story. The sum of a person's moral qualities; their unique stamp.

Character archetypes: The principal characters in a story which are the **metaphors** that represent the **archetypes** of the **conscious** and **creative unconscious self** — the **ego/hero**, the positive and negative **physical, emotional, mental** and **spiritual archetypes,** the **anima, animus, threshold guardian, trickster,** and **shadow.**

Charisma: The magnetic effect created by a **metaphor** that is making a powerful psychological connection.

Choices: The choices a person makes reveals their **character.**

Classic: Stories on the **upside** of the **storywheel** that relate the individual to the society in which they live.

Classical story structure: The structure of problem solving action in real life and story. Its components are complications, reversal, crisis, discovery, climax, and resolution.

Climax: See **classical structure.**

Comedy: A story that exaggerates the foibles and misadventures of its characters and ends happily. Cf. **tragedy, romance, drama.**

Comparing and selecting: A **creative technique** whereby you save the ideas that provoke the strongest positive feelings and discard the rest.

Complex: The archetypes of the **creative unconscious self** are divisible into subordinate functions called complexes.

Complications: See **classical structure.**

Conflict: A major factor in story, it is the natural struggle for influence, supremacy, and control that exists in the real world and between the different **conscious** and **unconscious** dimensions of our psyche.

Conjuring: A **creative technique** in which emerging metaphors are evolved into more perfect reflections of the underlying archetypes.

Conscious self: All of the things we are consciously aware of — our thoughts, feelings, mental images, etc.

Core element: The center or fascination of a scene. What the scene is about.

Creative process: The method used by storymakers to fashion great stories.

Creative techniques: The creative process described in this book utilizes six creative techniques — **probing the fascination, comparing and selecting, modeling, conjuring, testing,** and **problem solving.**

Creative unconscious self: The **hidden truth.** An ultimate creative partner, it is the source of all the higher, universal intelligence and wisdom we possess. The **archetypes of the creative unconscious self** guide us through the **passages** of the **Golden Paradigm** and are responsible for bringing potential consciousness to consciousness.

Crisis: See **classical structure.**

Curious tendencies of the mind: See **artistic tools of the imagination.**

Cycle: See **passage.**

Death: A stage on the **downside** of the **passage** wherein the **holdfast** and the **antihero** take actions which destroy the spirit and deaden consciousness.

Dialogue: The spoken words of a story. The principles of great dialogue are the laws of conversation in real life artistically treated.

Discovery: See **classical structure.**

Dominant plot: It is the story's most significant action, and it gives the story its genre.

Dominant trait: The outstanding quality a character personifies — greed, lust, loyalty, anger, etc.

Downside: The dark, negative half of the **passage.**

Drama: A serious story which can end happily or unhappily and presents its characters as they are generally found in real life. See **tragedy, comedy, romance.**

Dynamic cycle: The energy cycles of the **Golden Paradigm.** The rivalry between the **higher** and **lower self** to control the destiny of the entity is the engine that drives the cycles of transformation.

Ego: The center of consciousness.

Ego/hero archetype: The positive, constructive energies of the creative conscious mind. See **nascent ego** and **hero**.

Emotional: The part of our selves that manages social affairs and feelings.

Emotional archetypes: The archetypes created by the energies of the emotional brain (limbic system) and the source of our social feelings. In great stories, they are the positive and negative emotional father and mother figures.

Emphasis: Part of the **narrative structure**, it is the relative importance given to a story element.

Entertainment dimensions: The pleasant sensations an audience feels when it experiences a good story. Passion, suspense, excitement, magic, laughter and tears, fear, enchantment, and surprise are among the most significant and enjoyable.

Entity being transformed: The larger entity. A unified, human group (family, institution, corporation, tribe, government, city, country, etc.) that provides the larger context for the story. In a great story, it acts as a metaphor of the psyche.

Essence of story: That without which there would be no story. See **problem, change of fortune,** and **classical story structure.**

Evil: The uncontrolled or misguided expression of instinctual impulses that promote antisocial or illegal behavior.

Exaggeration: An **artistic tool of the imagination.**

Exposition: A structure of the **story focus** that links the focus to the whole story by revealing events that occurred outside the frame of the story being told.

Fairy tale: Stories on the **upside** of the **storywheel** which relate individuals to themselves, their families, or otherwise prepare them for life. This category includes all stories of childhood and youth, not just traditional fairy tales.

Fantasy: An artistic treatment of the real world that reveals the **hidden truth**.

Fascination: An idea or visual image that provokes strong feelings and inspires you to create a story.

Fear barrier: Fear thresholds that have to be crossed by the hero to complete the **passage**.

Feelings: One of the important ways the **creative unconscious self** communicates with **consciousness**.

Focus: See **story focus**.

Forces of assistance: The positive **archetypes** on the **upside**. The negative archetypes on the **downside**. See **forces of resistance**.

Forces of resistance. The positive **archetypes** on the **downside**. The negative archetypes on the **upside**.

Genre: The feeling quality given to an action or dominant plot by the emotional, physical, mental, or spiritual character of its objective.

Genre structure: The interacting plots and subplots of a principal action which reveal how the heart, mind, body, and soul work together. See **genre**.

Golden Paradigm: A model of the psyche created by patterns discovered in **great stories**. It contains the basic patterns that are repeated in all the stages of the **storywheel**, and when used as a **story model**, it helps create a bond between the **storymaker** and the **creative unconscious self**. See **Paradigm**.

Great story: A story that becomes powerful and endures or becomes a classic or megahit because it contains the **hidden truth**.

Group phenomena: The fact that organized human groups tend to have the same archetypal structure as the human psyche.

Handicap: See **inauthentic state**.

Hero: A **metaphor** of the ego archetype, the hero is, by definition, a person (in real life or story) who makes sacrifices and takes risks for the sake of others.

Hero's journey: The hero's progress through the upside of the **passage**.

Hidden truth: The ancient wisdom that has been accumulating in our DNA since the beginning of evolution. The **creative unconscious self** uses great stories and dreams to communicate this hidden knowledge to **consciousness**.

Hierarchy: The conscious and unconscious, archetypal energies have a pecking order and unequal strengths. The **primordial, physical**, instinctual self has been superseded by the stronger **higher self** and the **conscious self** is caught in the middle.

High concept: An intriguing story idea which can be stated in a few words and is easy for everyone to relate to and understand. The fewer the words, the higher the concept. Its four components are: the **threat**, the **hook**, the fascinating subject and the great title.

Higher consciousness: The quintessential, heroic consciousness that can be recovered by retracing the steps of the **Golden Paradigm**, which is to say our evolutionary path.

Higher self: The positive archetypes, governed by the **spiritual self**, working in concert to accomplish our highest aspirations and goals.

Holdfast: The negative, selfish side of the ego.

Hook: A component of the high concept, it is the unique aspect of the **threat** which is alarming and suggests intriguing possibilities. An intriguing twist given to the **subject** being explored.

Idealization: An **artistic tool of the imagination.**

Imagination: A largely unconscious, image-making function which helps the **storymaker** transform psychic energy into useful **metaphors**.

Inauthentic state: A state of incompleteness or stagnation that has to be resolved before an authentic, heroic state can be achieved. Any state that is less than our full potential.

Incident worth repeating: A significant, much talked-about event from which a **great story** can be evolved.

Inciting action: Downside actions which cause the problems in the larger, whole story and **story focus** are called inciting actions.

Initiation: A stage on the **upside** of the **passage** wherein the **ego** and the **hero** perform actions which strengthen **consciousness**. See **regression**.

Integration: A stage on the **upside** of the passage wherein the **ego** and the **hero** perform actions which bring about the synthesis of discordant aspects of the personality. See **alienation**.

Kali Yuga: According to the Hindu religion, the current age of alienation and discord.

Legends: Stories on the **upside** of the **storywheel** that relate the individual to the world at large.

Liberation: The goal of the **higher self**. It seeks to free the **entity** from the tyranny and corruption that caused the **state of misfortune** and create a new, unified whole.

Limbic system: The mammalian brain.

Love interest: The positive **anima** and **animus**. They act as go-betweens and are the **ego/hero's** guide to the soul.

Love story: A story whose dominant plot has an emotional objective which ends in reunion or separation.

Lower self: The negative archetypes, governed by the primordial, **physical self**, working in concert.

Major players: See **character archetypes.**

Make-believe: An act of pretending that creates a safe way of looking objectively at things that occur in real life.

Marvelous element: That without which the problem cannot be solved, they are the metaphors that reveal the vast, unrealized potential. Psychologically, they are the building blocks of consciousness. See **terrible element.**

Meaning: Another word for wisdom in a story. Cf. **moral**.

Meaningful connection: A realized parallel between the characters and events in a story and our real life situations.

Mental: The part of our selves that manages thoughts, memories, intelligence, and reason.

Mental archetypes: The patterns of energy in our thinking brain (neo-cortex) that create knowledge, intelligence and understanding. In great stories, they are the **wise old man** and **woman** (positive) and the **sorcerer** and **sorceress** (negative).

Metaphor: The symbolic, story language that reveals the **hidden truth**.

Miniaturization: An **artistic tool of the imagination**.

Modeling: A **creative technique** in which you associate emotionally charged images and ideas with the **archetypes** of the **Golden Paradigm**.

Moral: The lessons of a story's action. See **wisdom**.

Mozart effect: A creative stage in which ideas flow effortlessly.

Mystery: A story whose **dominant plot** has a mental objective and ends with a solution or an enigma.

Myth: Stories on the **upside** of the **storywheel** which relate the individual to the spiritual or cosmic self. See **anti-myth**.

Nadir: The lowest, most negative point on the **storywheel** or **Golden Paradigm**.

Narrative structure: The way in which the incidents of a story are arranged for the telling.

Nascent ego: The positive, unselfish side of the **ego**. The conscious element on the **upside** of the cycle that is about to be awakened and transformed into hero consciousness (a mature ego).

Negative: Serving or supporting the interests and objectives of the **lower self**.

Neo-cortex. The higher, thinking brain.

One and the many: The major **archetypes** have many separate functions and each of these functions can be personified as a different **character** (**metaphor**) or they can be combined.

Oral tradition: Stories that are passed verbally from generation to generation and not written down.

Overreach: Uncontrolled greed. A primary cause of the **antihero's** downfall.

Paradigm: A model.

Paradise: A **metaphor** for an optimum state of mind.

Passage: Known also as the **hero's** or **antihero's journey, the path,** or the whole story, it is the cycles of transformation outlined in the **Golden Paradigm**.

Path, the: The journey of our lives. The cycles of change and growth necessary to reach our full potential. See **passage**.

Perseverance: A component of the **universal structure**.

Physical: The part of our selves that manages the organs of the body and the needs of the flesh.

Physical archetypes: The motivating energies of the **R-complex** (the reptile brain) and the source of our most basic instincts, appetites, and drives. In great stories, these energies are personified as the positive and negative, male and female, physical parent figures.

Plot: A dramatic action. The virtues that give a story's dominant action its dramatic qualities.

Point-of-view: The vantage point from which a story is told or a problem examined.

Positive: Serving the interests of the **higher self**.

Possession: The goal of the **lower self.** It seeks to take control of an entity and redirect its goals toward those that fulfill its own desires and needs.

Potential: The vast potential is what we could gain if we followed the heroic **passages** revealed by story and outlined in the **Golden Paradigm**.

Precedent structures: Underlying motifs found in great stories that can be redressed to create entirely new stories.

Principal action: The central, unifying action that solves the problem and brings about a change to good fortune.

Principal (or Unifying) elements: The archetypal patterns (or threads) that create the Golden Paradigm.

Probing the fascination: A **creative technique** that involves working with a **fascination** in ways that bring other story-relevant ideas and images to the surface.

Problem: The central event of the story around which all of the action revolves. See **essence of story**.

Problem solving: A **creative technique** for solving the story problems that emerge when you **test** the **model**.

Protagonist: The character who initiates the action. See **antagonist**.

Psyche: The totality of all psychic processes, conscious as well as unconscious. According to Jung, a structure made for movement, growth, change, and transformation. An evolution towards self-realization is embedded in all psychic processes.

Quintessential: The ultimate example of something. The ultimate good or bad, best or worst example of something. All great characters are the quintessential personifications of some dominant quality or trait.

R-complex: The reptile brain.

Real life: The real things that are artistically treated to create **metaphors**.

Real life, imitations of: An artistic look at how people and other living things really act, communicate, and behave.

Rebirth: A stage on the **upside** of the **passage** wherein the **ego** and the **hero** experience an infusion of higher consciousness which gives them a sense of being reborn. See **death**.

Reflection: See **universal structure**.

Regression: A stage on the **downside** of the **passage** wherein the **holdfast** and the **antihero** take actions which weaken consciousness. See **Initiation**.

Relativity: The meaning of a metaphor is determined by its relation to the whole.

Resistance: A negative force, imposed by the **threat** to prevent a problem-solving action, which creates the **complications** and other components of the **classical structure**. A similar structure is created on the downside when the positive archetypes resist the problem-creating actions of the antihero.

Resolution: See **classical structure**.

Rivalry: The archetypes of the **higher** and **lower self** are competing for influence over the conscious self. See **hierarchy**.

Romance: A story that exaggerates the nobility and chivalry of its characters and ends happily. Cf. **comedy, tragedy, drama**.

Sacrifice: A selfless act that defines a **hero**. Without personal sacrifice there is no hero and no **higher consciousness**.

Satan: A metaphor of the lower, primordial self.

Scene: The most important **unit of action** in a story. It highlights the essential steps, gives them a dramatic structure and provides a setting that approximates **real life**.

Scourge: The scourge being avoided. One of the negative states (injustice, slavery, poverty, disease, death, ignorance, etc.) being created on the **downside** of the cycle. See **value**.

Self: The **creative unconscious**. A unifying principle within the human **psyche**. The sum of all the **archetypes** and our vast **potential**. According to Jung, it is the unity of the personality as a whole. An archetypal urge to coordinate, relativize, and mediate the tension of the opposites. It occupies the central position of authority in relation to psychological life and, therefore, the destiny of the individual. By way of the self, one is confronted with a polarity of good and evil, human and divine.

Separation: A stage on the **upside** of the **passage** wherein the **ego** and the **hero** venture out on their own seeking a solution to the problem.

Shadow: All of the undesirable and inferior aspects of our psychic selves which have been repressed into our personal unconscious. In a story these repressed elements appear as psychopaths, demons, monsters, and arch villains.

Shapeshifting: The ability of certain **metaphors** to change their shape or cast spells reflects the human mind's ability to adjust, change, shift, or be transformed.

Solution formula: The right combination of large and small actions used by the hero to solve the story's problem.

Sorcerer and sorceress: Negative mental archetypes.

Spiritual: The higher dimension of our selves that connects us to the mysteries of the universe.

Spiritual archetypes: The guiding spirits and hidden wisdom of the higher, unbounded cosmic self. They guard our destiny and inspire us to take positive actions. In great stories, they are the positive and negative, male and female spiritual parent figures.

State of good fortune: The positive state created within the entity by the **upside** of the cycle.

State of misfortune: The state of misery created within the entity by the **downside** of the cycle.

Story: The term I use to signify great stories collectively.

Story alchemy: The creative stage dominated by **conjuring**, **testing**, and **problem solving**.

Story focus: The aspect of the whole story being shown to the audience.

Storymaker: The creator of new stories. Cf. **storyteller**.

Storymaking: The art of creating new stories.

Story model: The **Golden Paradigm**, when it is used as a tool to assist storymakers.

Storyteller: Someone who relates stories that already exist. Cf. **storymaker**.

Storytelling: The art of telling a story that already exists.

Storywheel: A model that brings all the different types of great story together into one grand design. Viewed in this way, all of the cycles of change and growth we experience from birth to death are revealed, and it becomes apparent that the purpose of great stories is to guide us to higher states of being.

Structure: The arrangement of the incidents. **Actions** become structures when they have **meaning**. Structures become **plots** when they produce a dramatic effect.

Style: A quality that further defines a person's **character**.

Subject: An ultimate unifying force. What the story is really about.

Subplot: Subordinate actions necessary to accomplish the objectives of the **dominant plot**.

Sugar coat: See **entertainment dimensions**.

Technical dimensions: Craft dimensions like variety, contrast, proportion, symmetry, timing, and tempo that help create the **aesthetic dimensions**.

Technique: The conscious methods used by artists and **storymakers** to transform psychic energy into visual **metaphors**.

Tempter: The negative **animus**. He is the corrupter of the feminine **antihero**. Psychologically, he is a critical inner voice.

Temptress: The negative **anima**; the femme fatale; the **antihero's** guide to the underworld.

Terrible element: A metaphor for the destructive, negative powers coveted by the **lower self**. See **marvelous element**.

Testing: A **creative technique** that helps a **storymaker** test the **story model**.

Theme: The dominant character trait being explored in the **story focus**.

Threat: The cause of the problem. It is often the villain, but it can be an idea, a misunderstanding, or a non-human threat like a disease, an asteroid, a volcano, or a shark.

Threshold guardian: An archetype of the **creative unconscious self**. Threshold guardians stand in the way of the conscious archetypes and are there to test their readiness and resolve.

Tragedy: A story that exaggerates the nobility of its characters and ends unhappily. Cf. **comedy, romance, drama**.

Trial and error. Important component of the **universal structure**.

Trickster: An **archetype** of the **creative unconscious self**. Tricksters are troublemakers who goad the conscious archetypes forward when they are stuck.

Unconscious self: That part of the **psyche** that operates without our **conscious** awareness. In story, it is an unfamiliar, dark, or supernatural world and its denizens.

Unifying elements, see principal elements.

Units of action: The building blocks of action — the beats, shots, and scenes that make up a film or play, and the sentences, paragraphs, chapters, and books of a novel.

Unity: The thematic elements that make a story one. Ultimate unity, see the **subject**.

Universal structure: One of the four structures of a problem-solving **principal action**. Its key elements are trial and error, reflection and perseverance.

Upside: The positive first half of the **passage**. See **downside**.

Value: The value being pursued. One of the positive goals (justice, freedom, wisdom, life, health, etc.) being pursued on the upside of the passage. See **scourge**.

Victims: The casualties of the actions taken by the threat which create the **state of misfortune**.

Vilification: An **artistic tool of the imagination**.

Villain: See **threat**.

War story: A story whose dominant plot has a physical objective which ends in victory or defeat.

Whole story: The larger background or frame story that covers one complete cycle or **passage** of the **Golden Paradigm** and creates the context for the **story focus**. Understanding the dynamics of this structure can lead to an understanding of the world.

Wisdom: The special knowledge revealed by a story's action. The **hidden truth** concealed by a story's **sugar coat**. See **meaning, moral**.

Wise old man and wise old woman: Positive mental archetypes.

Yin and yang: The Chinese symbol of opposites.

Zenith: The highest, most positive point on the **storywheel** or **Golden Paradigm**.

INDEX

THE WRITER'S JOURNEY
3RD EDITION

MYTHIC STRUCTURE FOR WRITERS

CHRISTOPHER VOGLER

BEST SELLER
OVER 170,000 COPIES SOLD!

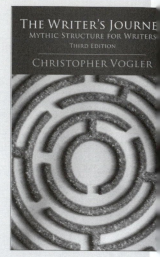

See why this book has become an international best seller and a true classic. *The Writer's Journey* explores the powerful relationship between mythology and storytelling in a clear, concise style that's made it required reading for movie executives, screenwriters, playwrights, scholars, and fans of pop culture all over the world.

Both fiction and nonfiction writers will discover a set of useful myth-inspired storytelling paradigms (i.e., "The Hero's Journey") and step-by-step guidelines to plot and character development. Based on the work of Joseph Campbell, *The Writer's Journey* is a must for all writers interested in further developing their craft.

The updated and revised third edition provides new insights and observations from Vogler's ongoing work on mythology's influence on stories, movies, and man himself.

"This book is like having the smartest person in the story meeting come home with you and whisper what to do in your ear as you write a screenplay. Insight for insight, step for step, Chris Vogler takes us through the process of connecting theme to story and making a script come alive."
> – Lynda Obst, Producer, *Sleepless in Seattle, How to Lose a Guy in 10 Days;* Author, *Hello, He Lied*

"This is a book about the stories we write, and perhaps more importantly, the stories we live. It is the most influential work I have yet encountered on the art, nature, and the very purpose of storytelling."
> – Bruce Joel Rubin, Screenwriter, *Stuart Little 2, Deep Impact, Ghost, Jacob's Ladder*

CHRISTOPHER VOGLER is a veteran story consultant for major Hollywood film companies and a respected teacher of filmmakers and writers around the globe. He has influenced the stories of movies from *The Lion King* to *Fight Club* to *The Thin Red Line* and most recently wrote the first installment of *Ravenskull*, a Japanese-style manga or graphic novel. He is the executive producer of the feature film *P.S. Your Cat is Dead* and writer of the animated feature *Jester Till*.

$26.95 · 400 PAGES · ORDER NUMBER 76RLS · ISBN: 193290736x

MYTH AND THE MOVIES
DISCOVERING THE MYTHIC STRUCTURE OF 50 UNFORGETTABLE FILMS

STUART VOYTILLA
FOREWORD BY CHRISTOPHER VOGLER
AUTHOR OF *THE WRITER'S JOURNEY*

BEST SELLER
OVER 15,000 UNITS SOLD!

An illuminating companion piece to *The Writer's Journey*, *Myth and the Movies* applies the mythic structure Vogler developed to 50 well-loved U.S. and foreign films. This comprehensive book offers a greater understanding of why some films continue to touch and connect with audiences generation after generation.

Movies discussed include *The Godfather, Some Like It Hot, Citizen Kane, Halloween, Jaws, Annie Hall, Chinatown, The Fugitive, Sleepless in Seattle, The Graduate, Dances with Wolves, Beauty and the Beast, Platoon,* and *Die Hard.*

"Stuart Voytilla's Myth and the Movies *is a remarkable achievement: an ambitious, thought-provoking, and cogent analysis of the mythic underpinnings of fifty great movies. It should prove a valuable resource for film teachers, students, critics, and especially screenwriters themselves, whose challenge, as Voytilla so clearly understands, is to constantly reinvent a mythology for our times."*
    — Ted Tally, *Academy Award Screenwriter,* Silence of the Lambs

"Myth and the Movies *is a must for every writer who wants to tell better stories. Voytilla guides his readers to a richer and deeper understanding not only of mythic structure, but also of the movies we love."*
    — Christopher Wehner, *Web editor*
    The Screenwriters Utopia *and* Creative Screenwriting

"I've script consulted for ten years and I've studied every genre thoroughly. I thought I knew all their nuances – until I read Voytilla's book. This ones goes on my Recommended Reading List. A fascinating analysis of the Hero's Myth for all genres."
    — *Lou Grantt,* Hollywood Scriptwriter Magazine

STUART VOYTILLA is a screenwriter, literary consultant, teacher, and author of *Writing the Comedy Film.*

$26.95 | 300 PAGES | ORDER # 39RLS | ISBN: 0-941188-66-3

24 HOURS | 1.800.833.5738 | WWW.MWP.COM

SCREENWRITING 101
THE ESSENTIAL CRAFT OF FEATURE FILM WRITING

NEILL D. HICKS

Hicks brings the clarity and practical instruction familiar to his students and readers to screenwriters everywhere. In his inimitable and colorful style, he tells the beginning screenwriter how the mechanics of Hollywood storytelling work, and how to use those elements to create a script with blockbuster potential without falling into clichés.

"Neill Hicks makes complex writing concepts easy to grasp, in a way that only a master teacher could. And he does so while keeping his book one hell of a fun read."
— Eric Edson, Writer, Lethal Vows
Executive Director, The Hollywood Symposium

NEILL D. HICKS' screenwriting credits include *Rumble in the Bronx* and *First Strike*.

$16.95 | 220 PAGES | ORDER # 41RLS | ISBN: 0-941188-72-8

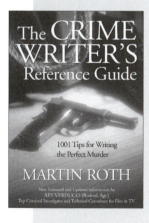

THE CRIME WRITER'S
COMPLETE REFERENCE GUIDE
1001 TIPS FOR WRITING THE PERFECT CRIME

MARTIN ROTH

NEW FOREWORD AND UPDATED INFORMATION BY SGT. REY VERDUGO, TOP CRIMINAL INVESTIGATOR AND TECHNICAL CONSULTANT FOR FILM AND TV

Here's the book no writer of murder mysteries, thrillers, action-adventure, true crime, police procedurals, romantic suspense, and psychological mysteries — whether scripts or novels — can do without. Martin Roth provides all the particulars to make your crime story accurate.

"Now you don't need a friend on the force, a buddy in forensics, a contact in the D.A.'s office, or a pal in the morgue — all you need is this book."
— Lee Goldberg, Two-time Edgar Nominee

MARTIN ROTH wrote over 100 TV scripts and several best-selling books, including *The Writer's Partner*.

$17.95 | 300 PAGES | ORDER # 105RLS | ISBN: 0-941188-49-3

24 HOURS | 1.800.833.5738 | WWW.MWP.COM

SAVE THE CAT!
THE LAST BOOK ON SCREENWRITING YOU'LL EVER NEED

BLAKE SNYDER

He's made millions of dollars selling screenplays to Hollywood and now screenwriter Blake Snyder tells all. "Save the Cat" is just one of Snyder's many ironclad rules for making your ideas more marketable and your script more satisfying – and saleable, including:
- · The four elements of every winning logline.
- · The seven immutable laws of screenplay physics.
- · The 10 genres and why they're important to your movie.
- · Why your Hero must serve your Idea.
- · Mastering the Beats.
- · Mastering the Board to create the Perfect Beast.
- · How to get back on track with ironclad and proven rules for script repair.

This ultimate insider's guide reveals the secrets that none dare admit, told by a show biz veteran who's proven that you can sell your script if you can save the cat.

"Imagine what would happen in a town where more writers approached screenwriting the way Blake suggests? My weekend read would dramatically improve, both in sellable/producible content and in discovering new writers who understand the craft of storytelling and can be hired on assignment for ideas we already have in house."
> *– From the Foreword by Sheila Hanahan Taylor, Vice President, Development at Zide/Perry Entertainment, whose films include American Pie, Cats and Dogs and Final Destination*

"Want to know how to be a successful writer in Hollywood? The answers are here. Blake Snyder has written an insider's book that's informative – and funny, too."
> *– David Hoberman, Producer, Raising Helen, Walking Tall, Bringing Down the House*

"Blake Snyder's Save the Cat! *could also be called* Save the Screenwriter!, *because that's exactly what it will do:* Save the Screenwriter *time,* Save the Screenwriter *frustration, and* Save the Screenwriter's *sanity... by demystifying the Hollywood process."*
> *– Andy Cohen, Literary Manager/Producer; President, Grade A Entertainment*

BLAKE SNYDER has sold dozens of scripts, including co-writing the Disney hit, *Blank Check*, and *Nuclear Family* for Steven Spielberg – both million-dollar sales.

$19.95 | 216 PAGES | ORDER # 34RLS | ISBN: 1-932907-00-9

SCRIPT PARTNERS
WHAT MAKES FILM AND TV WRITING TEAMS WORK

CLAUDIA JOHNSON AND MATT STEVENS
FOREWORD BY MARSHALL BRICKMAN

This book examines the role and the importance of collaboration, then illuminates the process of collaborative screenwriting itself. It includes revelatory interviews with such successful collaborators as Andrew Reich & Ted Cohen (*Friends*), Jim Taylor (*Election, About Schmidt*), Marshall Brickman (*Annie Hall, Manhattan*), Scott Alexander & Larry Karaszewski (*The People vs. Larry Flynt, Ed Wood*), and Larry Gelbart (*M*A*S*H*).

$24.95 | 300 PAGES | ORDER # 104RLS | ISBN: 0-941188-75-2

THE SCRIPT-SELLING GAME
A HOLLYWOOD INSIDER'S LOOK AT GETTING YOUR SCRIPT SOLD AND PRODUCED

KATHIE FONG YONEDA

Players understand that their success in Hollywood is not based on luck or nepotism; it's the result of understanding how Hollywood really works. *The Script-Selling Game* brings together over 25 years of experience from an entertainment professional who shows you how to prepare your script, pitch it, meet the moguls, talk the talk, and make the deal. It's a must for both novice and veteran screenwriters.

$14.95 | 196 PAGES | ORDER # 100RLS | ISBN: 0-941188-44-2

WHAT ARE YOU LAUGHING AT?
HOW TO WRITE FUNNY SCREENPLAYS, STORIES, AND MORE

BRAD SCHREIBER
FOREWORD BY CHRISTOPHER VOGLER AUTHOR OF THE WRITER'S JOURNEY

The definitive book on how to "write funny." Using principles developed in his popular UCLA Writers Program class on humor writing and his CBS Studio City seminars on screenwriting, Schrieber includes more than 70 excerpts from such top prose and screenwriters as Woody Allen, Steve Martin, and Kurt Vonnegut Jr.; unique writing exercises developed exclusively for this book; and vital information on writing comedy dialogue for TV, stage, and audio.

$19.95 | 278 PAGES | ORDER # 114RLS | ISBN: 0-941188-83-3

CINEMATIC STORYTELLING

THE 100 MOST POWERFUL FILM CONVENTIONS EVERY FILMMAKER MUST KNOW

JENNIFER VAN SIJLL

How do directors use screen direction to suggest conflict? How do screenwriters exploit film space to show change? How does editing style determine emotional response?

Many first-time writers and directors do not ask these questions. They forego the huge creative resource of the film medium, defaulting to dialog to tell their screen story. Yet most movies are carried by sound and picture. The industry's most successful writers and directors have mastered the cinematic conventions specific to the medium. They have harnessed non-dialog techniques to create some of the most cinematic moments in movie history.

This book is intended to help writers and directors more fully exploit the medium's inherent storytelling devices. It contains 100 non-dialog techniques that have been used by the industry's top writers and directors. From *Metropolis* and *Citizen Kane* to *Dead Man* and *Kill Bill*, the book illustrates — through 500 frame grabs and 75 script excerpts — how the inherent storytelling devices specific to film were exploited.

You will learn:
- How non-dialog film techniques can advance story.
- How master screenwriters exploit cinematic conventions to create powerful scenarios.

"Cinematic Storytelling scores a direct hit in terms of concise information and perfectly chosen visuals, and it also searches out... and finds... an emotional core that many books of this nature either miss or are afraid of."
> — *Kirsten Sheridan, Director*, Disco Pigs; *Co-writer*, In America

"Here is a uniquely fresh, accessible, and truly original contribution to the field. Jennifer van Sijll takes her readers in a wholly new direction, integrating aspects of screenwriting with all the film crafts in a way I've never before seen. It is essential reading not only for screenwriters but also for filmmakers of every stripe."
> — *Prof. Richard Walter, UCLA Screenwriting Chairman*

JENNIFER VAN SIJLL has taught film production, film history, and screenwriting. She is currently on the faculty at San Francisco State's Department of Cinema.

$22.95 | 230 PAGES | ORDER # 35RLS | ISBN: 1-932907-05-X

THE HOLLYWOOD STANDARD
THE COMPLETE AND AUTHORITATIVE GUIDE TO SCRIPT FORMAT AND STYLE

CHRISTOPHER RILEY

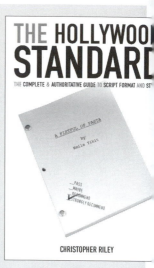

THE HOLLYWOO
STANDARD
THE COMPLETE & AUTHORITATIVE GUIDE TO SCRIPT FORMAT AND ST

CHRISTOPHER RILEY

Finally, there's a script format guide that is accurate, complete, and easy to use, written by Hollywood's foremost authority on industry standard script formats. Riley's guide is filled with clear, concise, complete instructions and hundreds of examples to take the guesswork out of a multitude of formatting questions that perplex screenwriters, waste their time, and steal their confidence. You'll learn how to get into and out of a POV shot, how to set up a telephone intercut, what to capitalize and why, how to control pacing with format, and more.

"The Hollywood Standard *is not only indispensable, it's practical, readable, and fun to use."*
— Dean Batali, Writer-Producer, That '70s Show; Writer, Buffy the Vampire Slayer

"Buy this book before you write another word! It's required reading for any screenwriter who wants to be taken seriously by Hollywood."
— Elizabeth Stephen, President, Mandalay Television Pictures;
Executive Vice President Motion Picture Production, Mandalay Pictures

"Riley has succeeded in an extremely difficult task: He has produced a guide to screenplay formatting which is both entertaining to read and exceptionally thorough. Riley's clear style, authoritative voice, and well-written examples make this book far more enjoyable than any formatting guide has a right to be. This is the best guide to script formatting ever, and it is an indispensable tool for every writer working in Hollywood."
— Wout Thielemans, Screentalk Magazine

"It doesn't matter how great your screenplay is if it looks all wrong. The Hollywood Standard is probably the most critical book any screenwriter who is serious about being taken seriously can own. For any writer who truly understands the power of making a good first impression, this comprehensive guide to format and style is priceless."
— Marie Jones, www.absolutewrite.com

CHRISTOPHER RILEY, based in Los Angeles, developed Warner Brothers Studios script software and serves as the ultimate arbiter of script format for the entertainment industry.

$18.95 | 208 PAGES | ORDER # 31RLS | ISBN: 1-932907-01-7

ce 1981, Michael Wiese Productions has been dedicated to providing both ice and seasoned filmmakers with vital information on all aspects of filmmaking. have published nearly 100 books, used in over 600 film schools and countless versities, and by hundreds of thousands of filmmakers worldwide.

r authors are successful industry professionals who spend innumerable hours ting about the hard stuff: budgeting, financing, directing, marketing, and ribution. They believe that if they share their knowledge and experience with ers, more high quality films will be produced.

d that has been our mission, now complemented through our new web-based ources. We invite all readers to visit www.mwp.com to receive free tipsheets sample chapters, participate in forum discussions, obtain product discounts — even get the opportunity to receive free books, project consulting, and other vices offered by our company.

r goal is, quite simply, to help you reach your goals. That's why we give our ders the most complete portal for filmmaking knowledge available — in the st convenient manner.

truly hope that our books and web-based resources will empower you to ate enduring films that will last for generations to come.

us hear from you at anytime.

Sincerely,

Michael Wiese

Publisher, Filmmaker

www.mwp.com

FILM & VIDEO BOOKS

Archetypes for Writers: Using the Power of Your Subconscious
Jennifer Van Bergen / $22.95

Art of Film Funding, The: Alternate Financing Concepts
Carole Lee Dean / $26.95

Cinematic Storytelling: The 100 Most Powerful Film Conventions Every
Filmmaker Must Know / Jennifer Van Sijll / $24.95

Complete Independent Movie Marketing Handbook, The: Promote, Distribute
& Sell Your Film or Video / Mark Steven Bosko / $39.95

Creating Characters: Let Them Whisper Their Secrets
Marisa D'Vari / $26.95

Crime Writer's Reference Guide, The: 1001 Tips for Writing the Perfect Crime
Martin Roth / $20.95

Cut by Cut: Editing Your Film or Video
Gael Chandler / $35.95

Digital Filmmaking 101, 2nd Edition: An Essential Guide to Producing
Low-Budget Movies / Dale Newton and John Gaspard / $26.95

Directing Actors: Creating Memorable Performances for Film and Television
Judith Weston / $26.95

Directing Feature Films: The Creative Collaboration Between Directors,
Writers, and Actors / Mark Travis / $26.95

Elephant Bucks: An Insider's Guide to Writing for TV Sitcoms
Sheldon Bull / $24.95

Eye is Quicker, The: Film Editing; Making a Good Film Better
Richard D. Pepperman / $27.95

Fast, Cheap & Under Control: Lessons Learned from the Greatest Low-Budget
Movies of All Time / John Gaspard / $26.95

Fast, Cheap & Written That Way: Top Screenwriters on Writing for Low-Budget
Movies / John Gaspard / $26.95

Film & Video Budgets, 4th Updated Edition
Deke Simon and Michael Wiese / $26.95

Film Directing: Cinematic Motion, 2nd Edition
Steven D. Katz / $27.95

Film Directing: Shot by Shot, Visualizing from Concept to Screen
Steven D. Katz / $27.95

Film Director's Intuition, The: Script Analysis and Rehearsal Techniques
Judith Weston / $26.95

Film Production Management 101: The Ultimate Guide for Film and Television
Production Management and Coordination / Deborah S. Patz / $39.95

Filmmaking for Teens: Pulling Off Your Shorts
Troy Lanier and Clay Nichols / $18.95

First Time Director: How to Make Your Breakthrough Movie
Gil Bettman / $27.95

From Word to Image: Storyboarding and the Filmmaking Process
Marcie Begleiter / $26.95

Hollywood Standard, The: The Complete and Authoritative Guide to Script
Format and Style / Christopher Riley / $18.95

Independent Film Distribution: How to Make a Successful End Run Around
the Big Guys / Phil Hall / $26.95

Independent Film and Videomakers Guide - 2nd Edition, The: Expanded and
Updated / Michael Wiese / $29.95

Inner Drives: How to Write and Create Characters Using the Eight Classic
Centers of Motivation / Pamela Jaye Smith / $26.95

I'll Be in My Trailer!: The Creative Wars Between Directors & Actors
John Badham and Craig Modderno / $26.95

Moral Premise, The: Harnessing Virtue & Vice for Box Office Success
Stanley D. Williams, Ph.D. / $24.95

Myth and the Movies: Discovering the Mythic Structure of 50 Unforgettable
Films / Stuart Voytilla / $26.95

On the Edge of a Dream: Magic and Madness in Bali
Michael Wiese / $16.95

Perfect Pitch, The: How to Sell Yourself and Your Movie Idea to Hollywood
Ken Rotcop / $16.95

Power of Film, The
Howard Suber / $27.95

Psychology for Screenwriters: Building Conflict in your Script
William Indick, Ph.D. / $26.95

Save the Cat!: The Last Book on Screenwriting You'll Ever Need
Blake Snyder / $19.95

Save the Cat! Goes to the Movies: The Screenwriter's Guide to Every Story
Ever Told / Blake Snyder / $24.95

Screenwriting 101: The Essential Craft of Feature Film Writing
Neill D. Hicks / $16.95

Screenwriting for Teens: The 100 Principles of Screenwriting Every Budding
Writer Must Know / Christina Hamlett / $18.95

Script-Selling Game, The: A Hollywood Insider's Look at Getting Your Script
Sold and Produced / Kathie Fong Yoneda / $16.95

Selling Your Story in 60 Seconds: The Guaranteed Way to get Your Screenplay
or Novel Read / Michael Hauge / $12.95

Setting Up Your Scenes: The Inner Workings of Great Films
Richard D. Pepperman / $24.95

Setting Up Your Shots: Great Camera Moves Every Filmmaker Should Know
Jeremy Vineyard / $19.95

Shaking the Money Tree, 2nd Edition: The Art of Getting Grants and
Donations for Film and Video Projects / Morrie Warshawski / $26.95

Sound Design: The Expressive Power of Music, Voice, and Sound Effects in
Cinema / David Sonnenschein / $19.95

Special Effects: How to Create a Hollywood Film Look on a Home Studio
Budget / Michael Slone / $31.95

Stealing Fire From the Gods, 2nd Edition: The Complete Guide to Story for
Writers & Filmmakers / James Bonnet / $26.95

Ultimate Filmmaker's Guide to Short Films, The: Making It Big in Shorts
Kim Adelman / $16.95

Way of Story, The: The Craft & Soul of Writing
Catherine Anne Jones / $22.95

Working Director, The: How to Arrive, Thrive & Survive in the Director's Chair
Charles Wilkinson / $22.95

Writer's Journey, - 3rd Edition, The: Mythic Structure for Writers
Christopher Vogler / $26.95

Writing the Action Adventure: The Moment of Truth
Neill D. Hicks / $14.95

Writing the Comedy Film: Make 'Em Laugh
Stuart Voytilla and Scott Petri / $14.95

Writing the Killer Treatment: Selling Your Story Without a Script
Michael Halperin / $14.95

Writing the Second Act: Building Conflict and Tension in Your Film Script
Michael Halperin / $19.95

Writing the Thriller Film: The Terror Within
Neill D. Hicks / $14.95

Writing the TV Drama Series - 2nd Edition: How to Succeed as a
Professional Writer in TV / Pamela Douglas / $26.95

DVD & VIDEOS

Field of Fish: VHS Video
Directed by Steve Tanner and Michael Wiese, Written by Annamaria Murphy / $9.95

Hardware Wars: DVD / Written and Directed by Ernie Fosselius / $14.95

Sacred Sites of the Dalai Lamas – DVD, The: A Pilgrimage to Oracle Lake
A Documentary by Michael Wiese / $24.95